REFORMING
CHILD WELFARE

Also of interest from the Urban Institute Press:

Child Welfare: The Challenges of Collaboration by Timothy Ross

Kids Having Kids: Economic Costs and Social Consequences of Teen Pregnancy, second edition, edited by Saul D. Hoffman and Rebecca A. Maynard

Meeting the Needs of Children with Disabilities by Laudan Y. Aron and Pamela J. Loprest

THE URBAN INSTITUTE PRESS
WASHINGTON, DC

REFORMING CHILD WELFARE

Olivia Golden

THE URBAN INSTITUTE PRESS
2100 M Street, N.W.
Washington, D.C. 20037

Library of Congress Cataloging-in-Publication Data

Golden, Olivia Ann.
  Reforming child welfare / Olivia Golden.
     p. cm.
  Includes bibliographical references and index.
  ISBN 978-0-87766-759-9 (alk. paper)
  1. Child welfare—United States. 2. Child welfare—Government policy—United States. 3. Family services—United States. I. Title.
  HV741.G587 2009
  362.7—dc22
                              2009020534

Printed in the United States of America

12 11 10 09   1 2 3 4 5

THE URBAN INSTITUTE is a nonprofit, nonpartisan policy research and educational organization established in Washington, D.C., in 1968. Its staff investigates the social, economic, and governance problems confronting the nation and evaluates the public and private means to alleviate them. The Institute disseminates its research findings through publications, its web site, the media, seminars, and forums.

Through work that ranges from broad conceptual studies to administrative and technical assistance, Institute researchers contribute to the stock of knowledge available to guide decisionmaking in the public interest.

Conclusions or opinions expressed in Institute publications are those of the authors and do not necessarily reflect the views of officers or trustees of the Institute, advisory groups, or any organizations that provide financial support to the Institute.

To my family, near and far,
for their love, encouragement, and
unwavering support

Contents

Acknowledgments

This book came about because of my three years as director of the District of Columbia's Child and Family Services Agency, which made me want to write about the struggles and successes of large public agencies. I owe enormous gratitude to every one of my colleagues, to the agency's hard-working social workers and supervisors, and to those who came before me and wrestled with the persistent difficulties in the agency's path. For the satisfactions recounted in the book, of good work accomplished by a dedicated team, and for insights generously shared during the years since, I particularly want to thank Uma Ahluwalia, Harold Beebout, the late Sharlynn Bobo, Ronnie Charles, Brenda Donald, Roque Gerald, Mindy Good, Carolyn Graham, Andrea Guy, Marti Knisley, John Koskinen, Janet Maher, and Michele Rosenberg, among many other District and CFSA colleagues. Of these talented public servants, four— Brenda Donald, Uma Ahluwalia, the late Sharlynn Bobo, and Roque Gerald—also deserve gratitude for taking on the difficult job of agency director after the years chronicled here.

For their thoughtful and constructive work while I was at CFSA and their wisdom since, I also want to thank Judith Meltzer, court monitor for the District's child welfare reform litigation; Marcia Lowry, lead plaintiffs' attorney; Margie Chalofsky, foster parent advocate; and Lee Satterfield, Chief Judge of the D.C. Superior Court. I owe special thanks to Mayor Anthony Williams, a former foster child himself, who cared deeply about the agency and trusted me to lead it. Most of all, I want to thank Grace Lopes. As the mayor's special counsel for receiverships and later general counsel, she was crucial to our work at CFSA. Since then, her unwavering interest and willingness to read, comment, and debate have kept me focused on the book's core questions.

For the District story, I could rely on my own records and recollections, tested at times against the recollections of others just mentioned. For the other case studies, though, I relied on the generosity and openness of those I interviewed, who talked with me at length and willingly shared materials. For the Alabama story, I am grateful to Margaret Bonham, Marty Beyer, Ira Burnim, Ivor Groves, Andy Hornsby, Jerry Milner, James Tucker, and Paul Vincent. For the Utah story, I am grateful to Richard Anderson, Robin Arnold-Williams, Ken Patterson, Leecia Welch, and, again, Paul Vincent, who never turned down my requests to ask him just a few more questions. In New York City, Linda Gibbs, John Mattingly, and Nicholas Scoppetta took time from demanding schedules to talk with me.

I owe an enormous debt also to the experts who offered insights and specialized knowledge essential to the book. To select the sites, I interviewed child welfare and family services experts with a broad national view, asking them to suggest locations and to comment on selection criteria. While none bears responsibility for my choices, all provided important insights: MaryLee Allen, Rob Geen, Marcia Lowry, Judith Meltzer, Wanda Mial, Jerry Milner, Jolie Bain Pillsbury, Matthew Stagner, Carol Spigner, Mark Testa, and Paul Vincent. MaryLee Allen also provided invaluable comments on the recommendations. Jolie Pillsbury clarified my thinking about the leadership chapter, and Marcia Calicchia spent innumerable hours suggesting sources and providing comments on the same chapter. Lively discussions with both of them, as well as their ongoing enthusiasm, helped keep me going. Robert Behn offered early advice on structure, and Shelley Metzenbaum provided insight about performance management.

Both experts and mentors, Lisbeth Schorr and Barbara Blum are sources of inspiration to me for their lifelong commitment to improving children's lives and were early advisors as I began to shape these ideas. Sadly, two other colleagues and friends whose ideas influenced the book are not here to see it published. Mary Bourdette's passion for the most vulnerable children and families shaped her career, and she was equally passionate about the District of Columbia. A colleague during my years at HHS, she helped persuade me to take the CFSA job and then put her nationally known talent for legislative advocacy at CFSA's service. Jane Knitzer gave generously of her unparalleled expertise about young children and made time to comment on the recommendations even while she was coping with terminal illness.

The Annie E. Casey Foundation and its president, Doug Nelson, as well as Frank Farrow, Michael Laracy, and John Mattingly, provided both financial and moral support. John Mattingly, at the Foundation before his appointment as New York City's children's services commissioner, first suggested the idea of comparing other case studies with my experience in the District. To that suggestion, I owe the structure of the book. Doug Nelson and Frank Farrow encouraged my writing from long before I had a coherent idea to share with them. I also want to thank the William T. Grant Foundation and its president, Robert Granger, for essential early support.

Since 2004, the Urban Institute has provided a wonderful environment to write and unstinting financial and intellectual support. I am particularly grateful to Robert Reischauer, the Institute's president, for welcoming me to the Institute not once but twice. Kathleen Courrier has been a stimulating and thoughtful editor, with a pitch-perfect sense of what advice would help most. Among many wise colleagues at Urban, I am particularly grateful to Jennifer Macomber for her deep knowledge of child welfare and willingness to share it. Pamela Holcomb, Pamela Winston, and Rosa Maria Castaneda contributed methodological advice and help with site selection; Laura Wherry tracked down newspaper articles; Erica Zielewski helped me sort out the federal data sources, and she and Amelia Hawkins checked and updated references. From the Urban Institute Press, Fiona Blackshaw, Serena Lei, and Scott Forrey and his production team have eased the process.

None of those who have helped so generously bear responsibility for the opinions expressed here, nor for any errors of fact or judgment. All are the author's alone.

Finally, I want to thank my family and friends. Many people helped me keep perspective during three intense years at CFSA, including Vicki Perry, a source of sanity over more than 30 years of friendship, and my brother, Dan Golden, and his family. My mother and late father, Hilda and Morris Golden, shaped my interest in what government can do for people who are struggling. Above all, I thank my husband, Bill Frey, for the inspiration of his intellectual creativity and curiosity, for his relentless determination that I would finish the book despite all distractions, and for his bottomless love and support.

1

What Does It Take to Reform Child Welfare?

Reforming Child Welfare is about what government can do for children in danger, children who have been failed by numerous public and private institutions and who have arrived at the last safety net—the public child welfare system. Society counts on parents to keep their children well and safe, but when parents can't or won't, then public child welfare agencies temporarily take on that responsibility.

This book is about how to deliver change in troubled public child welfare agencies. More broadly, it is about reform under difficult circumstances, including a history of failure, intense public scrutiny, and extremely limited resources. It is also about the national policy changes that would enable state and local agencies to reach a higher bar. Putting agency reform and policy together, *Reforming Child Welfare* is about why we should expect government to work better—and why we need to understand the time, persistence, and skill such improvement requires. Good ideas matter, but good ideas alone do not transform large organizations.

The job of the child welfare agencies at the heart of this book is summarized in federal law as "safety, permanence, and well-being."[1] To protect children's *safety,* agencies operate hotlines to receive reports of abuse or neglect, investigate the reports and assess the family situation in person, determine whether abuse or neglect has occurred, and judge what should happen next to protect the child. Services to protect children may be delivered in their own home, if possible, or through removing them

1

from the home. If children are removed from their parents and placed in temporary homes, then agencies are responsible for developing a plan and coordinating services so children can have *permanent* homes and families as soon as possible, whether with their biological family or through adoption or guardianship. Agencies must also attend to the *well-being* of these vulnerable children and families—their physical and emotional health, children's education and development, and families' stability. Finally, some public agencies, working alone or with community agencies, try to prevent child abuse and neglect by offering support services to families under stress.

A child whose experiences suggest the ways an agency can help is Lora,[2] one of several thousand children involved with Washington, D.C.'s public child welfare agency—the Child and Family Services Agency (CFSA)—in 2003:

> "Lora," age 13, is the oldest child in a sibling group of four. . . . In April 2003, [community agency staff] reported physical abuse of Lora by her stepfather. . . . Lora was removed by CFSA. . . . In June of 2003, Lora reported sexual abuse by the step-father during the time he still resided in the family home. [Her mother] currently is receiving treatment for a blood clot on her brain which resulted from a brutal incident of domestic violence by the stepfather. . . .
>
> [After her mother received a protective order against the stepfather] Lora returned to live with her mother and three siblings in late August 2003. . . . Both mother and daughter feel very positive about their experience with CFSA. They report their current worker has much empathy and concern for the well-being of the family. She offers advice and has provided financial help with school cloth-ing for the children. . . In addition to almost weekly visits to the family home, [the mother] reports that their worker frequently calls to check on the situation in the home. . . .
>
> Since the physical abuse incident in April 2003, many changes for the better have occurred for this family. Physical and financial stability have been achieved by their move to a Public Housing apartment and the beginning of TANF [Temporary Assistance for Needy Families] benefits and services. This mother has begun working on her GED and has clear plans to work toward employment, which will support her family without her having to work 14 to 16 hours a day . . . A wide array of services are being provided to this family . . . [including] family therapy and individual counseling for Lora. . . . Lora's transfer to a new school seemingly has enabled her to start with a fresh slate as far as her past behavioral challenges are concerned.

So far, intervention by the child welfare system in this case seems to have helped turn things around for the child and the family. Lora got back on track academically and emotionally, and the restraining order against her stepfather stopped further abuse. Intervention also influenced her mother's decision to seek help and counseling to keep an abusive partner out of the home, and possibly contributed to the emotional well-being of Lora's three younger siblings, who now grow up in a safer environment. Even if the system has not eliminated the underlying difficulties faced by a mother with very limited education and skills, struggling to support her four children, and wrestling with her past dependence on a violent drug-abusing partner, it has changed the odds in her family's favor.

If government intervention could make this kind of a difference in the lives of children and families routinely, that would be an important achievement from many different perspectives. We might care about the safety and physical and emotional well-being of Lora and other children like her because the test of a society is how well it protects the powerless. We might also care because research suggests links between the early lives of children and their future prospects. How well society responds may affect how well and how long children stay in school, how likely girls are to become teen mothers, and how much children will contribute to society, as workers and parents, when they grow up. Finally, we might care because we know that our families and friends might need such help some day. From all these perspectives, the importance of serving vulnerable children dwarfs the obstacles, however great.

Yet, child welfare systems far too often fail to make this kind of difference for children and families. Too often, children are seriously injured or die at the hands of their parents, sometimes in circumstances where the child welfare system should have known that something was seriously wrong. At the same time, too many children who enter the child welfare system leave it damaged by their experience. Some who are removed from their homes linger in temporary settings for years, grieving for the loss of their families, falling behind in school as they are bounced among foster care placements, and leaving care with no permanent ties. Other children find themselves trying to grow up in institutions, sometimes endangered by abuse from other children or staff, or deprived of caring, loving relationships. And too often, fragile families who look for help—substance-abuse treatment or help fighting depression—can't get it until the situation spirals into abuse or neglect, and maybe not even then. As a result of these problems and more, child welfare agencies in about 30 states have been ordered to operate under the supervision of a federal or state court (Child Welfare League of America and ABA Center on Children and the Law 2005).

Agencies operate in a delicate zone, where national and state legislation authorize intrusive government involvement in families only when children are seriously in danger. As a result, agencies may fail by taking too little action or too much. A Pulitzer Prize–winning *Washington Post* series in 2001 documented eight years of child fatalities in the District, offering an indictment of failure to act that is often echoed around the country:

> From 1993 to 2000, 229 children died after they or their families came to the attention of the District's child protection system because of neglect or abuse complaints. In dozens of cases, police officers and social workers responsible for the safety of children failed to take the most basic steps to shield them from harm. . . . at least nine D.C. children . . . perished after police officers and social workers conducted incomplete investigations or left the children to fend for themselves with violent, neglectful, or unstable parents or guardians.[3]

The same year, the *Salt Lake Tribune* described Utah state legislators angry about the opposite issue, excessive intrusiveness into families:

> More than 20 child welfare advocates, lawmakers, and attorneys are calling for sweeping changes in Utah's child welfare system . . . "We have a problem in this state," said Rep. Tom Hatch. . . . "We have several parents raising legitimate concerns that DCFS is removing children from homes unjustifiably . . . I've had constituents call me up with horror stories." Rep. Paul Ray (R-Clearfield) . . . said, "When we have an organization that's breaking up families, and we have to pass laws to protect people . . . it's time to reorganize."[4]

The intense public attention reflects the potentially devastating effects of both kinds of failures—children's death or injury when public help is too little, too late and family disruption and emotional devastation for children and parents when it is over-intrusive. One recent review of the national evidence argues that "It is hard to avoid the conclusion that the American child protective services system is investigating many families unnecessarily. . . . At the same time, however, CPS [child protective services] may be intervening too lightly, and providing too few services to some families" (Waldfogel 1998, 26–27).

Many of the most public tragedies and failures cannot be laid at the feet of a single agency; drug abuse, family violence, and troubled neighborhoods have complex causes and no simple solutions. Yet even if one agency could not have solved the problem, could the system as a whole have made a difference? The grave consequences of failure make any lessons that improve services critical.

With so much at stake, the task of improving child welfare services is urgent, and the scale is large. In 2007, state child welfare agencies received

3.2 million referrals involving 5.8 million children (U.S. Department of Health and Human Services [HHS], Administration on Children, Youth and Families [ACYF] 2009). After screening and investigation, the agencies found that 794,000 children had been abused or neglected, and removed about 21 percent of them from their homes for some period. The remaining 5 million children, who were referred but not found to have been abused and neglected, are often in very precarious home situations, and seriously behind other children developmentally and behaviorally.

How to Identify Lessons That Improve Agency Performance

This book offers lessons to help child welfare agencies to work better for children and families. Unfortunately, it isn't obvious how to identify which lessons will be effective in large organizations. Research on services and programs that work reveals evidence about how to help children and families that is important and useful in its context (see chapter 4 for a survey). But it falls short of this book's goal, which is to identify ideas that have been tested in large public child welfare agencies, not just small pilot projects. To find such ideas, researchers need to grapple with the agencies' real-life environment and scale: delivering services through hundreds or thousands of stressed frontline workers, in a tense public and political context, navigating complex relationships with a half-dozen big public agencies and private service organizations, and struggling to get city- or statewide personnel, budget, and contracting systems to help rather than hinder progress. Consequently, my interest is in ideas that have been tested in the worst large public systems, those with a history of persistent failure. As a former child welfare official, I want to understand how to raise the bar for all child welfare systems—how to make improvement possible for the most vulnerable families, even those in the most troubled settings.

Given my goal, a core method of this book is to analyze examples where a large and deeply troubled public child welfare system has turned around its services and results in measurable ways that outside observers can document. *Reforming Child Welfare* aims to delve beneath the surface in these turnarounds, examining the reasons for their historical failures, the multiple dimensions of the pattern-breaking strategies, the successes that they have chalked up, and their unfinished business. All child welfare systems have remaining failures, but those performing well should be aware of and striving to fix them. Exploring the patterns of change in different locations, and comparing the findings with broader research about what works in child welfare agencies and in other complex organizations, points to what must be done next to build on these still-too-rare successes.

I look closely at three examples but touch on several others. The first example is a personal account of change in the District of Columbia's child welfare agency during three crucial turnaround years. I was the director during those years as the agency moved from court-ordered receivership to much better, though still flawed, performance. Writing from the inside makes it possible to analyze, in retrospect, what we thought we were doing, what it felt like, and what led us to good or bad choices. The advantage of a personal story is its richness, leading to insights about both setbacks and progress. At the same time, the lessons might not apply to other places: child welfare systems differ considerably by jurisdiction, and the District of Columbia, with its unique legal structure and history, might seem the most distinctive of all. In addition, the subjectivity of a personal story, the flip side of its richness, might mean that the lessons I draw are biased or just wrong.

To complement the D.C. case study, I examine two other success stories in Alabama and Utah. These two additional case studies of child welfare turnarounds allow me to test my impressions and hypotheses in two different settings. I picked Alabama and Utah as the second and third examples after interviewing about a dozen national experts and reviewing court reports and other evidence. I was interested only in dramatic, documentable turnarounds: systems that had started off very bad and got better, not good systems that had enhanced the quality of their work. My criterion for a turnaround was evidence of great strides over time, not evidence that no problems remained, since even much-improved systems would still have problems to solve.

I initially chose three locations to study, mostly because information pointing to a turnaround was available and consistent. I narrowed the examples down to Alabama and Utah where I was able to interview 5 to 10 leaders and review media coverage, court filings, and published reports. In the third of the originally planned sites, New York City, I was able to interview only a handful of leaders, so I do not try to tell its full story.

I also draw on the national perspective I gained as the federal official overseeing child welfare policy in the Clinton administration,[5] on national data and research findings about child welfare and vulnerable children and families, and on research about management and leadership in public and private organizations. These broader perspectives help me frame and extend the site lessons, fill gaps, and distinguish between findings consistent with prior research and anomalies in need of additional exploration or interpretation. To address subjectivity, I used documentary evidence (court reports and newspaper articles) to supplement findings and interviews. I also tested my insights and lessons on colleagues from across the country, looking for hints about which findings had broad relevance and application. Most often, I found gasps of recognition, because while the specifics of the political and bureaucratic situation might be different, many failing agencies share the underlying problems—such as the inability to generate or use accurate data—that I found in the District.

It's Not Hopeless: Success in Child Welfare

Talking with many people about this book's theme, I have encountered two kinds of skepticism. First, many people suspect the situation is hopeless. If it weren't, how could it so often happen that newspapers report a scandal or tragedy, an agency vows to reform, and yet another tragedy occurs a year or two later, under circumstances that suggest nothing has changed? And if it weren't hopeless, why would we see the same recurring problems—social worker turnover, high caseloads, and failed decisionmaking, when children go home to dangerous parents or are removed from loving parents? Child welfare administrators can also come to feel success is impossible: they do their best, yet still find themselves failing and under attack.

The second kind of skepticism argues that success ought to be easy. Interestingly, the two views—that success is impossible and that a single obvious idea alone should save the day—sometimes coexist: it is impossible now, but it would be easy if only we had the political will or spent enough money to support reform, or if we replaced bleeding-heart social workers with tough policemen who aren't fooled by parents' promises to change.

Neither claim is true. Success in child welfare is not impossible, as evidenced by important recent progress, both local and national. And success is not easy, for a whole host of reasons. Understanding the complexity of the task is necessary to design and deliver the right local, state, and national policy and system changes to make things better for children.

Child welfare agencies can make a positive difference in individual cases, as suggested by Lora's story, and in children's lives across communities and states. Over the past decade, successful child-welfare reform strategies have emerged in both urban and rural systems that were once viewed as disastrous. While it is too soon to declare victory, these programs are much better than they were before, in significant ways that affect child welfare. Strong and credible evidence shows improvements in basic capacity, quality of services, and results for children and families. Improved capacity means, for example, lower caseloads for social workers and quicker investigations of abuse or neglect reports. Better quality means, for example, that families struggling to care for their children are more likely to find services and community support to help prevent abuse and neglect; social workers know children and families better, visit them often, and work with their extended families, teachers, and others active in their lives; and more children who cannot live safely at home live in nurturing foster families, not institutions. And in programs with better results, children who cannot live with their biological families are less likely to have to move among temporary foster homes and more likely to move quickly to a permanent home with a relative or adoptive family.

Struggles and Progress in the District of Columbia

In 1995, the District of Columbia's child welfare agency was removed from city government control and placed in receivership by the federal court, after a long history of failure—despite the best efforts of many deeply committed social workers, foster and adoptive parents, and community partners. But, in 2001, the commitment of a mayor, who had himself been a foster child, converged with the long-term involvement of the federal court to create an opportunity for change. I became director at that moment of opportunity, and by the time I left three years later, the agency had achieved measurable, though clearly incomplete and fragile, progress on behalf of children and families. During those years, I had the chance to work with an extraordinary team, in the agency and in the mayor's office. Together, we learned many lessons, often painfully, about striving to reshape a child welfare system so it can live up to the values of the individuals who work in it, the expectations of the citizens who fund it, and—hardest of all—the hopes and needs of the children and families it serves.

In August 2002, I got off an airplane at Washington's Reagan National Airport, fresh from a week of hiking in the mountains of Glacier National Park in Montana. It was the first real break I had taken in the 14 months since I had become director of the District's newly created Child and Family Services Agency (CFSA). The 100 degree blast of a summer heat wave hit me as I left the airport, and I came as close as I ever have to turning around, buying a ticket back to the mountains, and leaving Washington behind forever. More than just the sapping combination of heat and humidity, it was the feeling that I could no longer face what I knew lay ahead of me the next day at CFSA: the same internal and external battles that I had left behind a week earlier; the same dread of the next crisis, when we would discover once again that we had failed to prevent a tragedy; the same sense of responsibility for failing so many children; and the same anger of so many deeply committed social workers, foster and adoptive parents, and even members of my senior team, directed either at each other or at me when our best efforts failed to create the change we sought.

I feared that my staff and I were losing our struggle to keep ourselves focused on long-term change, on escaping the legacy of decades of neglect, and that I might be losing perspective and with it my sense of energy and joy in the work. Part of what had drained us all was the newspaper coverage of failures: in April, Maryland's threat to send children in foster families back to the District; in May, a child's death at the hands of her father; in July and August, a series of articles and commentaries on sexual activity among boys at a group home. There had been important successes over the past several months, too. Many more young children were living with families rather than in dormitory-like group homes, and early steps had been taken to develop new licensing requirements to protect children in group homes and foster settings. Even the situation in Maryland had been solved without uprooting the children. But none of us could savor the achievements, even for a moment. Two days after my return from vacation, I sat in my office waiting for union leaders to come by and tell me why their membership was so furious they were threatening a walkout.

A month after my vacation, in September 2002, we received some gratifying news. The court monitor, who conducted independent reviews of our performance for the federal court, told us we had passed our first test: we had met 15 of 20 measurable performance standards required by the Court. Among the most important changes were major improvements in the number of adoptions, the timeliness of abuse and neglect investigations, the proportion of children with up-to-date case plans, and the number of young children in family settings, rather than group homes. Sizing up these improvements, the federal judge ended our probationary status because CFSA had clearly demonstrated in 15 months that we could reform our system. After some very dark months, we had succeeded against all odds.

A year and a half later, in April 2004, I looked back on the summer of 2002 as a turning point in our ability to make significant agency changes that made a fundamental difference for children. In summer and fall 2002, we finally came up with the right recruitment and tracking strategies to sharply reduce social worker caseloads. While we couldn't yet see it, we were solving a painful problem that had devastated morale and services for years. In March 2003, we had about 270 licensed social workers on board, compared with about 240 in October 2002, and average caseloads declined from 36 to 24. By December 2003, the average caseload was down to 17—half of what it had been 14 months earlier. This sharp reduction in caseloads dramatically improved morale and created the potential for better services and results.

Over the same months, during the winter of 2002–03, we instituted rigorous new licensing standards for facilities that provided group care to children, closing a facility that was not on par. At last, people started to believe change was possible. By the following summer, we could honestly say that no child was staying overnight in the CFSA office building— a once-common practice in most overloaded child welfare agencies around the country. The stress in the pit of my stomach at four in the morning started to ease.

Our information system got better and better at telling us what was working and where we needed to change course. By mid-2003, we were regularly reviewing social worker visits to children in each of our units and our private partner agencies, licensing progress for our foster homes, social worker caseloads, and much more. In fall 2003, a team of outside experts examined 40 CFSA cases chosen at random, interviewing children, parents, foster parents, social workers, supervisors, and others involved in the cases. The team observed that, based on the reviewers' prior experience, CFSA had improved significantly in "many observable ways" (Center for the Study of Social Policy [CSSP] 2004b, 9).

In a summary report dated February 9, 2004, the court monitor gave an overview of agency performance:

> On balance, the record of accomplishments in the past six months is considerable and reflects an organization that is committed to positive change and has the leadership and skills to carry it out. . . . This is not to say that there are not serious issues remaining to be identified and resolved. However, the climate for working together on behalf of children and families is very different now than several years ago. (CSSP 2004a, 25)

So in April 2004, as I prepared to leave the agency, I could reflect on these recent reports and agree that there was much work left to do, but also that the agency's climate and approach had changed in fundamental ways that meant better outcomes for children. When the director of a well-respected private social work agency in the District told me at my goodbye party that the joy had come back to her job because "now, we are helping families, doing what we came here to do," I was deeply moved, and profoundly glad that I hadn't headed back to the mountains nearly two years before.

Turnaround in Alabama

Alabama's child welfare system was sued in 1988 on behalf of a young boy named R.C., who was removed from the home of his recently divorced father after the child welfare agency received a report of neglect. R.C., already distraught from the divorce, was further distressed by the separation from his father. As he grew more unhappy, his behavior got worse, and he was moved to more rigid and distant institutional settings and put on more medication. Each time, R.C.'s behavior worsened.

The suit was the culmination of several years of deepening dissatisfaction with child welfare in Alabama, including a governor's commission that found deep failures and made remedial recommendations, none of which were enacted by the legislature. To observers at the time, the R.C. case epitomized a system that damaged children deeply by treating families dismissively and failing to provide services that might have kept children safely at home. According to case reviews completed during the lawsuit's discovery phase, the system also removed children arbitrarily, moved them around frequently, placed them in faraway group homes, and did not hold social workers or the agency accountable.

After a consent decree settled the R.C. case in 1991, Alabama embarked on a path toward a very different kind of child welfare system. The path was certainly not smooth. One governor along the way tried to end the reform by appointing a commissioner who opposed it and appealing the settlement order that provided its framework. But when the federal courts threw out the state's appeal and the anti-reform commissioner resigned under pressure from many directions, reforms continued.

In 2007, 19 years after the case was filed, the court recognized the system's progress and ended the case. Measured results for children, and in-depth reviews of the work of social workers and the experiences of children and families, both suggested dramatic improvement. In 2008, the U.S. Circuit Court of Appeals supported this decision, rejecting the plaintiffs' appeal and ending the case. Everyone, including the plaintiffs, agreed that "We have a far, far better system in this state than we had 20 years ago when the lawsuit was filed."[6]

Transformation in Utah

Reform in Utah was also triggered by a lawsuit, filed in 1992, as widespread dissatisfaction with child welfare services came to a head. According to media reports, advocate observations, and the litigation itself, children were unsafe at home and in foster care, and workers had heavy caseloads and not enough training to make good decisions. Like Alabama's system, Utah's system was decentralized, "laissez-faire" in its absence of account-ability, and lacking consistent standards for all counties.

But Utah did not achieve immediate gains on settling the case in 1994. While the state enacted new child abuse legislation and hired many case-workers, juvenile court judges, legal advocates for children, and lawyers to represent social workers, progress on the measures in the court order stagnated. Morale was terrible, and despite threats of punishment for fail-ure to achieve the court-imposed standards, basic measures of quality—like the number of caseworker visits to children and success in foster parent recruitment—did not improve. Why didn't the court settlement have an early effect, as it had in Alabama? The reasons for this failure were a puzzle, especially since the state had just spent sizable sums to hire social workers and bring down caseloads.

By 1997, the judge, the plaintiffs, and the state all agreed that something needed to change. And it did. The judge appointed a court monitor, who proposed a somewhat different approach to state implementation of the settlement, and the governor's newly appointed cabinet secretary and child welfare director ended a run of short-timers. Ten years later, in May 2007, the parties to the Utah court case found that "significant reforms to Utah's child welfare system have been achieved" along with "significant progress in improving case practices and ensuring strong system performance."[7] The parties agreed that they would terminate the lawsuit in December 2008, if all went well in the last year. It did go well, so the judge ended the case for good in an order signed on January 5, 2009.[8]

National Examples of Success

Nationally, the child welfare system's persistent failures have driven repeated waves of reform. But if reform sometimes seems to be a constant cycle yielding no results, children nationwide are better off in several ways than they were a decade ago.

For starters, children have a better chance of living in a permanent family if they cannot go home to their biological family. Two important changes are the dramatic increase in adoptions of children from foster care—from about 25,000 in the mid-1990s to 50,000 or more each year from 2000 to 2006—and the expansion of subsidized guardianship programs, which now exist in more than 30 states and the District of Columbia (Children's Defense Fund 2004) and have just been incorporated into federal law.[9] Subsidized guardianship allows relatives to receive financial support to care for a child permanently, without completely severing the child's legal ties with a biological parent, as an adoption would. For example, a grandmother can become her grandchild's legal guardian and receive help from the child welfare system without cutting the child's parent out of the picture. Like adoption, guardianship offers a child a permanent, lifelong family.

Another national success is the dramatic increase in the quantity and quality of information available on the child welfare system and the children in it. When I started at the U.S. Department of Health and Human Services (HHS) in 1991, child welfare was widely regarded as far behind other human services fields in information collection. Some state and federal officials argued that it could never catch up, that the inherent complexity of child welfare made it impossible to collect useful management information that is well-aligned with goals.

But such worst-case thinking turned out to be false. Even though states and advocates have many legitimate criticisms of federal information collection and performance review, the improvements of the past 15 years are striking. First, much-improved automated information systems in many states now keep track of children and of agency actions, allowing accountability for such key performance measures as the number of temporary homes children live in, the likelihood that they are living in families and not group shelters, the number of children in a social worker's caseload, and the likelihood of repeat abuse. Second, qualitative reviews, modeled on Alabama's system, now offer a structured look at the quality of day-to-day practices in each state and the results, as seen by individual children and families. These reviews form the core of the federal government's official look at state performance, affording a far better glimpse of real-life practices than simply examining sample case files ever could. Third, new research tools—in particular, the National Survey of Child and Adolescent Wellbeing (NSCAW), a large national sample of children involved with the system—provide revealing data that can help policymakers improve child welfare services, such as how children are doing developmentally before and after they enter the system.

Yet It Will Never Be Easy

When I set out to write this book, one of the central puzzles that motivated me was why each step along the way to reform was so painful and difficult, despite the fact that agency staff and stakeholders agreed with the broad goals (if not the specific steps) of reform in the District of Columbia's child welfare system. It took 18 months to hire more staff and start reducing caseloads and improving social worker morale, even though I had resources and early commitment from the mayor and District Council to help with hiring. It took two and a half years to end the practice of children sleeping in the office building; social workers, foster parents, private providers, and police officers, desperate for help, continued to bring children in late at night, even though none of them would have said the office was a fitting place for children to stay. The system's failures were so complicated and persistent that they defeated the good intentions of many individuals. And, the resulting cycle of good people burning out and drifting away because they couldn't "do what we came here to do" only made things worse.

Trying to understand these patterns and the possible routes to a solution, I kept asking myself several related questions. What underlying forces push a child welfare system to this point of failure, where deeply committed people simply cannot make the system consistent with their values? How can you break such a cycle? What ingredients of reform finally crack the iceberg and make such systemic change possible?

As I began studying other successes, the theme of complex systems that defied simple solutions emerged. In Alabama, many of the same social workers and managers who drove the reform had been part of the old, failed system for years, always believing they were doing the best they could. What spurred the change if it wasn't new people? In Utah, major early steps by the state, including a sizable investment in hiring social workers and legal advocates for children, didn't help performance. What mysterious ingredient was added after 1997? Nationally, legislation that now pours hundreds of millions of dollars into subsidies for parents who adopt children from foster care was hardly used at all in its first decade. Again, what changed?

It is important to answer these questions, to better understand why changing failed child welfare systems is hard, and what pieces have to align to make success possible. If reform appears to rest on oversimplified solutions—the budget in one jurisdiction, the number of social workers in another, replacing the leaders in a third—yet never succeeds, then the public, the elected officials who oversee child welfare agencies, and the press are likely to become deeply cynical about whether anything can work. That risk makes it important to understand not only the individual components of success, but also how the pieces coalesce to change the patterns of failure.

Answering these questions requires looking not only at the world of child welfare itself but also at what researchers have learned about public and private organizations more broadly. Some of what is so difficult in child welfare can be found in the tragedies of the families involved, the challenges of achieving success on the timetable of a child's development, and the limits of knowledge about what works to prevent or stop abuse and neglect. But other answers are lodged in leadership and organizational challenges that cut across public and private organizations: specifically, how to respond and learn flexibly, when a history of failure colors everyone's reactions, when organizational goals and missions are complex and contradictory, when multiple partners have to work together to achieve desired results, and when multiple bosses mete out punishment for failures.

By taking this extra step and comparing the problems and the solutions from the child welfare sites with the problems and solutions researchers have noted in other organizations undergoing rapid change, we can understand better what strategies work in the child welfare context. For example, we can see how reformers' approaches to using information to change a stuck organizational culture compare with similar strategies in city governments, police departments, and private corporations. These comparisons also allow us to look for lessons from child welfare agencies that could, in turn, prove useful for reform of other troubled organizations. Because the child welfare settings are so hard, and in particular because they have such extreme public scrutiny and complex political settings, they offer insights that can likely help reformers in other tough public sectors orchestrate successful change.

The Personal and the Analytical in This Book

Since child welfare is about children and families who have often experienced devastating tragedy, even if they have also displayed astonishing resilience, it is by its nature very emotional for everyone involved. Many people who have encountered the child welfare system—whether as an abused child, a foster parent, a social worker, or a community advocate—have written powerful and deeply personal books drawn from those experiences. This book also offers a personal perspective, drawing on the experience of trying to spearhead change in an agency that had been under fire for more than a decade. Initially, I worried that it would be presumptuous to write about my own experience, when the real test of the system is the experience of the families and children in it, and of social workers on the front lines. But I concluded that just as the school principal's or the superintendent's experience offers insights into school reform, different from those of students or teachers, so my viewpoint that comes from trying to lead change provides unique lessons and insights.

The next challenge was finding out if those lessons and experiences contained some truth that was potentially applicable beyond my immediate context. My way around this dilemma was to explore and compare turnarounds in two other geographic settings. When insights in one setting didn't hold true in another, I looked for differences in the underlying circumstances (such as the political setting, the agency's history, or the characteristics of families) and in the leaders' strategies for change that might explain the apparent contradiction and lead to other lessons.

In addition, my experience overseeing child welfare programs in HHS also shaped my perspective. It gave me a sense of the context for child welfare in the 50 states and a perspective on which themes are national in scope and which are unique to a jurisdiction.

Even more pervasive as a theme in this book, though, is that my federal experience put children's development front and center in my thinking about child welfare. At HHS, I also oversaw the federal government's largest child development programs, particularly Head Start and child care. When we convened the nation's foremost researchers to help us design Early Head Start, a new program for babies and toddlers from the poorest families, I had a front-row seat as the experts laid out new scientific discoveries about children's early development. Their expert insights about what to do and what not to do when family settings are less than optimal have fundamentally shaped my perspective on child welfare.

Finally, having led at a time of change in a federal agency before moving to the local level, I brought many "compare and contrast" perspectives. What would it be like working with the District Council, compared to Congress? With the mayor's budget office, compared to the Office of Management and Budget? And perhaps most central to this book and to my task at CFSA, I wondered about the analogy to my experience with the federal workforce, where I had found that part of my job was to empower the many good people who came to human services work because they wanted to make a difference, yet had felt frustrated, stifled, and defeated over the years. Would I find the same thing with the District's social workers, who had chosen such a challenging job and work environment? Would peeling back layers of frustration and cynicism free up their original passion and motivation, so we could make far-reaching changes for the District's children? The next chapter begins that story.

2

Building the Airplane While Flying It
The District of Columbia

On May 14, 2001, I began working at the Child and Family Services Agency in Washington, D.C., in a transitional role. In mid-June, the receivership officially ended, and I became director. A half-dozen vignettes give the flavor of the agency in its early months, when every day brought a new emergency.

At 10:00 one night, I sat in an office with some of the agency's senior program staff trying to figure out what to do about the 20 children on the first floor of our office building. The boys and girls of all ages had either been taken from their parents or had left, or been ejected from, foster homes or group care facilities, and they had no place else to stay that night. They were crowded into a space filled with cots and staffed by two or three aides. A few weeks earlier, when I was downstairs late at night, I had seen the terror of the younger children as an older boy screamed in anger. It was not a situation that I wanted to be responsible for, but I was.

Nothing about the situation, or any of the choices available to us at that moment, was consistent with what we knew was best for children. We all knew that the trauma of abuse and neglect was compounded by chaotic settings and abrupt moves, that children did best in families, that all transitions should be prepared for, and that crowded settings with children of all ages and both genders posed additional dangers for children, beyond those that brought them there. Yet, we were not acting in accordance with any of those findings. Most likely, the children downstairs were going to spend the night either in the office building or in an emergency shelter. We just did not see any other choices at that moment.

Also in those early months, one of our lawyers burst into my office at 6 p.m. on Friday to tell me a local Superior Court judge had just sent a social worker to jail for contempt because she had failed repeatedly to submit a report on time. (State and local judges in every state make key decisions about children's removal from their homes and oversee children's care while they are in foster care, with child welfare agency social workers providing recommendations and reports.) The judge apparently believed that he had run out of options to get timely reports, and he thought he was doing the best thing for children. But the social worker was a single parent, unable to arrange for her own children's care on the weekend. And the decision represented the worst fear of the agency's social workers, who joked grimly about the need to carry a toothbrush for appearances before certain judges who were viewed as hostile.

As soon as I heard, I asked one of the mayor's most senior attorneys to join me and our agency attorney, and we rushed over to the court to talk to the judge before he left for the weekend. After we pleaded, he rescinded the decision, but by then, the social worker had already been processed at the jail. It took us until 10 p.m. to free her. When social workers heard the story Monday morning, they wanted to walk out in protest.

That first summer at CFSA, I spent an evening shadowing a night-shift social worker in the investigations unit as he responded to allegations of neglect called in to the agency's hotline. We drove across Washington to check out an allegation that a mother had left several young children, including an infant and a toddler, home alone for hours. She returned while we were at her building and said she had gone shopping with friends and had told her young daughter to ask a neighbor to look after her and her siblings. When we went inside, we saw that she was caring for the children in a grimy one-bedroom apartment filled with cockroaches, but she had food for the children in her refrigerator.

An old friend who had heard the mother was in trouble came looking for her and the children. He and his girlfriend had been neighbors to the young mother and her family until very recently, when they had moved several miles to a better apartment building. While living next door, they had spent a lot of time with the young woman and her children, taking the children on outings and babysitting when she needed a break—serving almost as surrogate parents to the young woman and grandparents to the children. Once they moved, though, the distance and logistics became a barrier to a family with young children and no car.

The social worker chose not to substantiate neglect, a reasonable decision based on the available information. He saw the adequate food in the refrigerator as evidence that the mother was caring for her children and not spending her money on drugs, and he saw the dirty, cockroach-filled apartment as mainly her landlord's failure. He also persuaded the mentoring couple to renew their commitment to helping the family. But even though taking the mother to court for neglect seemed inappropriate under these circumstances, the most powerful reaction I had that evening was sadness for the whole family: without some kind of intensive community services, it was hard to be optimistic about the children's future prospects, given their stressed and isolated young mother's dismal economic prospects.

In May, I found myself on a stage with the mayor, listening to foster parent representatives telling him their concerns. Foster parents recounted social workers who never returned calls or responded to crises; a lack of basic health and mental health services for children; arbitrary decisions about children's placement and removal; insensitivity by social workers, lawyers, and judges to the special circumstances of kin foster parents; and many other concerns. As I walked through the room afterward, I also heard individual grievances, like the grandmother battling for care of a child living with another relative she considered irresponsible. She had cast the social worker as the person who could solve everything, if only she would understand who was telling the truth and who was manipulating her.

As I met with agency staff to develop our responses to the foster parents' concerns expressed at the mayor's meeting, I was taken aback by their approach. Neither callous nor cynical, it was, however, unrealistic. I had assumed that with complex problems like these, we would have to pick one or two realistic changes, involve foster parents in a process that allowed us to achieve results together, and build trust and momentum, over time, for a bigger agenda. But CFSA staff proposed plans to solve all the foster parents' problems in two or three weeks. They were sure the mayor's office would accept nothing less, and they seemed to prefer a grand plan, whether or not it could realistically be implemented. I thought this might be because their prior experience counseled that nothing would work, so a grand plan at least showed good intentions. But despite the history, I would have to convince them, and the outside world, of my quite different conviction: that children would be better served by a realistic plan than by an ambitious one that never materialized.

The *Washington Post*'s view of reform in these early months reinforced the view that nothing could work. In September, the *Post* published a major series on the deaths of children associated with the District's child welfare system from 1993 to 2000.[1] The reporters who wrote the series continued afterwards to track children's deaths during the fall of 2001, leading to an October 27, 2001, editorial arguing that nothing had changed and nothing would ever change:

> The problem of small numbers of workers juggling larger and larger caseloads is at least 10 years old. So are the promises of reform. This week Olivia Golden, the Child and Family Services' latest director, said she is overhauling the agency and will use her increased budget to recruit more social workers and double the number of lawyers to back up her new team of managers. Sounds as familiar as the continuing accounts of children dying while under the city's protection.[2]

This editorial appeared just four weeks after the new CFSA Establishment Act transformed the District's system for responding to child abuse and neglect by creating a newly unified CFSA. It came just four months after the District resumed control of the agency and I was appointed. So, however poor the agency's historical record, it seemed early for the *Washington Post* to be so sweepingly cynical about change.

In the early weeks at the agency, I tried to find reliable information about agency performance and the circumstances of children. There wasn't any.

For example, we needed to know how many children under age 6 lived in group homes—dormitory-like settings that housed anywhere from 6 to 20 or more babies and young children—rather than families. (Whatever the number had been at the end of the receivership, the federal court required us to cut it in half because of the broad consensus that young children thrive best in families and that housing them in institutions could be damaging.)

That might seem like simple information to collect, but we could not produce an accurate number. An automated report supposedly tabulated the number every month, but it was clearly wrong: one large group home alone cared for more young children than were shown on the report. When the court monitor pulled together all our paper documents, she found that 99 children under age 6 were in group homes as of May 31, 2001, compared with a far smaller total shown on the automated report. I couldn't figure out why the reports persistently showed a number we knew was wrong.

A Brief History of Child Welfare in the District: How Did We Get Here?

Child welfare programs that failed to help the District's impoverished and vulnerable families went back decades, beginning well before the District gained some control over its own government and policy with home rule in 1973.[3] But after years of desperate failure and inadequate resources in the District's child welfare agency, the federal courts became involved when the *LaShawn A. et al. v. Barry et al.* litigation was filed in 1989. Federal District judge Thomas Hogan's 1991 opinion holding the District liable summarizes the case as follows:

> It is a case about thousands of children who . . . rely on the District to provide them with food, shelter, and day-to-day care. It is about beleaguered city employees trying their best to provide these necessities while plagued with excessive caseloads, staff shortages, and budgetary constraints. It is about the failures of an ineptly managed child welfare system, the indifference of the administration . . . and the resultant tragedies for District children relegated to entire childhoods spent in foster care drift. Unfortunately, it is about a lost generation of children whose tragic plight is being repeated every day.[4]

In response to the litigation, the District agreed in 1993 to comply with an 84-page consent decree that detailed every aspect of a successful system. But the District repeatedly failed to live up to these commitments. After trying unsuccessfully to work out an alternative arrangement, Judge Hogan felt he had no choice but to remove child welfare from District government oversight. In 1995, he appointed a receiver, who reported directly to the federal court, to head the agency.

This receivership faced major challenges from the start. The small child welfare division, removed from a larger cabinet-level agency, controlled only fragments of the total child welfare system. The widespread failures that had prevented reform went far beyond its limited reach; as a result, the receivers had only a few pieces of the puzzle in their hands. For example, unlike any state, the District's child welfare agency had responsibility only for child neglect, not abuse. The rules about who was responsible for which children were complex and filled with exceptions, and the whole structure was extraordinarily confusing. Other missing puzzle pieces—crucial responsibilities lodged outside the child welfare agency—were more typical of state child welfare systems, but no less damaging: legal representation for social workers when they went to court to remove a child or argue for a placement or services; authority to license foster or group homes; authority to work across state boundaries when children needed to be placed in Maryland or Virginia suburbs; responsibility for developing contracts to purchase services for children; authority to recruit and hire social workers; and budget and fiscal authority.

Fragmentation this great stymied all action. The head of the child welfare division, and later the receiver, did not control enough parts of the troubled terrain to move ahead, without involving perhaps a half-dozen other organizations in the executive and judicial branches of District government. And, with accountability so hard to trace, many of these organizations found it easier to avoid blame by fixating on the decades-old problems of the child welfare system than to collaborate.

By early 2000, five years of receivership had not resolved the agency's and the system's problems. The death of 23-month-old Brianna Blackmond at the hands of her mother's roommate, after a judge had ordered her back home from foster care in December 1999, highlighted the widespread systemic failures: the judge who sent the child home without a hearing, the social worker who missed the court's deadline for advising that the child should not go home, and a city lawyer who failed to appeal. The case received extensive coverage in the *Washington Post* and attention in Congress, which held hearings and set out to reform the local court system. Overseeing an agency accused of such devastating failure was painful for the federal court, which had become involved to prevent just such failures.

At the same time, the court had an opportunity to work with a new District administration that was committed to running the agency. New mayor Anthony Williams wanted to bring back under District control all the agencies then in court receivership, which also included mental health and corrections, on the grounds that the District should handle its own responsibilities. A foster child himself who was adopted at age 3, Mayor Williams also had an especially strong personal commitment to child welfare.

When Mayor Williams hired a special counsel for receivership to help him return these agencies to the District government control, the federal court monitor overseeing *LaShawn* was prepared to consider the idea. In a consent order issued in October 2000, Judge Hogan laid out the agreements on what the District would have to do to regain the child welfare agency. The requirements of the consent order reflected the structural issues that the judge and the parties to the suit thought most urgent for the District to remedy: passing legislation to unify a broad range of child welfare responsibilities under a stronger and more accountable Child and Family Services Agency, committing sufficient funds to meet the District's obligations, recruiting a new director, and requiring the director to hire a sufficient management team. New legislation to fix the structural problems, called the CFSA Establishment Act, was enacted in April 2001.

Of course, even with statutory changes, past experience fed skepticism about whether the District could do the job. So the court laid out in its October 2000 order a series of tests for the District to pass to end its receivership status. After the District had enacted the required legislation and hired the new director and management team, it would enter a "probationary period" during which it had to achieve 15 of 20 measurable performance targets. If the District met the targets, it would exit probation and resume its responsibility for complying with the 1993 consent decree, for which it would still remain under court supervision. If the District failed, the court would end the experiment with District governance and return the agency to receivership.

Opportunity for Change

As I thought about whether to take the job in the District, I knew that I somehow had to judge whether this history meant that success would be impossible, or just challenging. Were the changes big enough to make success possible? In the end, I decided that this was the right time to seize a rare moment of opportunity.

For one thing, the parties to the litigation, who were all realists, had identified the biggest obstacles to success, and the mayor and District Council had rapidly enacted legislation to remove every one of them. The mayor and the council had created a strong CFSA and solidified its long-fragmented authority, passed a budget increase, and committed to keeping the budget on track in the future. Important in themselves, these changes also made it possible for me to tell others why they should have hope, and invest their own energy in change, despite the perfectly plausible reasons for disbelief.

Second, the consent order required the new director to develop a new management structure and recruit a management team—explicit recognition that no one could do a job like this alone—and the budget negotiations had ensured enough resources for me to fill key jobs without having to let the current managers go. This cushion was especially important because agency morale was bound to be fragile, given the onslaught of public criticism over the past year. Without the additional monetary and staff resources, I might have doomed my relationships with staff, if I had asked competent people to leave in order to free up positions for critical missing skillsets.

Third, I was struck by the commitment of the mayor and his top team to the turnaround, and their willingness to stay with it for the long haul. Seasoned public officials, with experience in tough settings around the country, they understood how hard it was to turn around decades of failure. I wanted to make sure they also understood that the next Brianna case could happen at any time, and that even after a year, all I could hope to promise was that the response would be different. After just a couple of conversations, I was convinced that as long as they saw change and improvement, the mayor and his top advisors would stand by a new director, through the inevitable battles of reform, and even through tragedies. By my calculation, then, the only reason not to say yes was fear, and I wasn't willing to see myself as someone who would decline a chance to make a difference because of fear.

When the mayor announced my appointment at a press conference in late April, a fourth reason for optimism emerged from the participants' remarks: all the people and institutions—council members, community leaders, executive branch officials, local judges—whose battles had so often paralyzed the system were united, at least for a moment, in their pride that the court receivership was finally over and the District was about to regain control of its own affairs. "CFSA has been in foster care," a prominent community leader said. "Now we are all rejoicing that it has come home to a permanent family." At the same time, he asked everyone to join him in supporting me, rather than going back to the old ways of "looking for leaders and then destroying them."

That phrase had a vivid meaning for a longtime District audience, only too familiar with the pattern. Throughout District government, when something went wrong, outside observers and stakeholders rushed to protect themselves in the inevitable *Washington Post* article, which usually meant distancing themselves from the public agency. The article would spark oversight hearings by Congress, the District Council, or both; the agency would become further mired in responding to charges rather than fixing problems; and, eventually, the public agency's head would resign. Surviving enough cycles to make a long-run difference would not be easy, but the community leader's call to his colleagues, along with the genuine enthusiasm of so many for the District's new start, would be important assets.

Crises, Emergencies, Demands, and Expectations: The Early Months of Reform

Figuring out what lay in front of me meant untangling a knot of crises, emergencies, demands, and requirements. I had to recruit a management team and restructure the agency to meet its new responsibilities, meet a crucial legislative deadline to take over abuse cases from the police, close three emergency shelters, work with Congress and the local judges on legislation to reform the District's Family Court system, improve performance across the whole agency on 15 measurable court-set standards, reduce social worker caseloads, detoxify the relationship with the media, and prevent the state of Maryland from sending 1,000 children back to the District from Maryland foster homes.

At the same time, I had responsibility for about 3,000 children in foster care and 3,000 families caring for their children at home, and for the steady stream of tragedies and crises they experienced. I chose to spend more of my time trying to change the system rather than learning about individual children's circumstances, but I sometimes worried that I was wrong to do so. While I was pretty sure that no one could change the system just by fixing one case at a time, I hated being responsible for so much damage to children. When friends asked me in the early months what I thought about the job, I would often respond that I had predicted many of the challenges intellectually but had not understood the emotional toll of so much tragedy on my watch.

I also found myself starting to put into words my assessment of what had gone wrong over many years, and my vision and strategy for the future. As we struggled through the multiple pieces of the reform, I sought a way to talk about what these pieces had in common, and what whole they would build, once each piece was in place.

Building a Team for Jobs That Did Not Exist

My first challenge was to recruit a management team while designing a new structure to fit the agency's expanded responsibilities. In other words, I had to recruit people for jobs that didn't yet exist. I begged help from the mayor's top personnel official and was soon able to create the new structure, sketching out the broad responsibilities for each unit and promising the new recruits that they would have a hand in the design. Right at the beginning I added an office of clinical practice to focus on high-quality social work and to offer professional expertise in health and mental health, along with an office of licensing and monitoring to take on the new responsibilities created by the CFSA Establishment Act.

In recruiting, I needed to find people with the technical skills to do the new work—beyond the current staff's expertise in social work—and with the right temperament and backgrounds to succeed. That meant people with the maturity to handle a chaotic and troubled agency under enormous pressure, as well as people who could compensate for my own gaps: not being a social worker, not being African American or personally rooted in the District's neighborhoods, and not having District government experience.

I asked everyone I knew for names. A long-time community leader came up with my first success, my new chief of staff, recruited early in the summer to start in August. The rest of the new senior staff started work in the fall, four to six months after my appointment: five or six new senior staff members, in both program and administrative roles, and about the same number of senior staff from the receivership, who would stay on for at least the first year.

As the team assembled, I was proud of its talent, credibility, and breadth of background and experience. Team members were diverse on many dimensions—District and national; African American, white, and Latino; men and women; and social work experts, administrative specialists, managers, and a researcher. I was also optimistic about the new structure, which I hoped would give us at least a chance to meet the new expectations. But I was worried about still-unfilled gaps and conscious that the new, untested team was entering a very tough environment.

Taking on New Responsibility for Abuse Cases

Our next urgent deadline loomed: October 1, 2001, the effective date for unifying abuse and neglect services under CFSA's jurisdiction, was just three and a half months away when I took over. Before passage of the CFSA Establishment Act, the District's response to abused and neglected children had been split among the police department, which investigated reports of abuse; a special unit known as Court Social Services (a part of the local court system), which provided services to children who had been abused; and the child welfare agency, which provided both investigation and services in cases of neglect. The federal court monitor, plaintiffs, and most other observers thought that the division of responsibilities had made it far too easy for families and children to fall through the cracks. Now we had to fix those problems by making the new law's unified system a reality.

The stakes were high. Not only did the reorganization matter for children, but it was also a test case for the federal court's and the mayor's vision of reform, which relied on a unified, strong CFSA as the best route to successful reforms. But even though the legislation had passed, many local judges, the press, and others who had experienced CFSA's failures firsthand thought it was a mistake to add more responsibilities to a failing agency. The local judges feared that case oversight would deteriorate as responsibilities shifted from Court Social Services to CFSA, where social workers were overwhelmed by extremely high caseloads. They and others who were skeptical that CFSA could become a strong, successful agency expected that the October 1 deadline would be missed or implemented disastrously.

In a further complication, CFSA staff themselves expected to fail, or so it initially seemed to me. In our very first meetings, staff seemed ready to give up after each frustrating experience, explaining why there was nothing we could do if powerful people put roadblocks in our way. This expectation risked becoming a self-fulfilling prophecy: if we spent our energy lining up our excuses for why failure was someone else's fault, we wouldn't have enough energy left over to get the job done.

At the same time, staff anxiety was not irrational. Investigators who had handled only reports of neglect worried about their ability to investigate abuse cases that could be more serious and violent. And at this early point, the pace of hiring was barely allowing us to hold steady, let alone bring dozens of new workers on board to handle the abuse caseloads.

I knew we had to meet this deadline—and not only for the sake of the children who would be better served by a unified system. This first step would be closely watched to see if this was a new CFSA that could meet commitments and deadlines. As soon as my new chief of staff started in

August, I asked her to head the implementation. With less than two months to go, we had to hire and train enough workers to handle the abuse caseload, find space and support for the new workers and figure out who would supervise them, carry out a smooth transition for families and children now being served by Court Social Services to CFSA social workers, get caseload information into CFSA's computer system (especially challenging since neither the police nor Court Social Services had used an automated system before), and define our new relationship with the police and the courts.

While this was certainly a daunting agenda, we had powerful supporters and concrete resources on our side. The mayor's office, the federal court, and the council were all prepared to back us up when we needed them. For example, to address the staffing problem, we worked out an agreement with the local courts to temporarily transfer the Court Social Services staff handling abuse cases to CFSA. These staff did not have social work degrees, as District legislation required for CFSA social workers, so the District Council passed emergency legislation that grandfathered them in, based on their experience and performance.

To our enormous relief, a summer of late nights and frantic activity enabled us to complete the formal transition on time. The *Washington Post* took a negative view, suggesting a few days after the October 1 deadline that the agency was not ready for new responsibility:

> Another change designed to improve child abuse and neglect investigations is running into problems even as it goes into effect. . . . Child protection sources within the agency say that the transition has been chaotic and that they are unsure whether Child and Family Services, already understaffed, is prepared to take on more cases. Child protection workers said the agency can barely handle neglect complaints, let alone hundreds of new abuse cases . . . "It's mass confusion . . . ," said one social worker. . . . "It's been so disorganized," said another worker. "The transition is not going well at all," said a third social worker. . . . Golden and other child protection officials, however, are calling the consolidation "a huge accomplishment."[5]

True, the new system was still imperfect, but the old system had been broken beyond fixing, and the District's children deserved better, so I was willing to accept some confusion in early implementation. Then too, meeting the first of the court's and the statute's key deadlines represented a sharp break from the agency's past, providing early credibility with the federal court and the District Council. So although the *Washington Post*'s criticism dampened spirits, we felt great relief internally at accomplishing a major first step against considerable odds.

Closing Emergency Shelters

Just as we began implementing the unified system, the federal court asked us to resolve another issue right away. The court monitor recommended we immediately close the three emergency shelters set up by the receivership, through contracts with outside community organizations, to reduce the number of children in the office building at night. Temporary shelters, features of troubled systems around the country, are sometimes justified as settings where children can be assessed before a better permanent home can be chosen. But in even the best shelters, children already stressed from maltreatment and removal from their homes are plunged into another temporary setting.

Philosophically, the court monitor had always thought—as did we—that emergency shelters were a bad idea for children because of this added stress and instability. After a visit, however, her concern became more urgent. She worried about the risks of housing children of all ages together, from babies to teens, and she observed that school-age children were staying in the shelter rather than attending school.

Our senior staff had to decide what to do. We didn't want more children forced to stay on cots in our office building, and we already had to carry out very quickly a full list of court-mandated reforms that did not include shutting down these shelters. But we agreed with the court monitor that emergency shelters were an unacceptable way to house children. Pooling everything we knew about the risks of all emergency shelters, however well-run, and banking on the court monitor's experience and good judgment, we decided to try to move all the children out. We knew that if we could not find them homes, we would have to back off, since the office building was an even worse alternative.

First, we stopped admitting new children to the shelters and focused on placing the children who were already there in better settings—in families. It was one of the few times in our reform efforts that we found a change easier than we had expected. Some of the children's relatives had already expressed willingness to care for them, but the agency's cumbersome process had discouraged them. Once we reached out to these relatives, we were able to place many children in kin foster care.

In other cases, we found that once social workers knew a child had to be moved out of the closing shelter, they were able to quickly solve the problems keeping that child from moving to a foster home. The discovery that these problems could be solved fairly easily once they rose to the top of the social worker's pile of crises opened a window for us on the way emergencies drove the system. Of course, that meant that other children's problems were now on the back burner, so in the long run we had to change the system to go beyond emergencies.

We somehow managed, by luck and persistence, to keep the number of children housed temporarily in the office building about the same—even though it took another year and a half to reduce it to zero. We had not yet made the policy changes—like payment incentives to encourage more foster families to stand by on an emergency basis— that would eventually keep children out of the building at night, so we tried other ways. We elevated the level of approval staff needed to let any child stay overnight in the building, pleaded with foster families to offer emergency care, and relied heavily on the unbounded energy of senior staff who offered to be on call all night, to try to find homes for children.

We were less successful at handling the administrative piece of the problem: working out the most cost-efficient way to end the shelter providers' contracts. In closing the shelters, we were asking our contracts staff to do something new: specifically, to end contracts not because of poor performance but because we had decided not to purchase that service any longer. But the agency's contracts office was overwhelmed with trying to create order in the most basic contracts actions, let alone figuring out how to do something new. Fairly quickly, between the agency's and the District's contracts and legal staff, we determined that it was legal for the government to end the contracts for a policy reason, so long as providers were fairly compensated. But how much to pay them took years to figure out. Nonetheless, I did not regret my decision to close the shelters as soon as I knew it was legal.

By January 2002, all three shelters were closed. This was our first clear accomplishment to immediately affect children's lives. Closing the shelters also illustrated key principles behind our vision for CFSA: that children thrive in families rather than in institutions, and that they deserve to live in stable, permanent settings.

Reforming the District's Courts: An Unexpected Opportunity

When I arrived on the job, CFSA had about 1,500 court hearings a month in front of the local judges, equivalent to about one-quarter of our total child welfare caseload. So an individual social worker with a caseload of 50—not unusual then—would have had about a dozen court hearings a month, each one requiring a court report in advance.

Just days into my tenure an unexpected opportunity came up to improve this system. I found myself testifying before the U.S. House of Representatives on legislation to reform the District's local court system by creating a Family Court made up of judges specializing in child abuse and neglect, and other family matters. The mayor strongly supported the legislation because it fit so closely with the District's and the federal court's reform plans for the child welfare system. Driven by deep con-   .
gressional concern over the Brianna case, the bipartisan legislation was enacted a few months later.

Unlike the other early reform steps, generally driven by crises, emergencies, or requirements, my involvement in the Family Court legislation was driven by an unexpected opportunity. Before, all 60 judges of the Superior Court heard a mix of cases, including abuse and neglect, so the distribution of judicial expertise was spotty, and there were too many judges for us to build relationships or agree on common expectations. In addition, since judges heard such a mix of cases, our social workers and lawyers sometimes had to wait hours for a child welfare hearing while an unpredictable jury trial ended.

By contrast, under the new legislation, District social workers and attorneys would appear before a relatively small number of judges (about 20) who worked full time on child and family issues. That put reforms within reach that we could only dimly hope for before: more sensible scheduling of social worker appearances, more judicial expertise, joint training for judges and social workers, stronger relationships, and reduced frustration on both sides.

In addition, my appearances before Congress put me in a better personal position to strengthen judicial relationships. Because I testified on behalf of the mayor and had worked previously with the members of Congress who were involved with the legislation, the judges cared what I thought about their work and needed my help as a colleague—just what I needed from them, if CFSA was to meet the federal court's goals. As a result, our relationship began as one of mutual respect and mutual dependence, less one-sided than in the past.

That past relationship had been rocky. Superior Court judges oversaw every case in which a child was removed from home and many cases in which children were receiving services at home with their parents. While judges possess broad authority over out-of-home cases in every state—

to make sure the government's authority to remove children from their homes is not exercised arbitrarily or inappropriately—the District's judges were more deeply involved than in many jurisdictions. Many District judges believed that, aside from a few terrific exceptions, the typical social worker was at best overwhelmed and at worst irresponsible, and that the agency as a whole was a failure, requiring constant judicial vigilance. Social workers, for their part, felt disrespected, micromanaged, and talked down to.

As I mentioned earlier, this relationship faced an early test when a judge jailed a social worker, prompting a wave of anger and concern from her colleagues. The Monday after her Friday jailing, representatives of the social workers' union came to us to talk about what response by the judges would avert a staff walkout. The chief judge and other senior judges agreed to come to the agency offices for the first time ever to meet with social workers, hear the ways in which they felt disrespected in court, and in turn articulate what the judges expected. The meeting was a success, strengthening a critical working relationship. Perhaps paradoxically, the relationship would not have progressed without the crisis.

Just a couple weeks later, as if to prove that all steps forward had to be countered by steps backward, the *Washington Post* reported retrospectively on the action and interpreted it as yet another agency failure.[6] The stakeholders in the District's child welfare system had always fought their battles in the newspaper, so some in the agency thought that a judge must have called the *Post* to suggest the story. Whether that was true or not, the judicial leadership had taken a very different approach by reaching out to meet with us. I deeply appreciated that shift to direct dialogue and saw it as the only way to break with the District's grim history. As I was quoted telling the reporter, "We've done a great deal, but we have lots to do. . . . There's a history of mistrust. You get bumps in the road, and you solve them, and you move ahead."

Almost as soon as I arrived, the lead judge for the Family Court proposed meeting privately every two weeks, to make sure we had a direct line of communication as we initiated reform. We kept this schedule for three years, and it proved its value over and over.[7] The history of the Superior Court and CFSA had included many episodes of mutual blaming when under public pressure, and though the court had often won the immediate public relations battle, the damaged relationship had eroded both sides' ability to negotiate real improvements for children. Our twice-monthly meetings and commitment to communicate directly virtually ended the public wrangling and paved the way for substantial change.

Passing the Federal Court's Test: Improving Performance to Meet 15 Measurable Standards

While the Family Court was an unexpected opportunity and the closing of the emergency shelters an unexpected demand, I knew from the moment I was hired that our core work for the first year would be the task set before us by the federal court: to meet 15 of 20 measurable performance standards in just a few months. The required standards, listed in the court's consent order of October 2000, covered the A to Z of agency performance: staff training, foster parent recruitment, timely investigation of abuse and neglect reports, timely completion of case plans, visits to children, completed adoptions, and more. But the court had deliberately left the standards open to revision until the court monitor reviewed the agency's performance at the starting point, when the District took over from the receivership. If the baseline turned out to be a real surprise, the consent order included a sensible mechanism for renegotiating the standards.

In fact, the baseline review showed even worse performance at the end of the receivership than anyone had expected (Center for the Study of Social Policy 2002). Two examples follow:

- About 800 investigations of abuse/neglect reports were pending more than the allowable 30 days. Some had been the responsibility of the police under the old system, but in the new unified system, they were all ours. The original court order required reducing the baseline backlog to 50; the court monitor revised that requirement to 300 after seeing how vast the starting backlog was. Besides resolving the old cases, we had to keep up with several hundred new investigations a month to meet the standard.
- Only 5 percent of children had been visited monthly during the six months reviewed (45 percent had not been visited at all), and about a quarter of case plans for children in foster care were up to date. To meet the standard, we had to visit 35 percent of children monthly— that is, to improve sevenfold—and to have current case plans for 45 percent of children in foster care.

The original deadline for these improvements was six months after the receivership ended. But by the time the baseline report was completed and the new standards negotiated, the six months were almost over. With the judge's approval, the District, the court monitor, and the plaintiffs all agreed to add another six months for the change to happen, taking the drop-dead date to May 2002.

Even with the extension, November 2001 found us with grim news about our starting point, just six months left to reach rigorous performance requirements, and no idea whether we could do it. My first priority was to make sure that we were spending the scarce days we had on the right things. I had spent some of my past career working on campaigns, and I had learned that when you have to get everything done by the immovable deadline of Election Day, the overriding goal has to be using your limited time the right way. Working more hours just doesn't compensate for wasting time.

In a senior management retreat that fall, followed by a few more meetings over the winter, we translated the federal court's expectations into detailed performance plans for each senior staff member. This planning process had to translate goals immediately and seamlessly into action in sharp contrast to CFSA's history of plans detached from reality.

One reasonable worry for some team members—some of whom had left secure high-level jobs to take a big risk on the District—was how I would judge their performance if they couldn't achieve the requirements, no matter how hard they tried. Given the agency's history of failed administrative systems, program leaders worried in particular about whether they could succeed if administrative improvement failed. For example, the program leaders had to make visits to children far more frequent, case plans more timely, and investigations more prompt, all of which depended on the pace of social worker recruitment and on computer system support. So, could I give everyone a break if they failed for a good reason?

I understood the worries and considered them realistic, but I also felt the team had no choice but to take responsibility for results with no excuses, just as I had no choice but to be accountable to the mayor and the court for those same results. I even hoped that such a responsibility might prove exhilarating and lead us to scale the obstacles we saw at the beginning. This did not necessarily mean that I would judge all failures equally or by rote, any more than the mayor and the court would hold me accountable that way. But effort alone would not be enough: we had to live with the possibility that we might fail for reasons outside our control, and we had to use it to spur creativity and persistence.

We left the performance retreats with a shared sense of just how hard we had to work, and with a few key agreements about how we would work together. Every team member was expected to meet the deadlines. If, along the way, anyone found they couldn't, they were expected to tell others as soon as possible, so we could find another solution. Some team members feared that acknowledging the possibility of failure would only encourage it. But I believed the opposite: *not acknowledging* the possibility of failure would make it more likely, by reinforcing traditional counterproductive strategies for evading responsibility. Far too often in CFSA's history, individuals had committed to grand plans that had no connection to reality, and then hidden the inevitable collapse until other people's plans also went wrong and they could be blamed for the entire failure.

Besides a committed and capable management team focused on specific targets and deadlines, we also needed accurate, timely information on the measures. We couldn't wait two or three months for information if we were going to turn around performance in six months. Yet, high-quality information every month had simply not been possible in the agency as I found it in mid-2001.

When I first started, several outside observers had told me we might have to get a completely new computer system, surely a multiyear proposition, even though the receivership had just installed a sophisticated child welfare case-management system that other states were using with good results. But for reasons I could not yet diagnose, the information was universally believed to be useless, and agency decisionmaking felt like a "data-free zone." Without computer systems expertise, I had no idea how much of the problem was the agency's anti-information culture and how much was the system's technical shortcomings.

To answer these questions, I tried to learn as much as possible from the meetings and debates that first summer, when senior staff went through the agency's automated reports so we could tell the court monitor how much she could rely on the automated system for her baseline report. (In the end, she used a sample of paper case files instead.) But what I learned seemed contradictory. Sometimes, the senior team's distrust of the automated reports was justified; but other times, the court monitor's painstaking manual review yielded numbers similar to the automated reports, leaving me unsure about the root of the problem and what to do about it.

Then an unexpected opportunity put us on the road to solutions. Early in my management team recruitment, the top information systems job opened up. Swamped with recruiting for other vacant positions, I chanced upon exactly the right person. A nationally known researcher and long-time District resident, he had just left retirement to join us working part time on special projects. After watching him in action, our whole team knew that we wanted as much of his time as we could get. Eventually, I persuaded him to become our chief information officer (CIO) and postpone retirement for a few more years.

His early successes included fixing that frustrating report about young children in congregate care, which kept showing numbers that were far too low. After several monthly reports in a row failed to fix the problem, he plunged into the details and reported that a debate about whose fault the discrepancy was had kept us from being able to fix it. The social workers insisted that the computer system was just coughing up a "wrong report," while the information systems team claimed that social workers weren't entering correct information. Once the chief information officer and the new program leadership worked on the problem together, they discovered quickly that both complaints were right: there were programming problems and data-entry problems. Once both sides took responsibility, it took only a few months of comparing manual and automated reports to create a monthly automated count that could be used with confidence.

The long-standing stalemate over inaccurate numbers was understandable given the agency's historical incentives. I came to suspect that perhaps people preferred uncertainty to information for the same reason they sometimes preferred planning over action: their experience was that nothing worked and that every step toward taking responsibility inevitably led to failure and blame.

To cut through the stalemate, we had to start changing the incentives, and the federal court helped us do that. Between the baseline report, which meant the worst news was already out, and the short turnaround demanded by the probationary period requirements, staff started to see that information could help a lot more than it hurt. But another necessary ingredient was an early success so all could see that information could prompt solutions, not just reveal problems.

The newly improved information on young children in congregate care provided just such a success. I consulted the new automated report monthly, senior staff looked at it weekly, and specialists at our new office of clinical practice reviewed children's status daily, as they worked to find a family for each young child on the list. To reduce the number of new children on the list, we increased the pressure on social workers and supervisors to find better, case-by-case solutions when they first took children into care. We now required these staffers to get approval from the agency's top program official—waking her up from sleep, if necessary—before placing a child younger than 6 in a group home. With good information to track our progress, we were able to place children in families and bring the group home numbers down sharply within months.

Soon, the information system improvements gained momentum, and we could track such key indicators as visits to children and case plans developed on time, not just for the agency as a whole but by unit. Performance began to improve as soon as we started tracking the measures carefully, though social worker caseloads were not yet declining. The information system improvements probably helped just by shining a spotlight on performance. At a time of low morale, they also represented a bright spot for social workers, who could see that the information systems team was starting to listen to them and to clean up some smaller annoyances in the system.

We still didn't know if there would be enough improvement on enough measures to meet the court's requirements. Then, to raise the stakes, as winter slid into spring 2002, we hit another hurdle. We realized that we were behind on a standard we had expected to meet: increasing adoptions by 20 percent from 273 adoptions in the past year to at least 328 in the current year. Finalizing an adoption had so many steps that staff had long thought the unfinished adoptions were just stalled in paperwork, so at any moment the backlog would break and the numbers would jump up. By the time we finally realized that we were wrong, we were far behind the annual target. We needed local judges' help to get the job done in just a few remaining months.

Nervously, we asked the judges if they could help us move children through the process faster. Looking at data together, we realized that paperwork delays at the court were compounding agency problems; so we agreed on streamlined procedures for paperwork, a commitment by the court to more hours of judges' time, and a joint approach to detailed tracking and follow-up. Going into the last month, we knew we had at least an outside chance of reaching the target.

Struggling to Reduce Social Worker Caseloads

Central to all our reform plans was reducing the historically high caseload carried by each social worker. Everyone watching the reform and our progress, both inside and outside the agency, would use this indicator to judge our success. The court monitor's reports for years had highlighted the role of high caseloads in dragging down the agency's performance, and the *Washington Post* frequently pointed to impossible caseloads as a cause behind social workers' failures and children's deaths. Social workers spoke to me about the unbearable stress of knowing that any of your cases could blow up at any time, yet not being able to keep informed even by working full tilt. Bringing down caseloads was absolutely essential to changing the agency's performance and a critical step for me in demonstrating credibility.

Naively, I thought this goal would be easier to deliver on than other, more complex dimensions of performance improvement, since I had the resources and hiring authority. But nothing was easy, not even figuring out what caseloads really were to define the extent of the problem and track improvements. The *Washington Post* often cited individual social workers' assessments of their caseloads, sometimes in the range of 90 to 100 children.[8] Dividing the total number of cases by the number of social workers yielded about 35 cases or perhaps 50 to 60 children—still double the level set by the District's 1993 consent decree. But we really didn't know the number of cases, the number of social workers, or the typical burden, and social work staff insisted that we never would. They contended that the automated system couldn't track caseloads because the human resources office couldn't keep the list of social workers up to date or account accurately for workers on extended sick leave or non-case-carrying assignments. They also said it was impossible to resolve how to count cases, whether by number of children or number of families (despite clear definitions in the court order about which count fit which situations).

Over the next few months, as the new CIO and program director arbitrated these disputes, we clarified the problem enough to find out that the average of 35 cases concealed enormous disparities. Many social workers carried caseloads in the 40s or 50s, and some were even in the 60s and 70s while others handled very few cases because of disability, part-time or part-year employment, or perceived incapacity. Further, we found, some cases were theoretically being covered by supervisors or other staff with non-casework duties, and some cases were not assigned to anyone.

With burdens this large, social workers spent their time mainly on court appearances and on emergencies. Of course, failure to have regular contact with children, families, and foster parents only made emergencies worse and more frequent, creating a cycle of failure, more emergencies, and, in the end, higher caseloads as cases got worse rather than closing. A social worker who never got around to returning a foster parent's call, even if that call might give early warning of an avertable emergency, would then spend two or three days trying to find the child a new home after the foster parent decided no help was available and declared herself unwilling to keep the child. The planning that might have saved that placement, stabilized the child's behavior, and led to either a return home or an adoption by the foster parent always took a backseat to court and crises.

That first summer and fall, we tried everything we could think of to reduce caseloads. Our regular recruitment announcements did not yield enough candidates, and no one had an immediate plan to fix the process. I looked for solutions that could tide us over, such as seeing if the federal government's Public Health Service could assign us social workers on rotation for a year or two. A foundation agreed to fund a special project on recruitment and retention. And we opened our ranks for the first time to licensed social workers holding only bachelor's degrees in social work.[9] None of these steps had immediate effects, though some paid off later on.

In January 2002, we hired a staff person to focus full time on recruitment. For the first time, someone could explain to me the recruitment pipeline for social workers, analyze historical data, and develop and track a plan. Unfortunately, the data analysis revealed that we were not going to get results until late the following summer, and then only if we attracted a huge cohort of new entrants from the May and June social work graduations. The agency's historic recruiting networks were all with graduate social work schools, whose students started work in the summer upon graduation. With no recruiting networks in place to identify more than a handful of candidates during other seasons, we had to make a huge push for new spring graduates. And with a deeply demoralized workforce and federal court requirements to dramatically improve our work by May 2002, before the new graduates could even start training, this timetable seemed impossible.

Then it got worse. In the early spring of 2002, I heard that the local courts were going to pull out the case managers who had been temporarily assigned to CFSA from the Court Social Services unit. The temporary assignments were to last through the summer 2002, with the expectation that by then we would have new social workers on board; but now we heard that with only two weeks' notice, we would have to reassign hundreds of cases to overburdened CFSA social workers. Given that we had no hope of new staff until after the May graduations, I couldn't afford to lose anyone during the spring.

When I called the presiding judge to check the rumor, it turned out to be mostly true. While the judges were not forcing the staff assigned to CFSA to return before their assignments were completed, the court had made immediate offers to all of them for other jobs, and all were giving CFSA two weeks' notice. Losing the staff with so little notice would have undone our plans, devastated staff morale, and all but wrecked our chances of meeting the federal court's requirements. I badgered the judges to reverse this decision, even on pain of straining our relationship with them. In the end, the judges agreed to let us keep the social workers until summer, confirming, to my relief, that our long-run relationship and ability to work together were priorities for both parties.

After this close call, we decided that we couldn't just beef up recruitment and wait until our new hires arrived in the summer—we had to do something else immediately. The new program leadership team, on board since the fall, decided to assign both workers and cases more sensibly. To cut caseloads, they ended specialized units with extra-low caseloads and reassigned qualified social workers who had had non-case-carrying assignments (for example, working as a liaison to the court). Not surprisingly, these choices took a toll on morale since some talented workers had found a niche in the specialized units or no-caseload assignments that had enabled them to do good work somewhat insulated from the chaos of the rest of the agency. But we could not justify the damage done to children when caseloads got too high.

Our improved tracking system helped us reduce duplication of case responsibilities in situations where two workers, usually one public and one private sector, were both assigned to a case. Having the child on a public worker's caseload when the agency was paying for private case management contributed to the overwhelming burden on public workers and wasted money. In addition, workers sometimes were uncertain about who was responsible, upping the odds that a child would fall through the cracks.

But to our complete surprise, ending duplication also damaged staff morale. What the management team saw as clarifying preexisting agreements with private agencies, the union saw as an effort to privatize and threaten social worker jobs. The senior team saw the larger context as massive recruitment of public-sector social workers, leading to many more jobs rather than fewer, but the union saw recruitment as a promise rather than a bankable reality.

By mid-2002, despite all this effort, the typical social worker saw little if any progress, a year after expectations had been raised at the end of the receivership. The labor management partnership we had launched with great optimism hit shoals that summer, and the meetings grew grim and silent. As rumors about privatization flew and morale ebbed to perhaps its lowest point, I felt discouraged that after a year I had not yet eased the workload of the agency's social workers.

Talking to the Media, and Talking to Our Partners without Going through the Media

Given my observation that media coverage had contributed to the failures of the District's child welfare system—that the fear of bad coverage had led to passivity at best and to blaming rather than problem-solving at worst— I knew that I needed to reach out to the media myself. Purely defensively, I needed to communicate with the media to survive, but I also had higher hopes. I thought that maybe the press could get interested in systemic reform as a story and even buy into the goals that the federal court was holding us accountable for, so everyone would be measuring reform by the same standards and the public would understand what was really happening.

In the early months, we provided information and comments in response to a great deal of media coverage of the agency, particularly in the *Washington Post*. I also met early on with the *Washington Post*'s editorial board, to give an overview of the District's reform plans and strategy. The meeting helped me understand the perspectives of reporters and editors, but I was struck by the differences between their diagnosis of the problem (and, therefore, their interests for future reporting) and my own. To a considerable degree, they saw the problem as about incompetent individuals who needed to be fired, and they heard discussion of changing systems as an excuse for not firing enough people.

With somewhat more success, we also reached out to other media to explain reform. A public TV interview show on local politics and government twice invited me on for a long discussion of child welfare reform. And the local public access channel, which televised council hearings and replayed them at all hours to fill empty time, seemed to be surprisingly widely viewed.

But probably most important was the time we put into communicating directly with our key partners. In response to a suggestion from a "kitchen cabinet" of outside advisors that I convened in my first months, we decided to write a biweekly newsletter and e-mail and fax it to interested community members. While this was extremely time-consuming and issues were often late, the newsletter helped us communicate our plans, goals, and strategy to a broad audience. We also kept in touch directly with a wide range of colleagues, calling them whenever we expected a press story, for instance. As a result, stakeholders were much more likely to have a context for whatever information a reporter included in a story, and they called us if they needed to know more, rather than feeling they had to retaliate in the newspaper or conduct public hearings.

Eventually, we greatly reduced the use of the press by our partners as a bargaining chip to get an outcome they wanted or to derail a proposed change. In some cases, as with the Family Court, we agreed to talk directly and regularly rather than indirectly through the newspaper, and the agreements held. Sometimes, though, stakeholders had to try and fail at the old techniques before we could find new ways of working together. Our experience with Maryland was one example.

Negotiating with Angry Maryland Officials

As part of our plan for moving children out of the emergency shelters, in fall 2001, we thought it was time to restart conversations with Maryland that had begun during the receivership. We thought that one reason children ended up in emergency settings and group homes was that so many available families, including children's own relatives, lived in Maryland and were kept from caring for children by seemingly arbitrary rules about interstate placement. Unfortunately, the two jurisdictions' perspectives differed dramatically.

About half of District foster children lived in Maryland, either with extended family (kin foster parents) or, as the majority did, with unrelated foster parents. From the District's perspective, the large number of children living in Maryland was largely a consequence of the metropolitan area's history, family patterns, and housing markets. Most District households were either very poor or very well off, so most families of modest means, whether relatives of children in care or families serving as foster parents, lived in the suburbs. And if they were African American, like most of the District's children and its foster parents, they were most likely to live in Prince George's County, Maryland. Also from the District's perspective, the great obstacle to placing children quickly was that the bureaucratic rules governing interstate placement, which applied both to kin and to unrelated foster parents, seemed intolerably burdensome. The rules applied across the 50 states, but outside the District they typically applied to small numbers of children placed, for example, in a residential treatment program in another state, not to children moving in with kin or foster parents in a nearby suburb.

To Maryland officials, the problem was that far too many District children were in Maryland homes. Far from being bureaucratic, the interstate placement rules protected children, these officials believed, and the District's repeated failure to abide by those rules amounted to having children in Maryland illegally, endangering the children's safety. Given the District's abysmal record of visiting children and keeping track of them, Maryland officials foresaw a tragic death or injury to a District child, for which they might be blamed if they failed to enforce the rules. The match point, though, was that Maryland viewed the District's higher payment rates for foster parents—set by the federal court to ensure the availability of foster parents in the high-cost D.C. metropolitan area—as "stealing" homes in Maryland that otherwise would have been available for Maryland children.

In spring 2002, after a few months of inconclusive discussions, Maryland and Prince George's County officials presented a non-negotiable demand that the District pay foster homes in Maryland the lower Maryland rate rather than the rate required by the federal court order. I told them we couldn't. Soon after, I received a letter from the Maryland cabinet secretary expressing the state's intent to send back all District foster children placed in Maryland if we did not agree to reduce the rate within two weeks. And then a *Washington Post* reporter called us for comment on Maryland's letter, having just been briefed by state officials on their plans:

> Maryland officials yesterday threatened to return more than 1,100 foster children from the District, saying the city's repeated failure to properly monitor their placement may be putting many at risk. The unprecedented action, if taken, would throw the District's child protection system into chaos.[10]

I thought that both of Maryland's proposed alternatives were bad for children. I also suspected that taking more than a thousand children from their homes was not a realistic threat. So after consulting with the District's lawyers, I wrote back to the Maryland cabinet secretary explaining why I couldn't legally accept the choices in her letter, and offering to continue our work to find better solutions. At the same time, the plaintiffs sought an injunction against Maryland from the federal court because of the threat to the well-being of District children. The judge called us all in—officials from the District and Maryland, as well as the plaintiffs—heard the arguments, and ruled that he would hold the plaintiffs' request for an injunction in abeyance if we all worked together to come up with a resolution.

Using the *Washington Post* to force the District's hand had not worked, and Maryland officials did not try it again. To me, that change in approach was a prerequisite for real improvement. The substance of the interstate issue remained difficult, though. While we returned to negotiations and developed a far-reaching agreement, implementation never lived up to either jurisdiction's hopes.

Articulating and Fine-Tuning the Vision

Describing each reform, battle, and crisis separately leaves out the glue that held them together as a reform strategy: an emerging diagnosis of what had been wrong for many years in the District, a vision of what should be different, and priorities for reaching that vision.

As I talked more with foster families, social workers, managers, judges, providers, and the other caring people who were both part of the system and its greatest critics, my diagnosis of what was wrong came into focus, and I understood better why so many people saw the problems starkly but could never fix them. For one thing, the system had so many complex and closely linked parts, all failing, that no solution ever worked quickly. Each partial solution revealed more problems, exhausting the patience of reformers and, even more quickly, of outside overseers. For another, none of the partners in the system had much experience with cooperation or success, but they all had plenty of experience with public shame, criticism, and mutual blame. Under the dark shadow of this history, people could only see the dangers of action very clearly—it won't work, it will be sabotaged, it will only make the judges angry, it will show up in the newspaper—and hardly see the advantages.

An early glimmer of this diagnosis emerged when a long-time CFSA observer asked me in my first days what I would choose as my signature initiative. I didn't believe that any single initiative would make the difference, but instead that the whole system needed to change. I knew that the idea of "changing the system" probably sounded vague and unrealistic, but I also understood that nothing less would turn the tide. No one initiative could alter how people worked together across the system. CFSA's culture had to change: it had to become a strong, active, accountable agency with a management style focused on results, persistent in solving problems, hungry for information, honest yet optimistic, steady, and calm. I could see that those changes would require paying attention both to the outside world and to the agency itself, to change the environment of external hostility and criticism that had fed a cycle of despair, cynicism, and passivity.

This perspective was grounded in my own experience, but it also drew heavily on the conclusions of the federal court, the plaintiffs, and the mayor's office about the right way to bring the agency back from receivership. They had all agreed that a strong, unified, accountable child welfare agency was necessary to success, but this vision was still controversial both inside and outside the agency. It wasn't obvious or logical to some observers that the best way to fix an agency that has always failed is to raise the stakes even higher and give it more responsibility.

How could the vision of strength and accountability take root? For starters, I had to explain why this "moment of opportunity" really was different. To me, the answer lay in the dramatic structural changes that had already happened: the child welfare reform legislation that created a newly unified agency, the greatly expanded budget, the mayor's budget commitments for the future, and the Family Court reform. In speeches, testimony to the council,[11] and media interviews,[12] I repeatedly explained how these reforms transformed the playing field.

Second, it was crucial to success to model the new values, to act in the ways I was asking others to act. I knew I would not always be able to live up to this aspiration, but I also knew that if I wanted people to step forward, take responsibility, and meet their commitments, then I had to do the same—one reason I never considered trying to delay the October 1 effective date of the unification legislation. Similarly, if I wanted people to end the culture of blame, I had to avoid blaming others—hence, the somewhat bland *Post* quotes about how every reform encounters bumps in the road.

Third, people needed to experience success. Part of the challenge was that failure breeds passivity and blame, which compound the original problems. The judge who jailed the social worker probably would have made another choice had he believed collaboration could succeed and serve children. Foster parents who dropped children off at the agency at midnight would never have done it had they seen any other way to get attention and services. Agency staff who despaired of ever getting caseload data right might have solved the technical problems sooner had they seen the information as a tool for solutions.

My response was to look for early successes and celebrate them, but I soon saw that this strategy too would be difficult. When we met the October 1 deadline but the *Post* argued a few days later that we had failed, I saw that external cynicism made it hard to fight internal hopelessness. By the time we closed the three shelters, I understood that no single early win would save the day: the old patterns would give way only through persistence and, I hoped, by successes too big to deny. Passing the federal court's performance test would, I hoped, be big enough to break up old patterns—changing both how agency staff agency saw themselves and how the outside world saw them. As the deadline approached, we simply did not know if we would reach the required 15 of 20 performance standards.

Besides articulating a vision of an active and accountable agency, I also started early to articulate a vision of what we should be accomplishing for families and children. My years at HHS had taught me that persistence, the indispensible ingredient in changing a large bureaucracy, required staying focused on just a few themes, as media stories came and went and political winds shifted. So I wanted to identify priorities that could animate reform from beginning to end. The vision had to be consistent with the federal court's requirements, but at the same time, it had to be ours. The agency could achieve reform only if it took active responsibility for change. For that reason, I consistently avoided talking about "compliance": to me, the term smacked of passively doing someone else's bidding.

We needed to say what we believed in and then demonstrate how the court requirements helped us get there. Luckily, the links were easy to make because each court requirement sprang from a broader perspective that our senior staff generally shared about what children deserved and needed. For instance, the requirement that case plans be developed promptly came from the sound idea that it is simply not possible to help children find or return to a permanent family if years pass with no planning.

At my confirmation hearing on September 17, 2001, I laid out key themes that captured what our senior staff believed and matched the federal court's requirements, setting forth six priorities linked to the overall goals of "ensuring safety, enabling children to grow up in a permanent family, and promoting well-being for vulnerable children and families":

1. Recruit and retain enough well-trained, highly qualified social workers to keep caseloads at an acceptable level.
2. Provide timely and high quality investigations of allegations of abuse and neglect to ensure children's safety.
3. Increase the number of kinship, foster, and adoptive placements that meet children's needs, by recruiting more parents and by providing them with the supports they need to meet children's physical, mental health, educational, and developmental needs.
4. Plan quickly for children's futures in order to ensure they either return home or move to a permanent family if they cannot safely go home.
5. Build on the strengths of the existing Healthy Families/Thriving Communities Collaboratives to link CFSA's work to community supports for families.
6. Focus on our information systems, so we can make informed decisions and ensure that children never again fall through the cracks.[13]

I drew on these priorities repeatedly to explain recommendations or actions. When I testified before Congress on the Family Court legislation and again when I offered ideas to the judges on how to implement it, I focused on the fourth priority, our obligation to ensure children a permanent home. When we closed the emergency shelters and again when we reduced the number of young children in group homes, we drew on the third priority to explain how our actions followed from our vision, not from a desire to damage particular providers.

Early Results

Two excerpts from the *Washington Post* in the summer and fall of 2002 capture the mixed nature of this first year. An August 27, 2002, editorial criticized our early reforms:

No sooner had Carolyn Graham, deputy D.C. mayor for children, youth, families, and elders and Olivia Golden, director of the D.C. Child and Family Services

Agency, declared in an August 14 letter to the *Post* that the opportunity to change the city's shameful child protection system "has never been better" than new evidence of the system's endangerment of children materialized. Two days after they wrote their letter, an 8-year-old boy was molested by an 11-year-old in a city-financed facility. It was the third sexual assault of a child under the city's care to come to light in recent weeks. Only two weeks earlier, Ms. Golden had pledged to speed the removal of children under 12 from city-funded group homes to protect them from sexual assaults. . . .

In the wake of the latest outrage, and if past D.C. child protection performance is any guide, the public can expect to be told that reforms have been achieved—or are on the way; new regulations have been written—or are being drafted; new and better-trained staff are in place—or are "in the process" of being hired; and under the Child and Family Services Agency's new leadership, a brighter day for abused and neglected District children is right around the corner. It is a refrain that is old, familiar, and, by now, shopworn.[14]

Just a few weeks later, the court monitor announced that we had met the probationary period standards and recommended ending our probation. As the *Post's* news story noted,

The court-appointed monitor for the District's child protection agency is recommending that a federal judge terminate the agency's probationary period, citing significant improvements in its handling of foster care . . .

The report is important because it will place Child and Family Services firmly in the hands of city officials for the first time since 1995. . . . The report . . . found that the agency improved in 15 of 20 areas between May 31, 2001, and May 31, 2002. [Court Monitor Judith Meltzer] said the agency increased adoptions, improved its timeliness of child abuse and neglect investigations, and reduced the number of DC children living in institutions 100 miles from the city.[15]

Which picture was true, the "endangerment of children" and "shopworn" excuses, or the "significant improvements"? In fact, both were.

The tragedies that triggered the August editorial illustrated how fragile the system remained and how partial the fixes were. In April 2002, a CFSA worker sent a 7-year-old boy from foster care to a congregate care facility that mostly took in older children. There, two older boys (11 or 12) engaged in sexual activity with the 7-year-old. Some days later, the facility discovered the sexual activity but delayed reporting it. Eventually, the CFSA social worker found out and the agency removed the child. Despite all the institutional failures involved, the case did not capture the management team's attention until a court hearing and subsequent newspaper articles three months later, in July 2002. In the following days, another case of sexual activity among boys at a group home emerged in the newspaper, framed as an epidemic of sexual assaults in CFSA facilities.

Yet, the foundation already laid for reform helped us respond to the incidents far better than would have been possible a few months before. We had already successfully moved children under 6 to families from group homes, so we jump-started a further plan to move all children age 12 and younger. And we moved ahead on our first-ever licensing process, which imposed new, higher standards for group homes.

Our progress in articulating the reform vision and reaching out to stakeholders and political overseers also helped keep reform moving. I had feared that the negative press coverage would immobilize us, as it so often had in the agency's past, and that public and political reaction would follow the lines laid out in the *Post* editorial: this is the latest incarnation of a failed agency, and the reform is a sham. Instead, because we had an aggressive action plan, articulated the reform value that children should live in families rather than group homes, and retained the support of the mayor and other elected officials, the tragedies if anything helped us move faster on licensing and quality in group homes. The incidents and their press coverage helped convince providers, elected officials, and the public that tougher regulation and monitoring, a key part of our plan, were needed.

But the emotional impact was tough. Our senior team, still relatively new, hadn't anticipated the roller coaster of tragedy juxtaposed with success. We veered between deep sadness that we were responsible for the harm done to these young children, anger and frustration at what we saw as inaccuracies and unfairness in the news coverage, exhaustion because we had been doing everything we could for a year and it wasn't enough, and a commitment to learn from the failures and keep the momentum for improvement going.

How, then, to summarize the results of this first year? We met our most important target: improvements in 15 of 20 performance areas, as documented in the court monitor's report. For the first time, we had achieved measurable improvement across a range of performance measures linked to children's safety and well-being. Yet, those limited and fragile successes coexisted with failures that continued to damage children. And, the pattern of successes and failures was completely unpredictable. I had guessed that hiring social workers would be easy, but it was hard—so by summer 2002, caseloads were still very high, and an angry union leadership believed we were destroying the few islands of decent working conditions within the agency without improving the lives of most social workers. I had thought that we could not possibly meet the federal court's requirements unless we improved caseloads rapidly—but we did, despite the lag in caseload reduction. I had thought it might take years to upgrade our information system, but we saw dramatic progress in months. And our work on moving children from group homes to family settings progressed faster than I had expected and represented our most dramatic first-year achievement—except that the remaining failings of our group home placement system played out in tragedy for other children. In the short run, leading change means taking nothing for granted, expecting surprises, and understanding that nothing is predictable.

3

Children, Families, and the Child Welfare System
Alabama and Utah in the National Context

This chapter tells the Alabama and Utah reform stories while at the same time setting them in the context of the national child welfare system.

Alabama's story is set in the broad context of the children and families who come in contact with child welfare agencies. Many, but by no means all, of these families and children are deeply distressed, and their circumstances vary considerably within states and from one state to another. Alabama placed these variations at the center of its child welfare reform by embracing individualized response to each family rather than a standardized "one size fits all" approach.

Utah's story highlights the many parts of the child welfare system that extend beyond the child welfare agency itself, such as federal and state laws, local judges and lawyers, and state budget and contracting officials. The media often tell the story of a child's tragedy as if one social worker saved or failed to save that child, like a movie where one soldier's heroism wins or loses the war. But that picture is misleading. Closer to the truth, Mayor Anthony Williams once quipped that child welfare administration reminded him of a key lesson of military history: that the generals who win are those who get the supplies to the right place at the right time. This chapter explains all the parts—the supply train as well as the social worker and the general—and tells the story of Utah's child welfare reform, which used a practice model to align those different parts.

Ending One Size Fits All in Alabama

"All but two."—The response of a worker in rural Alabama to a question from Commissioner Andy Hornsby (Alabama Department of Human Resources) about how many of her 18 foster care children could go home to their parents if she had services to provide the families.

"Many families [in the District of Columbia] were dealing with multiple and complicated problems including substance abuse, lack of adequate housing, mental health concerns, and long histories of involvement with the child welfare system." —Center for the Study of Social Policy (2004b, 9)

In 1988, Alabama was sued because its child welfare system was damaging children in foster care. Neither the governor nor the legislature had acted on the findings of the Governor's Commission on Child Welfare, which had criticized the system and recommended funding increases and other improvements. R.C., a young boy whose treatment showcased the flaws in the system, was the lead plaintiff in this litigation. A local judge with personal knowledge of R.C.'s case reflected several years later on how the pre-reform system had failed the boy:

> While in the custody of the Jefferson County Department of Human Resources, [R.C.] was placed in a psychiatric ward and given powerful medication, which it now appears he did not need. R.C. had behavioral problems and divorced parents, who were not equipped to cope with the situation. He came to be in a locked mental ward because there was nothing else to do with him, and insurance or Medicaid would at least foot the bill for his stay there.[1]

How could this happen? How could a child enter the system because of "behavioral problems and divorced parents" and then receive treatment that further damaged him?

How Children and Families Enter the Child Welfare System

All over the country, a child's first contact with the child welfare system is typically a call to the agency's hotline. In 2007, just over half the calls to the nation's hotlines came from professionals, particularly teachers and police, about 8 percent were anonymous, and almost 20 percent came from friends, neighbors, parents, and other relatives (HHS, ACYF 2009). In R.C.'s case, the first call came while he lived with his mother, alleging that she was abusing him. After he was moved to his father's care, a later hotline call alleged that his father's utility service had been cut off (Bazelon Center 1998, 9).

The child welfare worker receiving the hotline call decides whether to refer the report for investigation. Of the more than 3 million referrals made to child-welfare hotlines nationwide in 2007, more than one-third were screened out without investigation. One reason might be that the caller was not alleging abuse or neglect but was asking for some other kind of help (HHS, ACYF 2009). The other two-thirds of 2007 referrals were investigated or assessed by the child welfare agency. The number of American children who have at least this fleeting contact with the child-welfare system is high and rising: about 47 per 1,000 children were the subject of investigated reports in 2007, compared with about 36 per 1,000 in 1990 (HHS, ACYF 2009; Macomber 2006).

These rates of alleged child maltreatment are high compared to other countries. While data problems can make comparison difficult, Jane Waldfogel draws on experience working with both British and American data to compare maltreatment reports among several countries. She observes that although the rates of abuse are about the same, the United States has a considerably higher number of reported cases of maltreatment than other comparable countries (such as Canada and Great Britain), mainly because it registers more neglect reports. In turn, she hypothesizes, more neglect reports may be filed here because family services outside the abuse and neglect system are not as available, or because the United States has more family and child poverty than comparable countries (Waldfogel 1998). Both these reasons zero in on a widely observed gap in the United States, one that may have contributed to R.C.'s entry into care: the dearth of preventive services that could help families deal with crises, stress, and chronic problems, like mental illness or substance abuse, before children are harmed.

Responding to Reports of Maltreatment

In some states, investigators will respond to all screened-in calls to determine if the child needs immediate protection, whether the alleged abuse or neglect really happened, and what the family's needs and strengths are, as the basis of a longer-term plan. Other states channel screened-in calls that they judge less serious through an "alternative response system" because they believe a more formal investigation would make it harder to build a relationship that could help get services to the family. Under this model, a social worker visits the family to find out what services the family needs and to involve family members, but the worker does not investigate the allegation.

When there is an investigation, the next step is to determine whether the allegation has merit. Data from these investigations reveal that 12 to 15 children per 1,000 have been victims of abuse or neglect, unchanged over the past dozen years (Macomber 2006).[2] But the number of child victims is probably higher because of unreported incidents, as consistently documented in research studies that include interviews with caregivers, professionals who see the children, and the children (when old enough) (Erickson and Egeland 2002).

Even when the investigator finds abuse or neglect, the family may still receive no services, as was the case in almost 40 percent of substantiated allegations nationally in 2007 (HHS, ACYF 2009). Providing no services at all when a child has been abused or neglected may seem unconscionable, but it is in fact common. In Alabama, the pre-reform system was said to have nothing to offer families between "aspirin and brain surgery"—that is, nothing between a very occasional social worker visit and removing the child from the home.

In the other substantiated cases, the family may get services for the child at home (almost 42 percent of the total substantiated in 2007) or the child may be removed from his or her home and placed in foster care (about 20 percent) (HHS, ACYF 2009). Annually, about 4 children per 1,000 nationwide enter foster care, while 6 to 8 children per 1,000 live in foster care (Macomber 2006).[3] The total foster care caseload has dipped slightly in the past six years, from 552,000 on September 30, 2000, to 510,000 on September 30, 2006 (HHS, Children's Bureau 2008b). States vary greatly in how much attention and how many family services they provide when the child stays at home, but all states dedicate a large share of resources and social worker attention to fostered children since the state is temporarily their parent—an enormous responsibility.

Each stage of this process is a judgment call, and in Alabama, before the reform, this subjectivity was part of the problem. Long-time Alabama attorney James Tucker, who monitored the settlement implementation, cited Alabamans' catchphrase for the disparity between jurisdictions: in rural counties, a child would be removed for having lice, but in Birmingham, broken bones would get no attention. R.C. may have suffered from the rush-to-judgment characteristic of the smaller communities, while children in the state's large cities got little protection. In Birmingham, chaos rather than rigidity reigned, with 1,000 uninvestigated cases in the mid-1990s and piles of unassigned cases. Ivor Groves, the court monitor, reported that in 1995, as reform began in Birmingham, he was told "See those cases there on that table? We don't know who they belong to."

Who Are the Children?

Children entering care are more likely to be very young or to be teenagers than to be children of 8 or 9, like R.C. The risk of reported maltreatment is by far the greatest for infants, in all income and racial groups. Smaller peaks occur for teenagers age 14 to 15 and for children just entering school—a peak often attributed to a "surveillance effect," when children are exposed to outsiders for the first time (Wulczyn et al. 2005).

School-age children in the child welfare system have a high level of behavioral problems, along with some (but more mixed) evidence of academic deficits. For adolescents, the issues are behavior problems, a greater likelihood than for younger children of having suffered physical or sexual abuse, and problems at school (Wulczyn et al. 2005). Infants reported to the child welfare system are far more likely to be developmentally delayed than infants in the population as a whole, with more than half "at high risk for developmental delay or neurological impairment," based on a national sample (Wulczyn et al. 2005, 82). Surprisingly, this very high rate of developmental risk is equally evident among children reported to the system whether or not they are found to be abused or neglected (Barth et al. 2008). While the full reason for this finding is not known, it could mean that such other features of a baby's home life as a chaotic or violent home or community are as damaging to development as actual incidents of abuse or neglect.

Who Are the Families?

There is no typical family involved with the child welfare system, though many families struggle with poverty, substance abuse, domestic violence, depression, and other mental and physical health problems. Poor families are disproportionately represented, but the reasons are complex (Macomber 2006). Poor families face more stress, which can push them over the edge into child abuse or neglect, and have fewer resources to use in a family crisis, where health care or counseling is often needed. The direct consequences of extreme poverty, such as homelessness or insufficient food in the house, may be defined by an agency as neglect, even though poverty alone is not supposed to establish maltreatment. Underlying problems, such as substance abuse, can lead both to child maltreatment and to poverty. And, poor families are probably subject to more surveillance and critical assumptions about their behavior by doctors, teachers, and other professionals than better-off families.

In Alabama before the reform, Tucker argues, such harsh assumptions about poor families particularly affected subjective child welfare judgments in some of the smaller, rural counties, where social workers had often grown up in more educated or well-off families in the same community where they worked. One complaint about lice in a child's hair might trigger long-held assumptions about poor white or black families, such as that they would never change and the children would be better off if removed.

Children and families in contact with the child welfare system nationally are disproportionately likely to be minority, particularly African American. The most recent summary of foster care children finds that in all but four states, a substantially higher proportion of children in foster care is black than in the general state population (HHS, Children's Bureau 2008a). African American children are more likely to come into contact with the system, more likely to be placed in out-of-home care, and likely to have longer stays in out-of-home care than white children. A review of the research concludes that "children of color and their families experience poorer outcomes and receive fewer services than their Caucasian counterparts" (Courtney et al. 1996, 99).

During the past decade, researchers have heightened their attention to the disproportionate representation and disparate treatment of children of color in the child welfare system and have sought to untangle the reasons behind them (Barth 2005; Hill 2006). Among the many likely reasons are differences in the attitudes and assumptions of child welfare staff and others who interact with families, along with real differences in family circumstances. In the words of one child-welfare official: "When a family presents as more articulate and can gather resources easier. . . .whether those resources are family or finances or provision of services, that changes the overall level of risk or the perceived level of risk."[4]

Besides poverty, many families in the child welfare system cope with such complex and often co-occurring challenges as family violence, substance abuse, and depression. For example, in the NSCAW sample of families investigated by CPS, 44.8 percent of caregivers have some experience with physical violence by their spouse or partner.[5] Almost one-third (32.6 percent) of the women have suffered severe violence (for example, being beaten up, choked, or threatened with a weapon) at least once (Hazen et al. 2004). These rates are consistent with other child welfare system studies showing that 30 to 40 percent of mothers have experienced domestic violence—about twice the rate for women in a typical community sample.

Depression is also widespread among women involved with the child welfare system. The NSCAW sample of caregivers for children investigated by the child welfare agency finds that almost a quarter have experienced a major depression in the past 12 months, almost twice the national percentage for all women (HHS, Children's Bureau 2005a). The proportion is even higher among women who have also been victims of domestic violence (Hazen et al. 2004). Other studies of low-income mothers have also found very high rates of depression, including a study of Early Head Start parents (who have income below the poverty level and at least one child under age 3), which finds that "a stunning 47 percent of the parents had depressive symptoms," and a study of homeless mothers with young children that finds that "more than 40 percent had a major depressive disorder" (Knitzer and Lefkowitz 2006, 14). These results are particularly distressing because so much evidence identifies the risks that maternal depression poses for the development of young children (Reder and Duncan 2000; Waldfogel 1998).

For substance abuse, the range of estimates is considerable, but all sources suggest that the problem is widespread. According to a recent review of cases sampled for the states' Federal Child and Family Services Reviews, substance abuse brings the attention of the child protective services agency in 16 to 61 percent of cases (Young et al. 2005). These estimates, however, are significantly lower than many other studies, possibly because child welfare workers have a difficult time identifying substance abuse during the rushed days of the initial investigation, and families have a strong incentive to conceal it. Another study of substance abusers in a child protective services caseload finds that 68 percent of the children have mothers who abuse alcohol or drugs (Jones ·2005). Many of these families are likely in the throes of other major problems, as a cause or an effect of the substance abuse. Other studies of low-income women who abuse substances find high rates of difficulties including "psychiatric problems, housing problems, legal problems, and domestic violence" (Morgenstern et al. 2003 in Morgenstern and Blanchard 2006, 64).

A detailed survey of birth parents in Washington, D.C., helps illustrate the range of practical challenges, such as income and housing, that troubled families likely also face. The proportion facing such great challenges may be higher in Washington, but gaps in housing, education, and work experience are major national issues as well:

> [Among birth parents supervised by CFSA in caring for children in their own homes], more than half does not have a high school diploma or GED, only 27% work outside the home, and only 4% are married. . . .Fully 25% of the birth parents surveyed reported having been homeless or living in a shelter before coming to CFSA's attention. (District of Columbia CFSA 2004, 9)

Two important caveats qualify this bleak picture. First, families are not homogeneous: some who find themselves caught up in the system have none of these additional risk factors. In a sample of Boston families involved with child welfare, one researcher finds that despite the patterns of high risk that characterize some families, others are involved with the system for different reasons and are hard to classify (Waldfogel 1998, 16). Similarly, in Washington, D.C., workers encounter many parents who are caring and effective but need specific and limited help, or who are suffering from a family tragedy—often a death or serious illness—that they cannot cope with alone. For example, a mother with mild mental retardation could have cared for a healthy child but could not safely handle a chronically ill child's complex medical needs without help. And a father who had been caring for a deaf and mute child with the help of his own mother could no longer manage once the boy's grandmother died.

The second caveat is that even families whose lives are overrun by serious and chronic problems should not be narrowly defined by them. Parents' courage, resilience, and abiding love for their children can coexist with drug and alcohol problems, emotional instability, or severe depression. Telling the story of one mother's probably doomed battle to keep her children from being adopted after many years of trying to end her dependence on drugs, a journalist sums her up as "a terribly flawed but fiercely determined mother," whose young son says of her after a visit, "If that was your mommy, you would be lucky."[6]

Children's Experience in Care and Afterwards

At the heart of R.C.'s tragedy was how the agency treated him after he was removed from his father's home. He was placed in institutions rather than in foster homes, and as he became increasingly distraught, he was moved farther away from his father and medicated more and more—leading to more emotional distress. Sadly, the system that was supposed to keep him safe damaged him further. That extra damage did not have to happen: children who encounter a better-functioning child welfare system ought to find a stable and loving home in their first foster family, live together with brothers and sisters and close enough for their parents to visit often, stay in a familiar school and neighborhood, and move promptly back home or to a permanent adoptive family.

Theresa Cameron, a foster child in the 1950s and 1960s, became a professor and wrote her life story *Foster Care Odyssey: A Black Girl's Story* about the damage that she, like R.C., experienced from a transient, unstable childhood in the system. She lived in foster care from early infancy with no adoption and no prospect of one, and her resulting grief, anger, and sense of displacement grew with each foster family, until she ended up running away, attempting suicide, and landing in an institution for delinquent girls. As she writes in the introduction,

> As I began to write this book, trying to find the right words to express myself, a story slowly took shape. At times, the pain stabbed through my heart, plunging me in depression. I hated reliving those memories. . . . Like most foster children, I had no choice with whom I lived or how long I would stay. . . . More than anything else, I wanted to be part of a family. . . . The transient nature of foster care . . . could not provide me with a sense of belonging. (Cameron 2002, x)

How frequently do children today have these deeply damaging experiences? While perhaps no longer typical, they are not as rare as they should be. In 2005, children in foster care for less than a year were far more likely to experience just one or two placements than three or more. But for children with longer stays in foster care, instability was more frequent. Among children in foster care for two years or longer, about two-thirds in the typical state had at least three placements. On the other hand, R.C.'s experience of placement in institutions rather than foster families is now relatively rare among children who enter care as young as he did: in the typical state, about 7 percent of children who enter foster care at age 12 or younger are placed in group homes or institutions (HHS, Children's Bureau 2008a).

Not only did R.C. have damaging experiences while in care, he was also left in limbo by the system, with no plan for a permanent home. Again, this is not how the child welfare system is supposed to work. All the adults in the system—the social worker and her supervisor, the biological parents and extended family, the foster parent, the judge, and the lawyers—should work together with input from the child to decide where he or she should live permanently. The child should move relatively quickly to a permanent and stable home, with help making a smooth transition and without ambiguity and mixed messages. But the system can and does fail in various ways at this delicate task of making prompt, yet sound decisions. It can take too long to decide about a child's future, the decision can be unmade repeatedly or not acted on, or the child can "age out" of the foster care system without any further support.

Every year, about 20,000 to 25,000 young people age 18 to 21 nationwide (26,517 in 2006) leave foster care because the state will no longer support them (HHS, Children's Bureau 2008b). Until recent legislation,[7] the federal government's regular matching funds for foster care ended when a child turned 18, though a few states provided longer support for some youth from other funds. When young people's lives have been disrupted, first by abuse or neglect, and then by repeated temporary placements, their prospects of supporting themselves alone and without a home at age 18 are grim. On average, they have also had poor educational experiences, putting them at a further disadvantage. Compared with their peers, former foster youth have higher rates of out-of-wedlock parenting, and many experience homelessness after leaving care. In addition, former foster youth frequently become involved in crime (Courtney et al. 2007; Pecora et al. 2005). This absence of support for youth who have grown up in the child welfare system is another widespread failure.

Unexplained Differences among the States

Many facts about the child welfare system, and the children and families who are involved with it, vary hugely by state. At the front end, the share of children with a substantiated allegation of abuse or neglect in 2007 ranged from less than 2 per 1,000 children in Pennsylvania and Arizona to 24 or more per 1,000 in the District of Columbia and Massachusetts. The explanations suggested by HHS include different definitions of child maltreatment (set by state law), different levels of evidence required for a substantiated or indicated finding, and the choice to serve some families through alternative response systems (which do not lead to a decision about whether an allegation is substantiated) (HHS, ACYF 2009; HHS, Children's Bureau 2008a).

Of course, differences in the real circumstances of families and children could also play a part, as could differences in the ways states implement their laws, not just the laws themselves. For example, if overloaded investigations units leave some referrals untouched, maltreatment rates will be lower than if all referrals were investigated. Possibly, differences in family circumstances and in state practice interact: states with more families experiencing dire problems might set the bar for abuse higher, as workers prioritize the most tragic cases, while states with fewer families in extreme distress might set the bar lower.

Children's entry into foster care also varies greatly. Rates of entry into foster care are less than 2 children per 1,000 in some states and over 10 in others. Most of the obvious explanations (such as explaining the patterns by rates of child victimization or demographics) are not borne out by the data. Another example with important policy and service implications is the difference in the proportion of children who are age 13 or older when they enter foster care. In Texas, it's 13 percent; in Delaware, it's more than four times as great at 56 percent (HHS, Children's Bureau 2008a). Such large unexplained differences suggest the need to understand particular state systems before diagnosing failure or prescribing solutions.

Diagnosing a Failed System in Alabama

In the early stages of the court case, Alabama officials were required to gather facts. As information piled up, the two senior officials who would lead the reforms—Andy Hornsby, commissioner of the Department of Human Resources, and Paul Vincent, director of the department's Division of Family and Children's Services—saw the damage that children were experiencing. Paul Vincent describes the cumulative effect of the evidence as leaving him "a different person." One study, for example, found that a third of the children entering foster care in Mobile could have stayed at home. Hornsby remembers a worker who arrived at a house on a bitterly cold day and found three adults down with the flu, at least a dozen children unsupervised because the adults were all sick, no food in the house, no heat, and "three-day-old diapers" on the youngest children. The social worker believed the adults in this family could have coped if they had a little money to rent a house where the heat worked, but instead the children were all placed in care—some of them 50 or 75 miles away.

Why had a system so flawed persisted for so long? Those I interviewed gave two answers. First was Alabama's long-standing political and fiscal neglect of child welfare and human services programs, coupled with a history of waiting to be forced, typically by the federal courts, before investing in any system that served vulnerable or troubled people. Commissioner Hornsby found a history of "political neglect, budget neglect, indifference" that affected the whole Department of Human Resources.

This pattern of refusing to act until forced by the courts was familiar in Alabama. According to the *Birmingham News'* editorial page,

> Near the end of U.S. District Judge Ira DeMent's ruling in a court fight over Alabama's shabby treatment of abused and neglected children, there is a list that ought to make all of us embarrassed about our state government. . . . [It includes] case after case of matters where a federal court had to order the state to meet its responsibilities to its own citizens. In fact, according to DeMent, the phenomenon is so customary, it has its own name: The Alabama Punting Syndrome.[8]

Second was the state system's culture, described by observers as made up of insularity, an absence of consequences for performance, passive acceptance of constraints, and low expectations. Both insiders and outside observers of Alabama's pre-reform child welfare system paint the same picture. Ivor Groves, who observed the state as court monitor once the lawsuit was settled, emphasized the lack of consequences for bad performance: "There were no clear expectations or accountability at all." With no information and no statewide standards, "counties performed as they performed" in a "laissez-faire" atmosphere, Groves said. Inside the agency, two longtime staffers described the pre-reform atmosphere as one of passive acceptance: people expected to do work the way they had always done it, meaning "always beleaguered, not enough resources."

Early Actions

In 1991, the court suit was settled. Rather than prescribe specific steps, the settlement agreement set forth goals to be achieved for children and families along with 29 principles for high-quality service delivery. The first goal was to protect children from abuse and neglect, and the second was to enable children to live with or near their families, "achieve permanence and stability in their living situation," succeed in school, and "become stable, gainfully employed adults" (Vincent 2006, 1). The 29 quality principles paint a comprehensive picture of an effective service delivery system. One ambitious principle represented a particularly large change from the pre-reform system: that services should be individualized to meet the needs of children and families, not "dictated by what services are available" (Vincent 2006, 2). The settlement also called for phasing in the reform by adding 15 percent of counties each year.

Hornsby and Vincent, the officials who would implement the settlement, brought different work experiences to their jobs, although they had known each other since meeting in the Army Reserve in the 1960s. Commissioner Hornsby was appointed in 1987, on loan from the federal government through the Intergovernmental Personnel Act. After considerable success in bringing order to the state's Food Stamps program and reducing its high error rate, he turned his attention to child welfare. Vincent remembers Hornsby as critical to the reform, ensuring sustained political support and marshalling resources through untiring "advocacy and cheerleading."

Commissioner Hornsby appointed Vincent, who had worked for the state's child support program, to head the child welfare agency just as criticisms of the system were mounting, shortly before the lawsuit was filed. Hornsby felt confident about Vincent's commitment to people in need and foresaw a strong and trusting working relationship.

Once the settlement was signed, Vincent convened a group of outside experts, hoping that someone could offer a blueprint for how to implement the ambitious vision it laid out. But Vincent soon realized that no one, including the top-flight talent gathered around the table, knew exactly how to achieve the new principles and desired results. Based on the group's advice, though, he decided to competitively select the early counties through an application process, to ensure that this first group would have the will and capacity to succeed. He also decided to deploy all the "modest" new reform resources within the pilot counties, rather than spreading them more thinly statewide.

In hindsight, Vincent sees the emphasis on "practice" rather than "systems" as the backbone of his strategy. That is, he focused more on how social workers did their jobs day to day than on such statewide administrative improvements as caseload reduction. Following this strategy, he carried out intensive off-site training for staff in the pilot counties and used outside experts to both design the training and serve as on-the-ground coaches for social workers, supervisors, and managers. Through the training and coaching, he hoped staff would learn by doing, so they could better design and perform their new jobs.

Zeroing in on a small number of counties made practice reforms faster to see, easier to finance, and easier to administer. The pilot began with only five or six counties serving a total of 700 to 800 children.[9] That small size meant that off-site training could be delivered quickly to the 20 to 25 social workers and supervisors involved. Vincent was able to trade off some of the procedural requirements to free workers up to attend training, yet still be able to respond to the true case emergencies because the smaller counties had less stress and chaos to start with.

Workers in the pilot counties responded enthusiastically to the new practices, particularly the stronger connection to families. One Shelby County social worker used her new skills to reach a father who had previously been hostile to intervention attempts. The social worker worked closely with the father and arranged for him to visit his children in foster care, which led the father to admit his failure as a parent and seek ways to change. "For the first time in his life, this man thought somebody cared for him, and he was empowered," the social worker told the *Birmingham News*. "I keep thinking, what if we had invested in that family 15 years ago?"[10]

While his reform strategy focused on the pilot counties, Vincent also had to move early to change the statewide contracting system, which was incompatible with the new, individualized plans for children and families. Under the old system, county social workers could use only those services the state had previously agreed to purchase, a one-size-fits-all approach. Vincent and Hornsby created and dispersed "flex-funds" that counties and social workers could spend as they saw fit for each family. At first, flex-funds came from a small amount of new money that Commissioner Hornsby squeezed out for the reform. As the reforms expanded, funds came from provider rate increases.

Although changing the system was difficult, the new flex-funds helped staff get results. According to Groves, outcomes for children started to improve once the flex-funds appeared. He thought there were two reasons: the money helped get the right services to families, and staff got the message that the agency was serious about the new practice model. As the *Birmingham News* reported,

> The reforms have given child welfare workers the freedom—and the money—to come up with creative ways of keeping families together and reuniting those that have been torn apart. . . . In Monroe County, a mother living on a limited budget was given stamps and stationery along with $50 a month in long-distance phone calls, so she could stay in touch with her 17-year-old daughter. . . . In June, mother and daughter were reunited.[11]

From the beginning, Vincent spread his new vision inside and outside the agency. Participants in the reform remember that his message was "unwavering," and the taproot of his leadership was "active engagement of all interested people." Ira Burnim, the lead plaintiffs' attorney, had originally expected that "changing hearts and minds would be hard, systems would be easy." But because of Vincent's leadership in changing staff values, it was the opposite: the administrative systems proved the greater obstacle. Inside the agency, a longtime staffer remembers that "Paul's leadership was critical . . . he made it not so scary."

By late 1993, reform had begun in the second group of counties, which included the largest and most troubled county, Jefferson County (Birmingham). At this point, strategies for spreading the reforms became crucial. As internal staff capacity improved, state office staff were paired with external consultants to provide assistance to the county offices. This expanded role helped engage state staff who had initially felt left out.

To assess how far along counties were on the path to reform, the reform team also invented the quality services review (QSR). Assessment was hard because the settlement agreement linked success to principles, not deadlines or tasks that could be tracked or counted. As team members struggled with this problem, Groves suggested building on a tool used in the developmental disabilities field. The new assessment tool scrutinized the quality of practice and the outcomes for children and families through structured interviews with the child, biological family, social worker, foster family, and others in a small sample of cases. A breakthrough in child welfare management, the QSR became a central part of Alabama's reform strategy because it linked the quality of practice to real accountability. According to Vincent, it served as "a powerful reinforcer of everything else" in the reform strategy because "you get what you measure."

When a county believed it had met the new criteria, it asked for a qualitative review by the court monitor. That review and other evidence, such as testimonials from staff and partners, were then used to demonstrate "conversion" to the new practice required by the settlement agreement.

The Reform Survives a Close Call

By November 1994, the *Birmingham News* reported that the court monitor's review of several counties in the second phase of reform showed progress. No county had achieved "conversion," but Groves was pleased with the trend in that direction. The article also reported that the new governor-elect, Fob James, was reviewing the R.C. case and other lawsuits against the state to determine the position he wanted to take.[12]

In the following months, Governor James's position became clearer. In January 1995, Hornsby left his job as commissioner, allowing the new governor to select his own appointee. A few months later, Governor James said publicly that he opposed the R.C. court settlement and was seeking a new commissioner who would too. In March 1996, he nominated Martha Nachman, the former head of a group home in Montgomery. Paul Vincent soon announced his retirement, citing conflicts of values with Commissioner Nachman.[13]

For the next year, differing views of federal court involvement, child welfare policy, provider roles and interests, and the role of child welfare officials clashed. Soon after Governor James took office, his legal adviser said he would try to end the child welfare settlement because it "diverts money from services and gives federal courts too much control of state agencies."[14] In May 1997, the governor and the attorney general asked the federal court to dismiss the settlement agreement. Explaining the action to the *Birmingham News,* the attorney general emphasized federal overreaching: "My job is to make sure the state of Alabama isn't run by federal courts. My job isn't to come here and help children."[15]

The governor and Commissioner Nachman also considered the settlement insufficiently focused on child safety. According to the local paper, Nachman linked the settlement to a series of child deaths dominating the news in order to "bolster her argument that the state should be allowed out of a federal court settlement she said has left battered children in unsafe homes." She was quoted saying about the reform, "Instead of having children placed where they are protected, they are being placed in graves."[16]

In accusing the child welfare agency of contributing to children's deaths through its reform approach, Commissioner Nachman tapped into a recurrent source of public anger. Child welfare agencies frequently weather periods of public outcry driven by child deaths. Sometimes the outcry leads to reform of a troubled system, as in the District after Brianna Blackmond's death, or in New York City, where the tragic death of Elisa Izquierdo led Mayor Giuliani to create a strong and independent child welfare agency under a new commissioner, Nick Scoppetta. Yet, public outcry can also lead to blame and staff turnover, without underlying reform. Reflecting back on child welfare in New York before the new agency was created, Commissioner Scoppetta pointed out that prior tragedies had led to frequent turnover of agency heads, which had stymied purposeful change. Thus, public criticism after a child's death is unpredictable as a driver of reform.

Worse, reformers worry that public anger after a tragedy can lead to responses harmful to the well-being of children. If criticism pushes agencies to remove too many children from their parents, it may increase the likelihood of the kind of trauma R.C. experienced, as children bounce around an overburdened foster care system. It may also increase the risk that the most serious cases will be lost in the sea of families brought into the system through excessive caution. Even for high-risk children—such as the siblings of children killed by their parents—removal from their homes is the beginning, not the end, of the story when it comes to their safety and well-being. A *New York Times* report following the siblings of Adam Mann, killed at age 5 in 1990, and the siblings of Elisa Izquierdo, killed at age 6 in 1995, demonstrates the point:

> Three years after Elisa's death, the four youngest had moved through four differ-
> ent homes, as ill-prepared foster parents gave up on them. . . . [In the Mann case],
> as the parents were nearing the end of their prison terms, all but the youngest, the
> only girl, were still being shuttled from foster home to foster home.[17]

Despite the intense public response to child deaths from abuse and neglect, there has been no reduction in the frequency of these tragedies nationwide. In 2007, an estimated 1,760 children died from abuse or neglect, up substantially from 2001, to a rate of 2.35 deaths per 100,000 children under age 18. More than 75 percent of these children were not yet 4 years old; infants had the highest rate of fatalities (HHS, ACYF 2009). The exact number is uncertain because it depends on a medical examiner's determination that a death was due to abuse and neglect. HHS attributes the rise in recent years to better reporting.

In Alabama, however, neither the fatalities themselves nor the commissioner's criticism ended the reform. The *Birmingham News'* editorial page argued forcefully from the court monitor's report on fatalities that the reforms were not the problem and, in fact, that child deaths were less common in counties that had started to implement the reforms than in those not yet there.[18] Some officials I interviewed agreed that the quality assurance information provided by the agency and the court monitor's report had discredited the view that the reform vision was unsafe and had demonstrated instead that workers inadequately applied the policy and needed more training and support. Others argued that the reform itself changed, pushed by the criticism to shift the balance between safety and family inclusion, somewhat more toward safety.

Commissioner Nachman's administration ended dramatically a year and a half after her appointment. In March 1997, both the county child welfare directors and the state House of Representatives voted no confidence after she reportedly blamed the county directors for child abuse deaths and told them they should be pallbearers at the next child's funeral.[19] In June, in a strongly worded opinion, the federal court rejected the state's argument for voiding the court settlement, attributing the request to "a shift in the political winds" and finding that "such maneuvering does not warrant the court's indulgence."[20] Nachman's resignation in November 1997 ended active opposition to the court settlement.

Those I interviewed draw various lessons from this experience. Some saw the deep commitment of the state legislature, the county directors, and the staff as evidence that the reform's basic philosophy had been strong enough to prevail. As Commissioner Hornsby said, "If a reform is strong enough, it can survive disastrous leadership." Others emphasized the central role of the federal court in creating continuity: as Groves pointed out, the court settlement has been a force for continuity through six or seven state commissioners and four governors. Those who stayed with the state agency through the turmoil thought reform was vindicated, but at a very high cost, through turnover in experienced staff and leadership.

Results

When U.S. District Judge Ira DeMent ended federal court oversight in 2007, after 19 years, Alabama's commissioner wrote that the decision affirmed that the state's child welfare system "not only met the high expectations of the court, it also demonstrated an unsurpassed, although imperfect, ability to provide for the safety and well-being of children and families in distress" (Walley 2007, 10). During the last phase of reform, all parties believed there had been great improvement, but plaintiffs and other observers thought the pace of reform had slackened. One longtime observer thinks the challenge was to sustain reform once the excitement of the early years gave way to the reality of policies and procedures needed for long-term operation: It "takes more energy to sustain an excellent child welfare program than to create it," this person said.

Nonetheless, all parties agree that Alabama's child welfare system today is far better than it was before the reform. Child abuse reports are investigated promptly, social workers carry fewer cases, children move around less from placement to placement, and many locations offer an array of family services to fill the gap between "an aspirin and brain surgery" for families. Between 1990 and 2004, Alabama quadrupled its investment in child welfare, from $71 million (of which $47 million was federal) to $285 million ($179 million of it federal).[21]

Synchronizing the Child Welfare System: Utah's Practice Model

> Organizations break down, despite individual brilliance and innovative products, because they are unable to pull their diverse functions and talents into a productive whole.—Peter Senge, *The Fifth Discipline*, 69

> Having a machine is not the cure; understanding the ordinary, mundane details that must go right for each particular problem is. . . . New laboratory science is not the key to saving lives. The infant science of improving performance— of implementing our existing know-how—is.—Atul Gawande, *Better*, 242–43

Utah's child welfare reform litigation, filed in 1993, addressed comprehensive failures in the state's child abuse and neglect investigations, child welfare services, and foster homes. Those I interviewed remember several reasons for these failures: high caseloads; complex and unproductive relationships with such key partners as the local judiciary; a cumbersome organizational structure that separated regional and state child welfare staff and pulled regional staff to work on other local priorities; and no interest from the governor's office before the 1993 gubernatorial election. As in Alabama, lack of accountability was a key problem, with a laissez-faire approach to regional office performance. Caseworkers and regional directors had no guidance or oversight on what constituted a good job, no consequences for poor performance.

But unlike Alabama, the signing of the court settlement in 1994 did not initially lead to reform. Today, the plaintiff's attorneys, state officials, and the court monitor all share the view that in the first three years after the agreement, performance stalled or even slipped backwards. A court-appointed monitoring panel found in 1996 that "the state had complied with only four of the settlement agreement's 95 areas."[22] Basic measures of quality (such as visits and foster parent recruitment) did not improve, and some measures deteriorated.

What was the problem? In Alabama and the District, a big problem going into the reform was funding, which is a shared responsibility of the federal, state, and sometimes local government (though not in Utah). According to an Urban Institute report on the cost of protecting vulnerable children (Scarcella et al. 2004), in 2004 the federal government paid just under half of the $23.3 billion total cost of the child welfare system, while the state (39 percent) and local (12 percent) governments split the rest.

But in Utah, while investment had been an issue in the past, it was not in those first years after the settlement. As part of Utah's reform, the legislature substantially increased the child welfare budget to hire caseworkers and bring caseloads down; hire and train new juvenile court judges; fully staff a children's division in the attorney general's office, to provide representation in child welfare cases; and create a guardian *ad litem* office staffed with public employees.[23]

If funding wasn't the problem, then what was? Even knowing where to look for the failure is difficult, because responsibility in the child welfare system is so fragmented. The federal and state governments split policy responsibility, while the state may split operational responsibility with city or county governments or, as in Utah, it may operate its own regional and local offices. State or local judges have important responsibilities, and so do public and private agencies that provide such services as medical and mental health care, education, and family support. And finally, because of the complexity of recruiting staff and developing, paying for, targeting, and monitoring services, child welfare agencies depend critically on their administrative systems—budgeting, contracting, licensing, human resources, information systems—to coordinate and support the day-to-day work.

State and Federal Roles in Child Welfare

State laws have historically set most parameters of the child welfare system, as they do for other aspects of family life such as divorce and custody. States vary in how they define child abuse and neglect, determine the roles and functions of the courts that make removal decisions, define the steps required to end a parent's rights and free a child for adoption, determine the child welfare agency's structure, and decide which services and funding will be available to which children and families. In one state, but not another, a baby born addicted due to the mother's substance abuse may be defined as abused. The child welfare agency in one state may be required to start investigating all reports of child abuse and neglect within 48 hours; in another state, some reports may not be formally investigated but instead handled through an alternative response system; and in a third, there may be no deadline for beginning an investigation.

The states' role compared with the federal government's is even greater when it comes to designing, organizing, and funding services to prevent maltreatment and help families strengthen their parenting skills. For example, substance abuse and mental health services receive far less federal funding than child welfare, and there is no consistent national approach to funding or organizing them. Informal, community-based family support services—such as help from a local neighborhood center, parent support groups, or mentors—vary even more in their funding and structure. Often the child welfare agency or other public agencies (public health, youth services, or early childhood services) are the main funder, but sometimes there is little or no public funding of any kind.

State values about families, both current and historical, can influence the legal framework and the context in which it is enforced. In Utah, the child welfare agency was criticized extensively for intruding into the rights of biological families, not just for failing to keep children safe. The press, the state legislature, and the Board on Children and Families (which oversees the child welfare agency) all frequently complained about intrusion. In December 2000, parents organized by Justice, Economic Dignity, and Independence for Women, an antipoverty group, argued in support of leaving children in their homes, calling foster care children "hostages . . . trapped in a complex and uncaring system."[24] Another group, led by the Utah Eagle Forum, argued that parents are targeted by false allegations: "All it takes is an anonymous phone call . . . you are guilty until proven innocent."[25]

While several people I interviewed agreed that such support for family privacy was part of Utah's culture, they disagreed about how it affected child welfare reform. One former official saw Utah's support for family privacy as a welcome contrast to other states, where few will rally to support families in the child welfare system. Others saw it as a backlash that threatened the crucial reform legislation. A third view argued that the support for family privacy was a sign of success because the public focus shifted from safety to government intrusion only when the agency started doing a better job on safety.

Yet while states have a great deal of policy leeway in child welfare, federal laws set key parameters and create financial incentives. First, all states seeking federal funding under the Child Abuse Protection and Treatment Act (CAPTA) must have state laws that define child abuse and neglect to cover at least the situations set out in the federal law: parental action or failure to act leading to death, serious physical or emotional harm, sexual abuse, or imminent risk of harm.

Second, states must provide specific protections and meet requirements in order to continue to receive federal funding for their child welfare and foster care programs. Federal legislation such as the Adoption Assistance and Child Welfare Act of 1980 (AACWA), which was modified by the Adoption and Safe Families Act of 1997 (ASFA), requires states to provide legal protections that govern children's removal from their homes, to ensure that a child's safety is paramount, and to move speedily to place children in permanent homes. By law, a judge must determine that removal is in the child's best interests and that the state has made reasonable efforts to keep the family together except under certain egregious circumstances (such as parents' murder of a sibling), where ASFA specifically states that "reasonable efforts" are not necessary. To ensure that children do not linger in the limbo of temporary foster care, ASFA sets tight deadlines for states to decide whether children can safely go home or should instead move to a permanent home with an adoptive family or a relative. While a child is in foster care, a judge must regularly review the case. After a child spends 15 of 22 months in foster care, states are required to either go to court to terminate parental rights (a legal proceeding that ends a parent's relationship with his or her child) or explain why this is not the best decision for the child.[26]

ASFA also added federal resources to help states promote adoption for children who cannot go home. AACWA paved the way in 1980 by providing federal reimbursement for states to subsidize the costs borne by families who adopt eligible special needs children from foster care. Previously, foster parents received such support but adoptive families did not. ASFA also rewarded states with a financial bonus—called the "adoption incentive"—if they increased the total number of adoptions of special needs children from foster care.

Further, ASFA called attention to the special role of kin in caring for children, identifying a long-term home with a relative as one outcome that child welfare agencies could aim at. Even though ASFA did not provide federal resources for permanent homes with kin, many states experimented with providing financial support to relatives even when they did not choose to adopt, primarily through subsidized legal guardianship.

Federal child welfare legislation has continued to evolve since these case studies. In 1999, the Foster Care Independence Act (FCIA) focused on young people aging out of foster care, providing states with modest additional resources to spend on young people just before and after they leave foster care, as well as the option to receive federal reimbursement for health insurance coverage for former foster youth age 18 to 21. In October 2008, President Bush signed the Fostering Connections to Success and Increasing Adoptions Act (FCSIAA), which builds on ASFA by providing federal reimbursement for subsidized guardianship and extends federal reimbursement to states that support youth beyond age 18.

After the Settlement in Utah: Why So Difficult?

When Ken Patterson arrived as director of Utah's Division of Child and Family Services (DCFS) in 1997, the state's reform legislation and the court lawsuit had further complicated an already complex oversight structure. The agency had to respond to questions, critiques, and suggestions from six outside authorities, while trying to improve day-to-day performance. The agency answered to the Office of Compliance in the Department of Human Services, home to the auditors who conducted case reviews; the Office of the Ombudsman, a largely independent entity with an investigative role including subpoena power; the Legislative Oversight Committee, a standing committee of the House and Senate created as part of the 1994 reforms; the Office of the Guardians *Ad Litem* and the Court-Appointed Special Advocates; the plaintiffs' attorneys from the litigation; and the Board of the Division of Child and Family Services, created by statute to set policy for the division.

My interviewees all thought that the legal process also contributed to weak agency performance in the three years after the settlement agreement was signed, but they interpreted the problems differently. The plaintiffs' attorney thought the state was preoccupied with litigation instead of the settlement in the early years and was "just trying to wait it out." Others cited personal tensions among the attorneys on all sides. Some state observers faulted the unwieldy settlement agreement itself, which had over 300 compliance provisions. Overwhelmed, staff viewed the agreement as the handiwork of lawyers—from the state's Office of the Attorney General and from the National Center for Youth Law, representing the plaintiffs—who had insufficient knowledge of social work or child welfare.

Management challenges at the department also hobbled compliance. Governor Michael Leavitt signed the settlement agreement immediately after taking office in 1994, and a stable team was not yet in place. In 1996, when Leavitt appointed Robin Arnold-Williams as the director of human services, she became the fourth director in two years. New directors of human services and child welfare rotated through the jobs, under intense pressure to comply with settlement requirements. Looking back, observers see some management strategies tried by these short-termers as counter-productive: one gained notoriety for reportedly taking a trailer around the state, setting up outside each local office, and interviewing workers and supervisors to see if they were committed enough to compliance to keep their jobs. Richard Anderson, a longtime, highly respected child welfare agency official working outside the division during this period, said he worried about his former colleagues because it was "a nightmare. . . . staff crying, thinking they're going to be fired."

In this setting, staff morale plummeted. Many in the agency resented the attempt to impose strict, even harsh, accountability for what they saw as the wrong things: a settlement agreement heavy on compliance and light on quality standards and results for children. The management strategies tried during this period did not increase compliance and drove people with more clinical expertise either into jobs where they could hide out unobtrusively or out of the agency entirely. As Arnold-Williams sums up this period, "Agency staff had no sense of control over their own destiny."

Patterson had a close-up view of this dark period's effect on social workers and families in 1995, before he became agency head. Brought in as a consultant to examine cases that had prompted complaints to the ombudsman's office, he found common ailments: children were moved among placements abruptly and arbitrarily, families were not involved in planning for their children, and "supervisors were missing." Caseworkers consulted mental health or other experts and made recommendations based on the "last and biggest degree" they had talked to, with no heed paid to the child's history and no family involvement. They then deferred the decisions to the lawyers in the courtroom.

Arnold-Williams remembers an experience during these years that shaped her picture of what was going wrong at the grassroots level. When asked why the number of visits to children wasn't going up, caseworkers told quality assurance interviewers: "We don't know what to do when we get there." Arnold-Williams concluded that even "with all this [extensive compliance monitoring], staff didn't quite know what we wanted them to do." And when you don't know what to do, "it's human nature to procrastinate."

Gaps in caseworker education and experience, meager on-the-job training, low salaries, and high turnover rates are frequent problems nationwide. Most often, though, these ills combine with excessively high caseloads. According to one recent study, child welfare workers typically have caseloads of 24 cases for investigation or 31 cases for ongoing case management—about twice the recommended number (Annie E. Casey Foundation [AECF] 2003). In Utah, though, caseloads had already been reduced by the time Patterson arrived, and there were no unassigned cases sitting on desks as in the extreme chaos of pre-reform Birmingham, Alabama, or Washington, D.C. Nonetheless, the concerns that remained mirror those associated with inexperienced and overwhelmed staff nationwide. These include bad decisionmaking about children, too often driven by emergencies; little or no ongoing monitoring of children's circumstances or planning for their future; and plans made without family input and firsthand knowledge of parents' and children's circumstances.

In addition, Patterson concluded that the very steps intended to reform the system instead sent it reeling backwards, creating a "perfect storm" of damage to children and families. When Utah enacted funding for quickly hiring many social workers and lawyers, for speed's sake it reduced the hiring standards for social workers. That produced a large class of new social workers without specialized training or "a social work understanding." At the same time, the state hired a fleet of lawyers whose training inclined them toward sanctions against parents. Pairing confident young lawyers with inexperienced and untrained social workers meant that decisions were driven "by the lawyers [because] the new workers didn't know any better"; social workers also internalized some of the attorneys' negative perspectives toward birth families.

The Roles of Judges and Lawyers in the Child Welfare System

Few Americans would want an agency to have the unfettered authority to take their child away, any more than we would want to empower police to send us to prison without a judge or jury hearing the case. So federal law and state laws require that judges make key decisions about children and families in the child welfare system. Judges determine when it is appropriate to remove a child from home, review case plans regularly, and, if necessary, terminate parental rights and create a new adoptive family. This judicial role reflects the grave decision to remove a child from his or her parents' home or to permanently terminate parental rights.

Consequently, legal decisionmaking and social work decisionmaking have to coexist in the child welfare system, with lawyers for each party playing a much greater role than in other human services programs. Lawyers representing the child welfare agency and its social workers and lawyers representing children, parents, foster parents, and prospective adoptive parents may all participate in a court hearing. A potential complication for child welfare agencies is that the lawyers who represent the state's perspective in court may be on staff, in a separate state agency (such as an attorney general's office), or in private practice, leading to potential coordination issues. Not surprisingly, a system with central roles for both the executive and judicial branches breeds conflict, as does a system in which both social workers and lawyers play major roles.

Local or state judges who hear individual children's cases play a completely different role from judges who hear cases arguing that a failed child welfare system violates state or federal laws or constitutions (called institutional reform litigation). Even though these two judicial roles are unrelated, it would be easy for the reader to confuse them because so many jurisdictions—about 30, including the District of Columbia, Alabama, and Utah—have, or recently had, institutional reform litigation targeting their child welfare performance. To avoid confusion in this book, the judges and the courts hearing institutional reform litigation are referred to as federal judges and courts, and the judges hearing individual cases of children are called local or state judges and courts.[27]

Starting Down the Path to Reform

As the parties to the Utah lawsuit found themselves three years into a four-year settlement and still not succeeding, they made a number of changes. The state filed an appeal arguing that the settlement was intended to end after four years no matter what the results, but at the same time, the governor appointed Arnold-Williams as the human services director in 1996 and stepped up the recruitment that led to Patterson's appointment as division director in 1997. Soon thereafter, Patterson recruited Richard Anderson, a respected Utah social worker and administrator who had just left the child-welfare agency, back to become his deputy. Meanwhile, the judge asked Paul Vincent (now a consultant) to conduct an implementation study and then join the team as ongoing court monitor. Vincent's initial charge was to work closely with the state team to develop a new implementation plan, to get the settlement agreement back on track.

The new team combined insiders and outsiders. Anderson and Arnold-Williams had both spent their whole careers in the department. Anderson came to Utah for college, received a bachelor's degree in social work, and worked his way up in the child welfare agency from a job as the only caseworker in a tiny rural office. Arnold-Williams came to pursue her master's in social work, started in the department's division on aging, and served in various policy, legislative, and administrative positions.

By comparison, Patterson was an outsider, though he too had ties to Utah and a long history in child welfare in the West. After many years heading up child welfare in Idaho, he left when administrations changed and accepted a prestigious fellowship from a national foundation, conducting a project in Utah along the way. After the fellowship, he headed child welfare in Nevada until Utah recruited him away with the draw of its major commitment to change: the state had doubled resources for child welfare to comply with the settlement.

At the same time, there were plenty of risks in taking on a system still in turmoil. Patterson didn't formally arrange a safety net in case the job didn't work out—unlike Andy Hornsby in Alabama, who remained on temporary leave from the federal government. But he recalls being glad that the people he had met during his foundation fellowship could be counted on to help him if something went wrong.

The new team's first charge was to develop the revised settlement agreement, the Milestone Plan. Patterson also believed that to succeed, the agency needed a practice model that would translate the Milestone Plan's broad themes into social worker practice, and he recruited Anderson to lead that part of the work. They worked closely with Vincent, a collaboration that was made easier by the vision the three shared. They all believed that the agency should move toward family-centered practice, a commitment to involving children and families in planning their own futures, and "clinically sophisticated" decisions that reflected an understanding of child and family strengths, challenges, and history, rather than just today's symptoms.

Patterson also wanted to reverse the agency's passivity by demonstrating that the plan was not imposed from outside but actively chosen by the agency. When the U.S. District Court ordered the state to remain under the court's jurisdiction—a decision appealed by the state—Patterson hammered home that the state's track to reform was the same either way.[28] As Arnold-Williams said, looking back, "The best way to handle a court order is to act as though you don't have it."

Another early step was creating an internal constituent services office to solve problems before they got to the external ombudsman. According to Anderson, the volume of individual complaints was so overwhelming that it was competing for attention with the development of the Milestone Plan and the practice model. The new office sprang from Anderson's concern and Patterson's conviction that the agency had to demonstrate it could respond effectively to citizens, directly. The new office resolved cases within the agency and halved the ombudsman's caseload. According to Patterson, this success built momentum and a sense that the agency could get things done.

But the biggest remaining step to reform was strengthening social workers' understanding of their job and their abilities to do it well. In Alabama, Vincent had hired outside consultants to develop training and consult with local offices, but Patterson and Anderson chose instead to rely on internal staff to develop a practice model that linked all elements of the work to the vision in the Milestone Plan. Patterson's idea sprang from his experience as child welfare director in Idaho, where the state had adopted a new family-centered philosophy, realized that the old state policy and practice no longer fit, and launched a project to translate the philosophy into policy and practice next steps. While it was tempting to imitate Idaho's model in Utah, he thought it wiser to engage the Utah staff to tailor the model to their needs. Involving staff in the work was part of the team's core strategy for both the Milestone Plan and the practice model, which Anderson describes as "attracting" staff rather than "driving them" through compliance enforcement.

The team also wanted external partners to feel that their ideas were reflected in the practice model. For years, Secretary Arnold-Williams had shared information about child welfare regularly with elected officials, so once her team began to work on the practice model, she was able to start a dialogue about its provisions that built on the officials' earlier knowledge. Her goal in explaining key elements of the model "up and down the decision and policy chain" was to make sure the governor and key legislators were confident enough in the model to refrain from scapegoating it, if a tragedy happened after implementation. At the same time, Anderson conducted 46 community meetings to gain public input to the model because he didn't want to build an approach that was "not supported by the people of Utah."

Tracking Progress

As in Alabama, the active development and use of data was a critical reform strategy—the single biggest change in the agency, according to Anderson. Patterson specifically emphasized the quality services review, arguing that it was essential to cementing the changes in the agency's outlook and practice. He embraced Alabama's QSR model because he knew that Utah's agency could not pass court compliance reviews unless the measurement approach reinforced the policy and practice approach. He was convinced the agency "wouldn't perform well on just process" without "the voice of the customer" in the evaluation process. Drawing on Vincent's experience, the team adapted Alabama's QSR model and found that it worked well, providing rich data and helping staff grasp how to use information to learn, rather than to target blame.

Utah's advances in data collection coincided with a national impetus to improve data collection. Fifteen years ago, the task of building strong agency information systems in child welfare seemed daunting. With a complex mission, rapidly changing caseloads, and overburdened workers leery of adding data entry to their other tasks, child welfare agencies seemed like poor candidates for automation, and their old computer systems were not easily adapted to meet caseworker needs. In 1993, however, Congress decided that better child welfare information was a national need and enacted legislation that enhanced federal reimbursement to states for developing and implementing state agency child welfare information systems (SACWIS). States could choose whether to develop and implement a SACWIS, but if they did, federal regulations defined requirements for the enhanced funding.

With new regulations and funding, several large private firms developed expertise in SACWIS systems that could be transferred from state to state. Today, 26 states and the District of Columbia have operational SACWIS systems as defined by the federal government, and 16 more have systems in development.[29] While there is plenty of room for improvement in SACWIS regulations, the change in data availability from a decade ago is dramatic.

But information systems that collect numbers are not enough, for Patterson's worry that quantitative information would fail to do justice to Utah's accomplishments is widely shared in child welfare circles. There is a related concern that if numbers drive out qualitative observations, then they will drive down the quality of practice—just as some school reformers argue that emphasizing test scores diminishes other ways of assessing teachers and schools. Luckily for child welfare agencies, tools for qualitative observation have gotten stronger and more widely used just as tools for quantitative measurement have improved.

Shortly after Alabama invented the QSR, Congress demanded that HHS revamp its approach to monitoring state performance. Nearly everyone hated the old HHS monitoring method, based heavily on review of paper case files: states, because it too often resulted in large fines for noncompliance; advocates, because it seemed to bear no relation to the actual results for children and families; and Congress, because of states' complaints about financial penalties. After freezing enforcement of the penalties for several years, Congress finally required the Administration for Children and Families (ACF), the part of HHS that I led, to develop a fairer method. Guided by Carol Spigner, associate commissioner for the Children's Bureau, a team scoured the country for assessment methods that best captured the results for children and families. After a careful review and several pilot tests, the QSR became a core component.

Moving from federal reviewers looking at files to federal reviewers talking to children, parents, and social workers has had big advantages but some minuses as well. To me, the biggest plus, far exceeding my expectations, has been the spread of qualitative review techniques to states and cities across the country, which use them in internal management and quality improvement, as well as to prepare for federal reviews and respond to litigation. Where the new qualitative reviews work best, they provide rich and detailed information about performance strengths and weaknesses, suggest insights for action plans, stimulate discussion among social workers and supervisors about the quality of practice, and bring stakeholders of all backgrounds into the process (most likely paired with an expert, fully trained reviewer), so they can more fully understand the dilemmas and judgment calls that are part of child welfare.

The minuses cited by states generally relate to the penalty process. While the new review process allows states a chance to improve before penalties are assessed, penalties in some states are now coming due, and some legitimately question whether the review methods are accurate and whether demanding penalties is the right way to improve the system. When we designed the system initially, the biggest concern was that doing such detailed reviews would mean looking at too few cases to have statistical validity. The information might be richer, more realistic, and more nuanced than in a case file review, but it would not necessarily be representative, so states worried that an unrepresentative sample might unfairly subject them to a penalty. Our response was a multi-method approach: the detailed case reviews would be combined with statewide statistics, and the state's performance rating and any possible sanctions would depend on both. Now that sanction decisions are approaching, the legitimacy of this approach will certainly be hotly contested.

Finally, besides qualitative and quantitative information for management, research data are also now easier to get and use, and far more comprehensive than previously, offering the potential for much improved knowledge. In 1996, Congress authorized and funded the NSCAW, which tracks a national sample of children and families over time and collects information on their experiences "drawn from firsthand reports from children, parents, and other caregivers, as well as reports from caseworkers, teachers, and data from administrative records."[30] For the first time, researchers can study how children are doing developmentally when they are first reported to the child welfare system, what circumstances they live in while in foster care, how their milieu changes over time, and what needs and strengths they and their families bring.

Results

In 2001, Richard Anderson took over from Ken Patterson as division director. He saw the reform through until his retirement in 2007, earning compliments from Leecia Welsh, the lead plaintiffs' attorney, when the agreement to terminate the litigation was signed several months later.

The 2007 agreement emphasized the dramatic improvements in case practices and in regular assessment that ensure that any drop-off in performance is identified and corrected. A news release from the plaintiffs' lawyers singled out key accomplishments, including doubling of the number of caseworkers and reducing caseloads to 13–15 cases per worker; extensive caseworker training; adoption of key practice skills that focus on addressing unique family circumstances and needs; dramatic improvements in data collection and assessment; and high-quality provision of health services to foster children.[31] The lawyers also cite the tripling of the budget for the Utah Division of Child and Family Services from $50 million in 1993, when the suit was filed, to $151 million in 2007.

As envisioned in the 2007 agreement, all parties agreed in December 2008 that the year had gone as planned and that Utah had complied with the settlement. Therefore, Judge Tena Campbell dismissed the case on January 5, 2009.[32]

Conclusion

Having sketched two successful child welfare turnarounds and set the national context, we now turn to the lessons that drive success. Chapter 4 hones in on research about effective programs and services. While good ideas are not sufficient for reform, they are necessary, so understanding what ideas work and how confident we can be about them provides the underpinning for change.

4

What We Know

How Research Can Contribute to Reform

> "In the varied topography of professional practice, there is a high, hard ground where practitioners can make effective use of research-based theory and technique, and there is a swampy lowland where problems are confusing 'messes' incapable of technical solution."
>
> —Donald A. Schon, *The Reflective Practitioner*, 42

So far, the stories of child welfare reform in the District of Columbia, Alabama, and Utah look a lot like Schon's lowlands, where messy problems bring together policy failures, complex and dysfunctional bureaucratic and political environments, and intense controversy. This chapter examines whether research can nonetheless play an important role in improving child welfare agencies, programs, and systems. What light does research shed on child welfare agencies' two central challenges: to enhance parenting so it is not dangerous to children (or, if enhancement fails, to protect children) and to support healthy childhood development? This chapter reviews the evidence needed to answer these questions, weighing what we know against what we don't know, to assess research's role in reform.

Research on Predicting and Preventing Parental Failure

Parenting failures extreme enough to damage or endanger children are child welfare agencies' core concern. But to fully protect children, the system needs to not only discourage bad parenting but also promote good parenting—the stable, consistent, nurturing, and stimulating relationship underlying a child's emotional and intellectual development. So we

85

might expect a solid knowledge base on the key questions: What shapes good or bad parenting? What does it take for parents to change? Does that answer differ for parents in different circumstances—for example, parents dealing with substance abuse or domestic violence, extreme financial stress, or uncontrolled anger or depression?

Surprisingly, research provides few clear answers to these critical questions. One problem is that there has been no top-level effort to integrate the insights from such diverse research fields as adolescent and adult development, early childhood interventions aimed at parents and children, parenting training programs, treatment for mental illness, substance abuse treatment, or domestic violence response. Without an integrated overview, child welfare research has focused on two specific threads: what is known about improving parenting and what is known about predicting parenting—in particular, predicting the risk of harm to a child. Child welfare research has also been limited by the agency's institutional role of short-term intervention after abuse and neglect occur, drawing many of its lessons from evaluations of relatively brief programs to improve parents' caregiving. Later sections of this chapter go beyond the child welfare research to identify additional tools drawn from related fields, including two-generational early childhood programs that provide services to young children and their parents and programs that treat maternal depression among low-income women.

Improving Parenting: What Works?

Although concrete evidence from child welfare interventions is sparse, it hints that interventions can change the behavior of even highly challenged parents. But not every intervention works, and the principles that would help predict whether an intervention is likely to work are still emerging.

For years, child welfare researchers studied an approach to changing parenting that showed early promise: intensive family preservation. Programs based on this premise delivered short-term (e.g., 90-day) intensive services to parents faced with having their child removed from home. These programs used that risk to change parents' behavior and avert a crisis. Workers were to have a handful of cases so they could be available to parents around the clock, visiting their homes, providing practical help like cleaning a filthy apartment, and building a relationship that could motivate change. The initial hope was that children who would otherwise have been removed would be able to stay safely at home, thus reducing the number of removals and the resulting trauma.

But rigorous evaluations show that family preservation programs did not work as initially envisioned for most families. Families referred to family preservation services are no less likely to experience removals than a control group that receives the child welfare agency's usual response, according to highly reliable random assignment evaluations of family preservation programs. Some studies of family preservation interventions tailored to very specific populations (for example, older youth with behavior problems) have, however, found successful outcomes (Pecora et al. 2000).

Pecora and colleagues (2000) put these findings in context. First, the success of specific interventions like family preservation programs depends on the broader context of services available within a community. For example, a brief intervention might work in one site where longer-term medical or mental health services are available through other programs but not in another site where a family is unable to get mental health or medical services after 90 days. Second, "some families need services on a long-term basis and are not well-served by a short period of intensive work" (Maluccio 1991 in Pecora et al. 2000, 284). This conclusion, that families' deep-seated problems typically require long-term attention, is consistent with findings from other policy areas. But it challenges child welfare agencies, whose mission often limits the time for serving parents.

At the same time, rigorous research finds positive results for other parenting programs. Three recent reviews identify programs that improved key aspects of parent-child relationships, helped parents prevent or respond better to the behavioral problems of troubled children, or led to more positive, less abusive parenting. Most of the available evidence does not directly address whether interventions reduce the frequency of abuse and neglect reported to child welfare agencies (Center on the Developing Child 2007; Hurlburt et al. 2007; Johnson et al. 2006). Promising programs occur in many settings: in the family's home, a classroom or parents' group, nursery schools or child care centers, a substance abuse or methadone maintenance program, or a therapist's office. Home visit programs for parents with very young children draw special attention from the reviews for their range of effects (Johnson et al. 2006), though the programs supported by the strongest research evidence target narrow populations such as "young first-time mothers living in poverty" (Center on the Developing Child 2007, 13).

An encouraging finding is that some parenting programs can improve parent-child interactions even among parents with substance abuse and mental health problems (Hurlburt et al. 2007). In a Head Start program serving very poor families, a parent training program was tested on a group of mothers, some of whom had depression, substance abuse problems, and other difficulties. The program worked equally well for mothers with and without the risk factors (Baydar, Reid, and Webster-Stratton 2003). However, getting these results with the most troubled families may require supplemental services to meet other needs (Chase 2002 in Johnson et al. 2006).

Unfortunately, most parent training programs used by child welfare agencies bear little resemblance to the proven, effective programs (Hurlburt et al. 2007). Unlike most agency programs, the successful initiatives require parents to devote many hours and become intensively involved through techniques like role-playing, and highly trained and well-supervised therapists are required to teach and oversee these programs. Successful home visit programs also require "well-trained and adequately supervised professional staff" with clear goals structuring their services (Center on the Developing Child 2007, 13).

Programs may be most effective when they recognize the complex causes of parenting difficulties and avoid one-dimensional solutions. One review identifies "five core domains of parenting difficulty" (such as impulse control, parenting skills, and stress management skills) and argues that programs that address several of these dimensions will likely have the biggest impact. But most programs identified by researchers address just one factor (Johnson et al. 2006).

Thus, successful interventions are not casual or easy to deliver; rather, most are intensive, entail high quality standards, and combine clinical expertise with relationship-building and outreach. In addition, some evidence indicates that the gains of short-term interventions will erode and that the most troubled parents may not experience gains without additional backup services to address their underlying problems.

Predicting Parental Failure: Research about Risk

Throughout its involvement with a family, the child welfare agency tries to predict the risk of future child abuse or neglect. As soon as an investigator finds that a child has been abused or neglected, he or she will try to predict the risk of future harm in determining whether to remove the child from the home. If the child is placed in foster care, the agency and the local judges will decide whether and when the child can return home, based on predictions about when parents will be able to keep the child safe. If a child stays at home while the parents receive services, agency staff need to assess the constantly changing situation and, again, predict future harm to decide whether the danger has disappeared and supervision can be ended or whether the danger is increasing and removal is necessary.

High-profile tragedies frequently call into question the accuracy of these predictions. A major debate among child welfare researchers is whether (and how much) sophisticated risk assessment tools can make prognostications more accurate. These tools require workers to assess specific risk and protective factors and then take actions based on the boxes checked off—increasing consistency in decisionmaking and reducing the role of individual discretion and judgment. Do these tools work in the real-life circumstances of child welfare? Or is improving prediction an unrealistic goal? Would it be more realistic to acknowledge the limits of information and focus on the best services and policy choices given those limits?

Advocates for risk assessment tools make two broad arguments. First, without a structured tool, even expert social workers fail to take all relevant factors into account to predict the danger to a child because of limits in human decisionmaking. Second, risk assessment tools (or at least the best of them) predict well. Child welfare experts can have difficulty balancing the impacts of multiple factors, some helpful and some harmful—for example, substance abuse coupled with a strong social network—or considering evidence systematically or consistently. Tools developed from case data provide more consistent results (Shlonsky 2007).

Research on families characterized by repeated and chronic neglect illustrates social workers' difficulties in using evidence to predict risk. Suppose an investigator responding to a neglect report finds the children dirty, hungry, and wandering in the neighborhood. Even if this is the third or fourth such report, if the investigator is not using an assessment tool that forces attention to the pattern of multiple reports, he or she may not open the case. The children have not been physically harmed, the parents are likely to acquiesce to the child welfare agency's directions, and the information about past neglect reports may not be available or seem relevant at the moment. Or the investigator may tackle the immediate problems—the empty refrigerator or the dirty clothes—even though researchers find that in some chronically neglectful families, current stress is not the core problem (Pecora et al. 2000).

Unfortunately, as both fatality reviews and broader research suggest, misreading these situations costs children dearly. The risk of a child's death or injury, as well as the damage detached parents do to children's development, can be obscured for workers if these parents are not resistant or angry. Yet, parents' compliance may reflect not a desire to change but extreme passivity or depression, which endangers children's well-being (Pecora et al. 2000; Waldfogel 1998). For example:

> Child welfare expert Patricia Schene, who reviewed the handling of [a St. Louis child fatality] case. . . . concluded that the agency misread the parents' lack of resistance, interpreting it as a positive indicator when in fact it was merely symptomatic of their generally neglectful parenting style and in particular of the mother's depression. (Schene 1996 in Waldfogel 1998, 3)

The second point proponents make is that risk assessment tools outperform unstructured decisionmaking. The evidence comes from studies of the relationship between structured tools and re-referral (a later report, whether or not substantiated, of abuse or neglect). A study in Illinois finds a drop in re-referrals after a structured safety and risk protocol was implemented. A study in Rhode Island finds that "63% of families classified as high-risk had a subsequent substantiated report of maltreatment and only 6% of families classified at low-risk had a subsequent substantiated report" (Hollinshead and Fluke 2000 in Kluger, Alexander, and Curtis 2000, 71). Comparing risk assessment tools, researchers find that "actuarial" models, derived from data about past cases, are far better at predictions than models that rely on a consensus among clinical experts (Gambrill and Shlonsky 2000).

On the other hand, critics argue that overreliance on risk assessment *reduces* workers' ability to engage parents and work with them to improve the family setting; that tools require more information than workers can collect; that badly structured tools may lead to worse, not better, decisions; and that no tool can predict risk with even near certainty. Emphasizing risk assessment may reduce social workers' ability to change the outcome by casting them as distant experts whose job is to document everything wrong with the family. Unfortunately, "in such a paradigm it is fairly easy to see how parents can be relegated to a supporting role and become bystanders as the worker becomes solely responsible for the child's safety" (Berg and Kelly 2000, 16–17).

Another problem is that information entered into even the most sophisticated tool may have gaping holes, because social workers are frequently unable to identify the most challenging problems facing families.

In a study of domestic violence using a national survey of child welfare families, 31 percent of female caregivers reported experiencing partner violence in the past year, but child welfare workers identified it in only 12 percent of these families (Kohl et al. 2005). Another study using the same national sample found that 43 percent of children under 3 were identified as developmentally delayed through a screening, but only 21 percent of these cases were identified as special needs children by intake caseworkers (Rosenberg, Smith, and Levinson 2007).

A review by Illinois' inspector general of how the state's assessment tool functioned in child death cases underlined this issue: in nine cases, workers failed to identify domestic violence, substance abuse, or mental health problems that later took a terrible toll. While the reviewers clearly believe that every worker should pay attention to all the information at hand, they also find it unreasonable to expect an investigator to make judgments about all these issues in the press and heat of a child abuse investigation: "many of the factors ask workers to make determinations that are beyond the worker's competence" (Illinois Department of Child and Family Services [DCFS], Office of the Inspector General 2005, 11). The report recommends revising the Illinois form, which at the time required yes/no answers, to allow workers to say they don't know if a factor is present and then resolve the uncertainty later. Similarly, Nancy Young and coauthors from the National Center on Substance Abuse and Child Welfare advise that no substance abuse assessment tool can replace a team of experts that works together over time, since problems such as mental and physical illness, domestic violence, and substance abuse come "jumbled together" and are difficult and time-consuming to understand accurately (Young et al. 2007, 4).

Finally, the evidence on how well risk assessments predict endangerment is mixed. A study of fatal versus nonfatal child abuse in New York City finds that even with 11 distinguishing criteria, 17 percent of the fatalities would have been missed (Pecora et al. 2000, 141). In addition, if agencies use risk assessments to make high-stakes decisions, such as removal, then there is clearly a cost to false positives as well as false negatives. We need to know how many errors a tool makes in both directions to judge its accuracy. If almost 40 percent of families rated high-risk in the Rhode Island study did *not* have a re-report, that is a high proportion of false positives—families flagged as risky who never engaged in further abuse. An agency would certainly not want to remove children based on that assessment.

Can these conflicting views be reconciled? Improving risk-assessment techniques is valuable; it can structure social worker and team decision-making. Instinct is not a good enough guide through the thicket of information that a social worker must continually process. Yet, we should be conscious of the limits of risk-assessment tools used in the real world, where information is hard to gather, ambiguous, and constantly evolving. We should expect them to play a useful supporting role in keeping children safe, not to bear the whole burden. We should also see risk assessment as an ongoing process, not a one-time event, particularly when it comes to substance abuse and mental health issues. And we should think of assessing risk as intimately related to designing effective services, not as a substitute for services—just as medical tests do not substitute for treatment but rather help select or fine-tune it. If research identifies programs or interventions that work for some parents, then wise decisionmakers might shape risk assessments to help identify parents who could benefit.

How Well Does the Child Welfare System Measure Up to the Evidence?

Two national measures of child welfare performance relate most directly to strengthening and predicting parenting. One assesses how quickly and safely children are reunified with their parents after they have been removed, and the other assesses how likely children are to be re-abused.

To safely reunite children in foster care with their parents, child welfare agencies have to both predict and strengthen parenting effectively. But data suggest that national performance has been weak. The number of reunifications since ASFA has held steady, with no improvement, and reunification continues to be unstable. HHS data show that in 2004 and 2005, about 15 percent of children reunified during that year reentered foster care less than 12 months later (HHS, Children's Bureau 2008a). HHS's analysis concludes that states that reunify children more quickly also have more reentry to foster care, raising two concerns:

> (1) children are reunified with their families before all of the problems that resulted in the child's initial entry into foster care were adequately resolved, and/or (2) at the time of reunification, new problems emerged that were not sufficiently addressed. (HHS, Children's Bureau 2008a, vi)

Most likely, one reason that the frequency and safety of reunification are not improving is that very few parents are benefiting from effective interventions. When children stay home after a substantiated report of abuse or neglect, about half of their families receive no services at all.[1] Even if they do, few child welfare parenting programs resemble the higher-quality, more strictly designed programs known to get results.

Performance on the other measure, the proportion of children re-abused, has improved in recent years, though there are reasons to question the data. Specifically, re-abuse (measured by the percentage of children with one substantiated report of abuse or neglect that have a second substantiated report within six months) dropped from 8.5 percent in 1999 to 6.6 percent in 2005. However, HHS notes several reasons for caution about the data. The measured level of re-abuse could be affected by, for example, state practices to screen out more or fewer cases before they are investigated, state adoption of alternative response systems (under which workers who respond to the call often do not determine whether abuse occurred), and state choices about how to handle reports on open cases (some states do not formally investigate these reports but simply route them to the caseworker) (HHS, Children's Bureau 2008a).

Research on Children's Development Sets a High Bar for Successful Child Welfare Reform

The considerable literature on child development tells us much about what children need to grow and thrive. These principles are central to thinking about how a child welfare system should work if it is to avoid damaging children and, ideally, provide them with the opportunity to heal and develop to the fullest.

What Children Need

Children develop in the context of stable, loving, dependable relationships with a small number of caregivers. The circle of important relationships widens as a child ages, with a very small number of caring adults anchoring the development of a baby or toddler and a larger number—coaches, teachers, neighbors, and peer groups—assuming importance as children get older. Youth do best when family and other important relationships work together (Wulczyn et al. 2005).

A seminal National Academy of Sciences review of the literature summarizes the developmental needs of young children:

> Children grow and thrive in the context of close and dependable relationships that provide love and nurturance, security, responsive interaction, and encouragement for exploration. Without at least one such relationship, development is disrupted and the consequences can be severe and long-lasting. If provided or restored, however, a sensitive caregiving relationship can foster remarkable recovery. (Shonkoff and Phillips 2000, 7)

Two characteristics of the relationships here bear repeating: stability over time (dependable relationships) and quality or depth of the relationship ("love and nurturance, security, responsive interaction, and encouragement for exploration"). Evidence of stability's importance in children's lives comes from many sources, with researchers finding that "children have much better outcomes if their family lives are stable, despite the overwhelming influence of poverty and associated risk factors" (Harden 2004, 33–34). A study of the effects on children's well-being of a range of disruptions, such as a change in schools or child care providers, notes that all entail negative outcomes (Moore, Vandivere, and Ehrle 2000).

Similarly, researchers who study parent-child interactions looking for a mix of nurturance and stimulation find that the quality of parenting and the home environment predict child well-being. In one study, researchers exploring a dataset that tracks children over time report that "the most consistent relationships found were those between learning stimulation and children's developmental status" (Bradley et al. 2001 in Barth et al. 2007). Thus, to develop fully and to thrive, children need more from parents or caregivers than freedom from abuse or neglect. Young children especially risk developmental lag when they miss out on close interaction because, for example, parents are too depressed or caregivers too busy with other children to smile at and talk to a baby.

Children need these stable and loving relationships throughout their development and will likely have a tough time catching up if they miss that support at a critical stage, especially in the first few years of life. While research emphasizes that there are no absolute timetables, and positive, protective factors such as a nurturing, stable caregiver can make a difference at any point in a child's life, a child nonetheless risks losing ground without a stable loving relationship at key stages of development (Shonkoff and Phillips 2000).

The developmental literature suggests that risk is cumulative, so children most damaged in their early life are likely to be most gravely harmed by future traumas. Children who have experienced both neglect or abuse and then removal are more vulnerable to future moves or disruption of close ties because their harsh start in life hinders the development of emotional buffers needed to cope with later tragedies (Shonkoff and Phillips 2000). Recent research on the science of brain development indicates that excessive stress in a young child "produce[s] an internal physiological state that disrupts the architecture and chemistry of the developing brain" (Center on the Developing Child 2007, 9). For these reasons, the most fragile children need the most skilled staff and caregivers and the best services to thrive and develop fully (Shonkoff and Phillips 2000).

Implications for Child Welfare Agencies

These findings about child development have important implications for the day-to-day operations of child welfare agencies. First, they suggest that unstable and temporary settings can be deeply damaging. Second, the quality of the relationships children have while in care, particularly with foster and kin caregivers but also with other adults, may be instrumental in their recovery and development.

Stability and Permanence. Research about child welfare placements confirms that children do better in stable settings and worse when they are moved from one home to another. Moving quickly into a stable setting and staying there seems to lead to the best outcomes. One recent literature review concludes that earlier research has shown "increased rates of mental health problems, homelessness, and incarcerations particularly among children who experienced multiple placement changes" and that the most rigorous study, which sorted out the role of the child's initial state when entering the system from the impacts of subsequent instability, confirmed the independent effect of instability on behavior (Rubin et al. 2007, 4). In their own study, Rubin and colleagues (2007) find that among children whose behavior is rated as normal when they enter care, 85 percent of those who achieve early stability still score as normal three years later, compared with 60 percent of those who never achieve stability.

Child development literature also suggests the importance of a permanent relationship that the child can count on. This inference is reflected in the Adoption and Safe Families Act requirement that agencies move children promptly to *permanent* homes, whether reunification with parents, adoption, or subsidized legal guardianship.

The research base on permanence is weaker than that on stability, partly because permanence is a newer concern and partly because[2] it is hard to generalize about permanent settings as different as adoption and reunification. In general, though, the evidence from child welfare studies fits the conclusion of child development experts that permanence is important. According to several literature reviews, children's sense that they live with a family permanently rather than on sufferance matters for their well-being and sense of security and satisfaction (Barth et al. 2007; Pecora and Maluccio 2000). The predictability and security of a permanent family enable a child to "form a more secure sense of the future and . . . better weather other difficulties and changes in childhood and adolescence" (Pecora et al. 2000, 12). A child who moved from foster care to guardianship puts this into her own words:

> I used to have nightmares before every court hearing and I could not concentrate in school for a month before each hearing. I was afraid I would have to move. Now, I don't have to do that any more. (Quoted in HHS, Children's Bureau 2005b)

Another advantage is that permanence makes parents more committed because "their role is secure," and "children need parents who are fully committed to caring for them" (Pecora et al. 2000, 11–12). The likelihood of disruption is much less in adoption than in long-term foster care, consistent with the idea that permanence strengthens parents' commitment. Agencies and workers often believe that a foster home is stable because a child has resided there a long time, but in fact, many long-term foster care placements fall apart, often when a child hits the turbulence of adolescence (Barth 2000).

Besides direct research on children's satisfaction and well-being and on parents' commitment, researchers also give more common-sense arguments for the value of permanent settings. A permanent home means no more bureaucratic and fragmented decisionmaking with the child's agency worker, the foster parent, possibly a service provider, and the biological parent all weighing in. Instead, the family is able to make its own decisions (Pecora et al. 2000). (A recent *New York Times* article described the benefits from the viewpoint of a teenager thrilled to go on a sleepover without having to wait for a criminal record check of all attending.)[2] And children don't "age out" of a permanent family. "Given the lengthening preparation to adulthood that children are now experiencing, the value of a permanent family that can support them until they are on their own is growing" (Pecora et al. 2000, 391).

The research on permanent settings also delves into the consequences for children of reunification and adoption, as well as very early findings about permanent guardianship. The reunification literature is inconclusive. Children generally report being pleased to go home, but the mixed evidence on how they develop after being reunified contains some red flags (Pecora and Maluccio 2000; Pecora et al. 2000; Rubin et al. 2007). Some methodological problems make the study of reunification difficult—for example, if reunified children on average enter care later than children who get adopted, they may have experienced more damage early on—but common sense suggests why the effects might be mixed. For example, given the evidence described earlier that parents are unlikely to receive effective services for such underlying challenges as depression, mixed results for children should not be surprising. In addition, biological families are typically poor, children in poor families score lower on developmental assessments, and biological families typically do not receive subsidies after reunification, unlike adoptive or guardianship families.

The evidence on adoption's benefits to children is strong, though the dramatic rise in adoptions in the past decade awaits full study. One survey finds that, "in general, the value of adoption and the relatively modest disruption rates (about 10%) shown in several studies make adoption the clearly and convincingly superior plan over foster care" (Pecora et al. 2000, 395). Another review of the research on adoption dissolution finds that as adoptions of special-needs children from foster care have increased, the percentage of failed adoptions has declined—the opposite of what might have been expected with more difficult children (Barth 2000; Golden and Macomber forthcoming; Smith et al. 2006).

Researchers have just begun to study the effects of permanent guardianship, which enables relatives to offer a permanent home to a child without terminating parental rights. In 1995, the Children's Bureau within ACF, using waiver authority that allowed certain child welfare experiments, allowed states to try subsidized guardianship programs as long as they included rigorous evaluations and were cost-neutral to the federal government. The federal government would share in the cost of subsidies to families taking on guardianship of children leaving foster care— before that, a relative who chose not to adopt could receive help only as a foster parent. In response, 11 states implemented subsidized guardianship waivers. Three states showed an improvement in children's movement to permanent homes. Four states tracked measures of children's safety and well-being while in guardianship and found that these children did at least as well as children who were adopted or returned home (HHS, Children's Bureau 2005b; James Bell Associates 2007).

A third implication of the role of stable adult relationships in a child's development is that removal from the home is traumatic and potentially damaging even when there is no other way to protect children and see to their long-term well-being. Social work experts suggest minimizing damage by giving children a basic explanation of what has happened and what the future might hold and addressing their likely feelings of rejection (Pecora and Maluccio 2000). Child welfare reformers generally emphasize reducing the trauma and upheaval by keeping the rest of a child's life as stable as possible—maintaining close relationships (especially with siblings) and continuing ties to the neighborhood and the school.

Children's need for stability and permanence means that delaying decisions about their lives is harmful because being in limbo jeopardizes healthy development. Because child welfare agencies and judges have traditionally done a poor job of this—both bureaucratic and judicial processes can move glacially, especially when the decisions are tough—ASFA specifically requires sped-up decisions when a child has been in foster care for 15 of 22 months. Even though waiting for new information may in some cases produce a better decision, the ASFA requirement reflects the judgment that the benefits often prove illusory and the delays better serve the judges, lawyers, and social workers involved than the children. The particular challenge of child welfare is that red tape or courtroom delays may simply annoy adults, and seem a reasonable price to pay for thorough vetting or due process, but waiting actively damages children.

Quality of Settings. Along with stability and permanence, the quality of a child's close relationships with adults and peers figures centrally in healthy development. When a child's home setting features close relationships that balance nurturing and challenge, the child is far more likely to thrive and develop fully. For fragile infants, children, and adolescents in the child welfare system, with their "extraordinarily high levels of behavioral and developmental problems," a "curative" home environment is especially important (Barth et al. 2007).

A first major issue is whether children live in families or in group homes. In group homes (or "congregate care"), a number of children—six or eight in a small group home, possibly dozens in a large one—are cared for in a dormitory-like facility by staff working in shifts. In some child welfare systems, children may also live in emergency shelters or emergency group homes, a setting meant to be temporary but sometimes lasting weeks or months. Since the late 1970s the proportion of children in out-of-home care who are in group care has remained at close to 25 percent (Pecora et al. 2000).

The broad developmental evidence suggests that, typically, children thrive best in families. For very young children, the research consensus approaches unanimity. Even in clean and healthy group settings with well-trained and stable staff, infants and children can lose developmental ground. Babies find it deeply disruptive to adapt to a new caregiver every time the shift changes. In a group home with three eight-hour shifts and weekend staff, each baby experiences the equivalent of four or five different placement settings just from the shift changes—more if staff turnover is high. For older children, group homes are widely used, but researchers remain concerned about their risks. A recent literature review concluded that "children living in institutions felt less comfortable, not as happy, less loved, less trusted, and less cared about than did children in other forms of out-of-home care" (Pecora and Maluccio 2000, 143). Advocates for group homes argue that some children, especially troubled older ones, cannot thrive in families and do better in a structured group setting. While the research on group homes is inconclusive, the developmental literature as a whole suggests that children generally do best in families.

Researchers who assess the quality of the family settings children live in have found strengths as well as room for improvement. Using a standard assessment of parenting quality that has been linked convincingly to children's developmental outcomes, studies of foster parent samples have shown that both kin and nonkin homes score lower than a national average group of families and that a substantial proportion of children in foster care have a caregiver who demonstrates punitiveness (Barth et al. 2007). However, one recent study that traces children's developmental status before and during their experiences with kin and nonkin foster parents finds that both settings appear able to help youth reduce the trauma that they experienced before entering care (Barth et al. 2007).

How Well Do Child Welfare Agencies Meet the Challenges of Children's Development?

During the past 10 years, the response of child welfare agencies to children's need for permanence and stability has improved greatly for a subgroup of children: those who cannot go home and who used to linger in foster care. These children are now more likely than before the mid-1990s to be adopted or to live with a relative who has permanent legal guardianship. The economic circumstances of children living with kin have improved over the past decade, as has the likelihood that young children will be placed in families rather than group homes. However, in crucial ways, the system continues to fail the larger group of children whose goal is to reunify with their birth families.

Doubling of Adoptions from Foster Care. National evidence and detailed studies of particular states show a major increase in adoption of children from foster care since the mid-1990s and particularly after enactment of the Adoption and Safe Families Act in 1997. The total number of children adopted annually from foster care doubled between the mid-1990s and mid-2000s, from about 25,000 to about 50,000 a year. Adoption also increased as a proportion of children's exits from foster care, from 15 percent in 1998 to 17 percent in 2006, and the time to adoption appears to have decreased. Several in-depth studies using data from one or several states confirm that since ASFA, children are more likely to be adopted and take less time to navigate the process (Golden and Macomber forthcoming).

To achieve this improvement, federal and state investment and legislative action during the 1990s built on a foundation set more than a decade earlier. The Adoption Assistance and Child Welfare Act of 1980 paved the way by providing federal reimbursement of state subsidies for families who adopt special-needs children from foster care (previously, foster families received such support but adoptive families didn't). Yet this subsidy, vital in retrospect, did not stimulate immediate change, as federal spending remained extremely small ($0.5 million in 1981) and adoption rates remained low. But by the late 1990s, several legislative, policy, and cultural changes came together to transform the picture. ASFA required states to speed up decisionmaking and move toward adoption when children could not go home, and it rewarded states with a financial bonus—called the "adoption incentive"—if they increased adoptions of special-needs children from foster care. By 2004, federal plus state funding of adoption subsidies to families totaled more than $1 billion (Scarcella et al. 2006). The state adoption incentives totaled about $200 million cumulatively paid from the federal government to the states from 1998 through 2006.

Expansion of Guardianship. The expansion of legal guardianship (mostly with relatives) as a permanent option for children has been even more dramatic.[3] In the decade since ASFA, the number of children leaving foster care for guardianship each year has more than doubled from about 5,900 in 1998 to over 15,000 by 2006. In 2006, guardianship represented about 5 percent of exits from foster care, compared with just 2 percent in 1998 (Golden and Macomber forthcoming).

Behind this expansion were the federal waivers just described and the pressure that ASFA placed on states to achieve permanent homes for children—in particular, to terminate parental rights if children could neither go home nor live in a permanent home with relatives. In the years following ASFA, many states—30 in one accounting (Allen and Bissell 2004), 35 in another (Jantz et al. 2002)—implemented subsidized guardianship for some children to give relatives the financial support they needed to take on permanent responsibility. Where states did not have federal waivers, they used state dollars or other federal funding sources, but this mixed picture meant that children's access to permanent homes with relatives varied greatly depending on state finances and policy choices. Going forward, however, children and families in all states will have access to subsidized guardianship, with the costs shared by the federal government, as a result of the Fostering Connections to Success and Increasing Adoptions Act of 2008.

Improved Finances and Access to Health Care among Kin Caregivers. A series of Urban Institute briefs allows us to track trends in economic security and health care access from 1997 to 2002 for children living with kin caregivers, including those in formal kinship care arranged by the child welfare agency and those in more informal arrangements.[4] The most recent brief finds that "the financial circumstances of children in kinship care improved significantly," especially for children in public kinship care (that is, coordinated with the child welfare agency). In 1997, children living with kin caregivers had extraordinarily high rates of poverty—35 percent for children in public kinship care and 42 percent for children in private kinship care. These rates fell sharply five years later. The 2002 poverty rate for children in public kinship care (18 percent) was just slightly higher than the rate for children living with their parents (15 percent).

Over the same period, health insurance coverage for children in kinship care also grew dramatically, with the greatest improvements again in public kinship care. Only 6 percent of children in public kinship care in 2002 were uninsured, down from 23 percent in 1997, and less than the 9 percent rate for children living with their parents.

What drove these improvements? While it is hard to be sure, the researchers find that these improvements in children's well-being may trace back to such policy and practice changes as the ASFA requirement that states license kinship caregivers to receive federal matching funds. Once licensed, caregivers typically receive the state's foster care payments, usually higher than the welfare and other public payments that unlicensed kin caregivers might have received. States might also be more attentive to licensed rather than unlicensed caregivers, helping them link to other supports, such as health insurance (Main, Macomber, and Geen 2006).

Fewer Young Children in Group Care. From 2000 to 2005, the proportion of foster children under age 12 living in group homes fell from 9.6 percent to 7.2 percent in the median state. Over the same period, 40 states improved on this measure and only 8 got worse (HHS, ACYF 2006; HHS, Children's Bureau 2008a).

Instability, Long Stays in Foster Care for Many Children, and No Improvement in Reunification. Yet these new successes, important as they are, have left many children behind. Children who stay in foster care longer than a year or two often move through many different placements, and states appear to be getting worse on this measure, not better (HHS, Children's Bureau 2008a). And when we zero in on children who go home, not to an adoptive family, their prospects of prompt, stable, and safe reunification are not improving. Reunification numbers have remained stable between 1998 and 2006, dropping steadily as a share of exits from foster care from 60 percent in 1998 to 53 percent in 2006 (Golden and Macomber forthcoming). HHS's review of state-by-state data concludes similarly that there has been no improvement (HHS, Children's Bureau 2008a). Thus, children whose plan is to return home are not reaping the developmental benefits that permanence could offer.

In addition, while children are in care, there is little information about the quality of the settings they live in. Most likely, far too many extremely vulnerable children and the families that care for them miss out on basics like good health care and schools, let alone the top quality services these children need to thrive.

The Tool Kit: Evidence from Effective Services for Troubled Families

Child welfare reformers trying to solve these problems rely on their own values and on the best judgments they can find about what makes services effective. Certainly, reforms need to embody our values about families and children, but evidence of results matters too. This section hones in on four broad strategies that characterize many recent reform efforts, drawing on insights from research in child welfare and related fields.

Supporting High-Quality Social Work by Supporting Social Workers

At least two reform threads focus on the individual caseworker: improving such working conditions as caseloads, pay, and supervision and changing daily practice and decisions through training and supervision (Annie E. Casey Foundation 2003; Center for the Study of Social Policy 2006). Common sense argues that more skilled social workers with better training, smaller caseloads, and more stable working conditions could better help children. Certainly, in extreme examples of overload the damage seems obvious: in, say, Birmingham, Alabama, or Washington, D.C., before the reforms, children were being completely ignored because they had no social worker or because the worker had no time for anything except emergencies. Beyond these extreme cases, though, what does the evidence show?

In other child and family service programs, researchers find that staff qualifications and working conditions directly affect results for children. Studies of early childhood education and related programs find measurable differences in children's performance depending on teacher qualifications, teacher skills, the number of children in the group or classroom, and staff turnover (Adams, Zaslow, and Tout 2007; Shonkoff and Phillips 2000). Research on effective parenting programs also suggests that high skill levels (and intensive supervision) are closely linked to results for parents and children alike, and research from several fields suggests that the most fragile children need the most skilled service providers.

However, early childhood caregivers and other service providers spend a lot more time in direct contact with children than social workers do. This is important because researchers studying service delivery to young children find that intensity—the number of hours spent a week or a month—counts too. For example, no matter how qualified, a home visitor who sees a child two or three times a month may exert little influence on the child's development (Shonkoff and Phillips 2000; HHS, ACYF 1994).

More persuasive is the idea that social workers may interact intensively enough with parents and extended family to affect their behavior and choices. These interactions in turn affect children, by ensuring that they live in safe and nurturing settings surrounded by adults committed to getting them what they need. This role seems more attainable, though not easy, and it is the goal of most of the reforms.

A recent project called Community Partnerships for Protecting Children tested such an approach, seeking to change social worker practice as part of a broader child welfare reform in four urban neighborhoods. The initiative aimed to draw a broader range of family, community, and public partners into keeping children safe—a departure from the old approach of the child welfare agency acting unilaterally. The new approach also shifted from a one-size-fits-all service plan to one tailored to individual families, involved families more actively in decisions, and retrained social workers to support the new expectations and skills. An evaluation of the project found some evidence of positive effects, but only when families also received needed services:

> When service plans addressed a family's needs and when new services were provided in response to those needs, that family was more likely to see a reduction in depression and parental stress, as well as an increase in overall progress. However, when a service plan did *not* deal with a family's concerns, or when the worker was not responsive or services were not provided, the results were not as positive. (Center for Community Partnerships and Center for the Study of Social Policy 2006, 17)

Thus, supporting social workers should certainly be part of the tool kit for child welfare reform, but evidence so far suggests that improved social worker practice and support alone are insufficient. Unskilled or overwhelmed social workers can damage children's prospects, but even the best trained and most supported social workers probably cannot solve a child's or family's deep-seated problems on their own. The availability and quality of services and of family settings likely affect results above and beyond the quality of social workers. Research and experience both caution against heaping all credit for success or all blame for failure on individual caseworkers.

Engaging and Empowering Families

Many child welfare reform strategies make families a central theme. Strategies seek to help workers understand and build on family strengths (not only needs) by involving biological, extended, and foster families in planning for the child; drawing on extended families for support for children; minimizing the use of group homes, shelters, and residential treatment centers; and offering family services at convenient times and places, including in the home.[5]

Since the child development literature emphasizes the important role parents play, it is not surprising that a broad research consensus beyond child welfare experts finds that involving parents in services wherever possible can improve results for children. In child welfare, one researcher finds that evidence from Great Britain as well as the United States supports this conclusion (Waldfogel 1998). Experts in early education also highlight the robust research finding that programs work best with a dual focus on parent and child (HHS, Administration for Children and Families [ACF] 2002; HHS, ACYF 1994; Shonkoff and Phillips 2000). Given what is known about the centrality of close relationships in a child's development, this finding could plausibly be extended to kin, foster families, and other people who care about a child.

Yet, despite the expert consensus about the broad theme, research and clinical experience both suggest the care it takes to strike the right balance between engaging parents and responding to children. The most detailed evidence comes from evaluations of early childhood development programs that recommend, in the words of one home visiting checklist, that the service provider "should not lose sight of the child's needs," however overwhelming the parent's needs (Leventhal 1996 quoted in Pecora et al. 2000, 244). Even though the child's and the parent's needs may converge in the long run—a healthy, loving parent is what the child needs most—in the short run, competing needs may pull the service provider in different directions. For example, an early case management intervention for young children and their families, the Comprehensive Child Development Program, did not show significant impacts on child development, and one possible reason was that case managers spent too little time on direct services to children in the face of parents' extensive needs. As a result, the parents' behavior may have changed in time to enhance later siblings' development, but the children initially targeted for help fell behind. The Early Head Start program was able to learn from that mistake, requiring in its program standards focused attention to the child as well as the parent (Golden 2006).

This research provides a context for the experiences of child welfare practitioners, who report that finding the right balance is essential to improved child development and child safety. One big-city child welfare director described a case where workers visited frequently and sought doggedly to respond to the mother's needs for day-to-day services and protection from domestic violence, yet did not see the mounting evidence that her children were dangerously affected by her substance abuse and depression. In the end, the mother's baby accidentally drowned in the tub while she was distracted.

To find the right balance, clinical experts focus on social worker skills such as being able to speak directly and honestly with the parent about the child's safety needs, no matter how much is going on in the parent's life. Marty Beyer, a national expert involved in the Alabama training, notes that without strong training and support, workers may spend too much time addressing families' concrete needs (such as overdue utility bills) rather than zeroing in on what families need to keep their children safe. In Alabama, she sought to teach workers to keep the child's needs front and center, using that focus to engage the parents.

Thus, the research supports family engagement as an essential part of a two-generational strategy for child welfare reform that focuses explicitly on children's safety and development. But building such a strategy, the evidence suggests, requires sophisticated skills and considerable staff and service resources.

Tailoring Services to Individual Families

A number of reformers echo Jane Waldfogel's criticism of child protective services agencies for "adopt[ing] a 'one-size-fits-all' approach, whereas both family preservation and child protection principles emphasize the need for a more nuanced, dynamic, and individualized approach"

(Waldfogel 1998, 72). The Alabama consent decree takes this principle as central. But what does the research say?

In child welfare and other child and family services fields, professionals and clinicians broadly concur with this principle. For example, the home visiting program summary cited above concludes that "home visiting . . . should be tailored to the family's needs" (Leventhal 1996 in Pecora et al. 2000, 244). Similarly, Pecora and colleagues find that adoption research demonstrates the importance of finding the right fit between characteristics of the parents, those of the child, and available services (Pecora et al. 2000).

But does individualizing services mesh with the well-supported principle that to succeed programs need to stay close to evidence-based program models, approaches, and curricula? Should we worry that agency workers free to choose how to deliver services may dilute the response's effectiveness—by, for example, accommodating a parent's wish for parenting classes that are less demanding than those researchers have found to pay off? In principle, commitment to evidence-based services need not be at loggerheads with customizing services: for example, evidence from rigorous research could provide guidance about how to adjust services for different families But in practice, the two principles may conflict. If an agency chooses to embrace both, it needs to send a clear message to workers about how they are expected to balance the high-quality delivery of services against the design of unique services for each family.

How should reform-minded agencies balance these principles? First, when customization's alternative—"one size fits all"—reflects the convenience of providers or the patterns of history instead of evidence, individualization that responds to families is surely an improvement. As the Institute of Medicine says about this same dilemma in health care, providers' idiosyncrasies are not good reasons for health care to differ (Institute of Medicine [IOM] 2001).

Second, practice models or similar guidance for social workers about how to deliver services need to reflect the agency's best understanding of which program approaches, principles, and curricula bring desired results, what should stay the same no matter what, and what adaptations to family needs and strengths are acceptable. Sometimes, researchers have explicitly examined what aspects of programs can be adapted while retaining good results. For example, in the Early Head Start program, home-based and center-based services to families with young children were tested through rigorous research, in the hope that the service location could be adapted to parents' work schedules and needs without losing effectiveness. It turned out that as long as other quality standards were kept consistent and rigorous, both locations yielded positive effects. In other cases, agencies will not have this specific research support for their conclusions but nonetheless need to draw on clinical and professional experience to articulate which services should be used as is agency-wide and which can be adapted.

Agencies should be particularly cautious about individualization that leads to less rigorous services or less qualified staff as a substitute for (rather than supplement to) more intensive services. Researchers from the Center on the Developing Child conclude that evidence from many different fields demonstrates the need for highly qualified staff:

> Home visiting programs staffed by nonprofessional staff would be grossly inadequate for mothers coping with serious depression, substance abuse, or family violence. Stated simply, programs that cost less because they employ less skilled staff are a waste of money if they do not have the expertise needed to produce measurable impacts. (Center on the Developing Child 2007, 22)

Creatively Combining Formal and Informal Services

When families are truly involved in designing their own service plans, reformers believe the result is new services, not just referral to a potpourri of existing services.[6] Families and skilled social workers planning together often come up with creative ways to use informal supports— that is, people already trusted by the family or services already available to the whole community—to help the family solve its problems. For example, a neighbor or extended family member might help a parent cope with stress, and dance lessons or sports coaching might help an abused child regain confidence.

This approach draws on several themes in the research literature. For parents, research on social support and the prevention of abuse and neglect suggests that troubled families are often isolated and benefit from help linking to such positive supports as family or friends, though informal connections can be negative if they generate conflict (for example, if a mother has a deeply confrontational relationship with her own siblings or mother) or reinforce negative behavior (Pecora et al. 2000; Waldfogel 1998). For very young children, evidence already cited on the crucial role of close and stable relationships fits well with a service-delivery strategy that builds on interactions with familiar people, such as a child care provider or neighbor. For older children, the approach is certainly consistent with research findings that underscore the importance of a widening circle of relationships and a sense of achievement and belonging in the community.

Yet informal supports will often be incomplete: services aimed at such deep or complex problems as parents' depression or substance abuse or children's developmental lags may require intensive, long-lasting services delivered with careful quality control by skilled clinicians. In an ideal world, services would be available in convenient and familiar settings and would combine trusted informal supports with more formal expert help. Experts have recommended that broadly available and familiar services—like child care programs, or pediatricians in a health clinic—should screen families and link them to more intensive services. The National Center for Children in Poverty recommends nesting more formal and intensive services within a broader, less stigmatized setting to reach the most vulnerable babies and toddlers and their families:

> Over the past decade, there have been major developments in infant and parent family therapies. Using this knowledge base not just in clinical settings, but embedding more intensive interventions into core infant and toddler child development and family support programs appears to be one of the most promising strategies in which states and communities might invest. (Knitzer and Lefkowitz 2006, 19)

When this ideal combination is not available, the evidence suggests that reformers' commitment to invent creative approaches to fill in the gaps should be tempered by a sense of what it will take to solve the more difficult problems. Because child welfare agencies and workers seldom directly control the design or availability of formal services, it is tempting for them to hope for more results from informal supports than is really possible. Perhaps the best way to interpret the research as a whole is that informal supports belong in the reform tool kit, but so do high-quality, intensive formal services.

The Tool Kit: Promising Programs for Parents and Children

Research on troubled families and vulnerable children outside the child welfare system can also generate reform strategies. Among the most promising insights are those drawn from evaluations of Early Head Start, studies of maternal depression and its treatment, and evaluations of substance abuse treatment for parents.

Early Head Start

Research on Early Head Start (EHS) is especially relevant to child welfare reform for several reasons.[7] In some ways, EHS families are similar to many families in the child welfare system: poor families with babies and toddlers who score far below national norms on child development measures and, often, parents in the throes of depression, substance abuse, or family violence. The program has demonstrated success on both of the big challenges facing child welfare systems: improving parenting and supporting children's development. EHS research has been unusually thorough, tracking the effects on both children and parents from birth or entry into the program until age 5.

Early Head Start's goal is to enhance the emotional development and learning of low-income babies and toddlers, narrowing the gap with better-off children and improving poor children's chances of starting school ready to learn. Its approach to this goal is two-generational, focusing on young children and on their parents and caregivers. Teachers and home visitors interact with the babies and toddlers in a child care center, in a family child care home, or through frequent home visits to parents. At the same time, the program works with parents on their needs, including their approach to parenting. Early Head Start also ensures comprehensive health care for young children enrolled and links parents to services ranging from counseling to job training and education. Based on lessons from past research, EHS has tough standards for the number of teachers in a program, for their educational background and continuing education, and for the curriculum they and the home visitors use.

Early Head Start's rigorous evaluation of program effects, which compared children and parents who entered EHS with a control group who did not, found that by the time the children turned 3, EHS programs had small positive effects on many aspects of children's development, including cognitive, social, and emotional development, and on parenting (such as less harsh discipline). The positive effects were largest for families classified as moderate risk (even though very poor) and for local programs that were more consistent with national EHS standards for structure and curriculum (HHS, ACF 2002).

Two years later, as children turned 5, the follow-up evaluation found positive effects for the highest-risk group of families, who had shown no effects two years earlier. Children were doing better, fewer children lived with someone with an alcohol or drug problem, and fewer children witnessed violence in the home. The effects were stronger if the children attended Head Start after Early Head Start, so families had five years of comprehensive services. At the later evaluation, programs were also reducing the level of maternal depression compared to the control group, whereas at the earlier evaluation, depressed mothers were showing improvements in parenting but remained just as depressed (HHS, ACF 2002, 2006).

These findings suggest opportunities for child welfare reform and point to what it takes to achieve success: high-quality, long-term, continuous services that reach and engage children and their parents. Programs that followed Early Head Start's stringent regulations produced better results for children than did less well-implemented programs. And while the findings offer some hope that parenting can be improved before parents' underlying problems (such as depression) begin to yield, the largest effects for the most troubled parents and their children came after five years of comprehensive services.

Other EHS research findings underline the difficulty of keeping struggling families engaged for several years given the turmoil in their lives. In fiscal year 2002, HHS funded a small pilot project to encourage links between EHS programs and child welfare agencies (James Bell Associates 2006). Unfortunately, one of the most striking findings of the pilot evaluation was how fleeting services to families were. All but one program reported an average length of enrollment of under one year, in some cases less than six months. Parents' reluctance to participate and policy constraints on the EHS or child welfare agencies apparently accounted for the brevity. For example, "In Tulsa, the grantee reported that many families are referred to the project when they are close to having their CWS case closed . . . when their CWS case is closed, the families are no longer eligible to participate in the EHS/CWS project" (James Bell Associates 2006, 47). Other programs reported difficulty engaging the many families who moved frequently or had mental health or substance abuse issues.

The Early Head Start research contributes insights that refine child welfare reform strategies: for example, blending informal supports for all parents with more formal services to help those with the greatest needs. Like child welfare reformers, EHS practitioners sometimes see the approaches as mutually exclusive, but researchers recommend combining them:

> As program staff have long believed, focusing on relationships does translate, down the line, to reducing depression. But more can be done. Linking families with mental health services and other approaches . . . can lead to a reduction in depression sooner. (Chazan-Cohen et al. 2007, 167)

The Early Head Start research also offers a new twist on the value of a two-generational approach—that improving children's development can have positive effects on parents. In other words, parenting a thriving child is less stressful than parenting a troubled one and may in turn improve parents' mental health and parenting skills. Researchers evaluating Early Head Start conclude what other studies have also found: that "child behaviors and abilities do contribute to or exacerbate later depression . . . and, conversely, interventions that improve child outcomes appear to have an indirect effect on maternal well-being as well" (Chazan-Cohen et al. 2007, 166).

Effective Treatment for Parental Depression

Research on effective treatment for parental (particularly maternal) depression also offers important opportunities for child welfare reformers. Considerable evidence documents the prevalence of maternal depression among low-income women with young children and the threat it poses to children's emotional development, health and safety, learning, behavior, and later school performance (Isaacs 2004; Knitzer, Theberge, and Johnson 2008; Onunaku 2005). Researchers have found that maternal depression shortly after birth is a risk factor for abuse or neglect in a child's early years (Kotch et al. 1999). A mother's depression erodes "two core parental functions: fostering healthy relationships and carrying out the management function of parenting" (Knitzer et al. 2008, 2–3). Damage is greatest when a mother is depressed during her child's infancy because "the primary ingredient for healthy early brain development is the quality of the earliest relationships from a baby's primary caregiver" (Knitzer et al. 2008, 2–3).

This widespread illness's sometimes devastating consequences can be avoided because "depression is in general a highly treatable disease" (Knitzer et al. 2008, 4), but far too few women in low-income communities receive effective treatment (Isaacs 2004, 2). One initiative to expand treatment included an array of support services to buttress strong clinical interventions: "intensive outreach, child care and transportation to care when needed, and encouragement to comply with evidence-based treatment regimens. Without these adaptations, the research team believes that few impoverished women are likely to receive appropriate treatment for depression" (Isaacs 2004, 24). An evaluation found that the initiative led to a significant decrease in depressive symptoms.

More broadly, large-scale programs to treat low-income mothers' depression need to address at least two major barriers: the women's reluctance to seek treatment (for reasons including the disease itself, as well as their distrust of mental health agencies) and their lack of health insurance. In most states, the primary health insurance program for low-income children, Medicaid, does not cover parents above very low levels of income. According to the National Center for Children in Poverty, some states and communities are addressing the first barrier by making screening easily available to mothers (for example, at their child's pediatric clinic), communicating that treatment for depression is something a mother can do for her child, and embedding specific interventions for preventing or reducing depression into early childhood programs (including home visiting programs and EHS). However, only a handful of states have addressed the second barrier through expanded funding for treatment. In North Carolina, mothers of Medicaid-eligible children are able to receive six mental health visits as part of the health and developmental package for babies. Unfortunately, "few states have the capacity, nor are there federal incentives, to take research-informed practices to scale" (Knitzer et al. 2008, 11).

Effective Treatment for Parental Substance Abuse

Finally, evidence also suggests that intensive substance abuse treatment programs can engage and help low-income parents, including those involved with the child welfare system. A review of substance abuse services targeted to women concludes that numerous effective programs yield considerable improvement (Wingfield and Klempner 2000). A recent summary of substance abuse treatment programs for welfare recipients finds that while more research is needed, "evidence from a rigorous random assignment study indicates that more intensive interventions can yield better treatment engagement rates and substance abuse outcomes" (Morgenstern and Blanchard 2006, 66). Fully 43 percent of those getting the intensive intervention were abstinent after 15 months, compared with 26 percent of the control group.

Evidence about the results of state child welfare agencies partnering with substance abuse services comes from four state experiments supported by HHS child welfare waivers. The projects taken together yielded some promising results, particularly in Illinois, yet highlighted the operational challenges of linking substance abuse services and child welfare. One program in Maryland was terminated early because of implementation difficulties. The other three used substance abuse experts to provide some mix of intensive support to families and better expertise to child welfare workers. The Illinois pilot led to substantial reductions in children's time in placement (from 563 days for control group children, whose families did not have access to the services, to 421 days for experimental group children, whose families did) and in repeat maltreatment (from 15.3 percent of control group families with a maltreatment report after they entered the demonstration to 11.2 percent of experimental group families). Delaware and New Hampshire also found some, though less certain, evidence of improvements (HHS, Children's Bureau 2005b; James Bell Associates 2007).

However, gaps in the availability of substance abuse services posed a problem, as did other implementation challenges. Delaware found that "the limited availability of appropriate treatment options" seriously constrained its ability to get parents into treatment under the waiver program. In child welfare monitoring assessments submitted to the federal government, states frequently report that substance abuse services aren't always available, though states do not always fully explain whether policy, practice, or resource barriers cause the problem (Young et al. 2005).

Other implementation challenges arise from the child welfare agency's incident-driven mission, its charge to investigate a specific report of child abuse or neglect. When agencies define screening, assessment, and referral as a one-time process that occurs when the investigator first sees the family, they are unlikely to learn much about substance abuse. Instead, because few families disclose their substance abuse early, and few workers are likely to pick up cues amid the early confusion, the child welfare and substance abuse agencies need a joint approach to screening and assessment that lasts as long as either agency is involved with a parent (Young et al. 2007). Differences in mission and culture, which plague all big system collaborations, also need attention. The reports on waiver implementation showed that in one state, child welfare workers took some substance use (alcohol, for example) more lightly than substance abuse counselors did; in another, child welfare workers thought the substance abuse counselors did not care enough about children's safety.

The Tool Kit: Emerging Knowledge on Safety in Complex Systems

As we have seen, children supervised by child welfare agencies are not always safe, and agencies are repeatedly thrown into turmoil when a tragedy strikes and public outrage follows. So it's clearly worth trying ideas from other fields—including airline safety, nuclear plant operations, and health care—to help improve children's safety and mitigate the toll that public outcry takes on agency effectiveness. The following discussion draws on the insights of child welfare researchers who have been studying and applying some of these ideas[8] and on the much more extensive research and practice experience in applying safety lessons to health care.

Why health care? Medical errors now receive considerable attention, driven by the large number of deaths and injuries that they produce— "at least 44,000 Americans die each year as a result of medical errors" (IOM 2000, 1). As a result, considerable resources have been devoted to research on safety in health care, so there is already a major body of work that child welfare reformers can build on and adapt. A panel of experts convened by the Institute of Medicine to help distill emerging knowledge published their findings in 2000 as *To Err Is Human: Building a Safer Health Care System* and in 2001 as *Crossing the Quality Chasm*. In both books, researchers draw insights from studies and successful safety innovations in commercial aviation and manufacturing that apply to health care. Subsequent case studies of the health care applications of these insights provide further refinements, along with evidence that medical errors can be substantially reduced.

How similar are the health care and child welfare systems? Both rely on professionals who may resist structure and believe that their own skills are enough to vouchsafe safety; in both, complex interactions among different kinds of professionals can lead to confusion or gaps in communication; and both serve vulnerable people. One difference of concern to child welfare reformers, though, is the historical tension in child welfare between supporting families and removing children—which can leave reformers worried that a focus on safety by definition would lead to more removals. (That is, they fear that the traditional way to achieve safety in child welfare has been to remove more children from their homes, despite the emotional toll.)

But some evidence suggests that the safety lessons identified below could have just the opposite effect: they could jolt the child welfare debate out of the old way of thinking and suggest a wealth of smaller, more specific, more practical changes. Further, the health care evidence suggests that such changes could both improve safety and change perspectives on prevention. McCarthy and Blumenthal, through case studies of successful health care settings, find big improvements in safety problems long considered intractable once the methods described below are applied systematically, and they find that this success in turn engages staff much more in prevention (McCarthy and Blumenthal 2006). Deaths or injuries that seemed purely random when clinicians thought only about what was in their own power to do or change now seem preventable when they imagine systemwide responses.

Transferred to child welfare agencies, this finding seems profoundly important. One reason child tragedies play out in such a damaging way is the polarization of responses. Child welfare staff, feeling under attack and misunderstood, conclude that nothing they can ever do will keep children safe, while the press, public, and political officials conclude that all death or injury would be averted if staff did their jobs right. By contrast, if safety analyses led to rigorous, well-documented recommendations and, in turn, to documented success in reducing deaths or at least serious injuries, both outside and inside attitudes might start to change. Staff within the agencies might start to understand that with a broader, systemwide concept of prevention, and with the support they need to put that concept into practice, they can prevent some bad outcomes. And outside observers could place an individual tragedy in a much broader context, rather than simply assuming that the problem is a worker or supervisor who needs to be fired.

How could this happen in practice? Six lessons from the safety literature in health care seem particularly useful to child welfare reform.

Punishing or Retraining People Distracts Attention from the Underlying Systemic Flaws

A central but perhaps counterintuitive finding of the IOM's review of the safety literature is that improving safety is *not* about punishing individual people for errors or even retraining them. Focusing on individual fault is both ineffective and dangerous because attending solely to the human error that is most obvious leaves the underlying problem untouched and ready to cause another error (IOM 2000). For example, singling out a nurse who sets a machine wrong overlooks a confusing or badly designed machine or ambiguity about the roles of different members of the operating team.

James T. Reason puts the same point more vividly:

> Unsafe acts are like mosquitoes. You can try to swat them one at a time, but there will always be others to take their place. The only effective remedy is to drain the swamp in which they breed. In the case of errors and violations, the "swamps" are equipment designs that promote operator error, bad communications, high workloads, budgetary and commercial pressures, procedures that necessitate their violation in order to get the job done, inadequate organization, missing barriers, and safeguards. (IOM 2000, 155)

Applied to child welfare, this finding means that the typical focus of press and public attention (and often of agency investigations) on the mistakes or failures of individual social workers does more to damage than to improve future safety. If, for example, a child dies after a social worker fails to pick up hints of substance abuse in the family, it may be much more valuable to respond differently to substance abuse than to punish or retrain the individual social worker.

The System Is Too Complicated for Even Caring and Capable Professionals to Foresee the Consequences of Each Action

Researchers studying medical errors note that experienced clinicians may believe that if they were left alone to do their best, patients would be safe. But health care is such a complex system that individual commitment is not enough. One survey of successful patient safety initiatives concludes that health care professionals often cannot see how their actions affect patient safety within such a complex system. "The goal of patient safety is to rectify this system 'blindness' by providing the means to detect and eliminate or mitigate system vulnerabilities that could harm patients" (McCarthy and Blumenthal 2006, 173–74).

Child welfare too offers many examples of such hard-to-manage complexity—of situations where individuals have highly specialized roles, depend on actions by many other people, and cannot see how the other parts of the system will interact. For example, suppose that one social worker doesn't enter a child's age into the computer because the shift is ending, a second looks at the child's record and places him in a group home for much older children based on a mistaken impression, the group home takes the child thinking he is older, and by the time the first social worker comes back on duty, she is on to the next emergency, knowing only that the child has been given a place to sleep. If the child is later assaulted and injured by the older children, each person's actions contributed, yet no one saw exactly how the interaction would play out.

Rigorous Data Collection and Analysis Are Essential to Finding and Fixing a System's Vulnerabilities

The Institute of Medicine offers several lessons about how successful safety programs collect and analyze information. First, error analysis needs to be structured with sophisticated knowledge of underlying causes. If individual incidents are reviewed naïvely, then the only causes identified will be the immediate ones, and little will be learned. In a more sophisticated systems approach, human errors are the starting point for inquiry, not the end: we want to know why a given worker did or didn't do something, what organizational factors contributed, why that worker and that organizational unit were involved rather than others, and what other factors fed into the result (Munro 2005).

Applying this lesson to child welfare, Dr. Tina Rzepnicki has introduced root cause analysis—a way of working backwards from events to the "changes, conditions, and inactions" that set the stage—to review child fatalities for the Illinois Department of Child and Family Services Inspector General's Office (Rzepnicki and Johnson 2005, 400). Using the root cause approach, Rzepnicki found many examples of child fatalities where workers failed to gather and use information about domestic violence, substance abuse, and mental illness in assessing family risk. Rather than stopping there, the new approach prompted further analysis that led to recommendations for rethinking the department's unrealistic expectations of workers (as embodied in its risk assessment form) and strengthening supervision (Illinois DCFS Inspector General 2005).[9]

Second, understanding system vulnerabilities requires gathering information on "near misses"—where workers made mistakes but nobody got hurt—as well as damaging events. Absent a specific focus on these near misses, they are not likely to show up in a database, even though they are important early alerts of danger (IOM 2000, 95–96). For example, if nurses routinely cannot read the doctor's handwriting and rely on other clues to decide how much medication to dispense, each incident must be reported so the problem is flagged and can be fixed before an unwitting patient pays the price. While it's harder to define a near miss in child welfare, reviewing deaths and injuries will suggest what to look for in cases without injuries: for example, parental substance abuse or serious mental illness that became evident during the first year of services but was not flagged during the investigation.

Third, an effective reporting system includes enough incidents to reveal patterns. Expanding geographical scope and including near misses help to achieve scale: for example, airplane crashes are infrequent, but adding to the database equipment malfunctions that were successfully managed may allow underlying patterns to emerge.

Taken together, these recommendations could palpably improve child welfare practice. Typically, state or city child fatality review teams fall far short of successful safety initiatives in other fields in the scope of information collected and the depth of analysis. Too often, these teams analyze fatalities one by one or in clusters too small to yield useful lessons. Too often, the teams follow their own intuition in analyzing the stories, rather than a structured process intended to assure that systemic lessons emerge. And a team reviewing a high-profile event generally gets public pressure to pin blame, never mind the hindsight bias that the Institute of Medicine notes frequently clouds analysis of safety cases (IOM 2000). By contrast, the data collection and analysis needed might cover multiple jurisdictions throughout a large state or even the whole country, use a rigorous approach to examine causes, identify patterns from many cases at once, and include not only child deaths but also serious injuries and near misses (Wilson 2005).

Organizations That Have Improved Safety Have Developed Safety Cultures, Which Share Important Characteristics

McCarthy and Blumenthal find that in case studies of successful health care safety improvement, all the programs cited a shift to a patient safety culture as "critical to making patients safer" (McCarthy and Blumenthal 2006, 170). In such a culture, leaders make safety a priority, the approach to mistakes is open and non-blaming, and the focus in collecting and analyzing information is on learning. Five interrelated features of this culture have been found across industries, such as nuclear power and aviation, wherever safety has been greatly enhanced: "an informed culture, a reporting culture, a just culture, a flexible culture, and a learning culture" (McCarthy and Blumenthal 2006, 173). In a just culture, as defined by the researchers, actions that will be disciplined or treated as blameworthy are clearly defined (for example, deliberate damage or actions under the influence of alcohol), so people know they will not be punished if they report ordinary errors.

Applied to child welfare agencies, these findings would all but transform the current culture. For one thing, the "safety culture" encompasses values and techniques meant to enhance *any* clinical approach, unlike child welfare's history of associating safety with just one approach—removing children from their homes. For another, the safety culture contrasts starkly with the culture of blame characteristic of child welfare. Eileen Munro notes that "the public's emotional responses to child abuse deaths are complex and powerful and seem to include a deep need to find a scapegoat" (Munro 2005, 378). Not surprisingly, the agencies blamed and pilloried often become defensive and reluctant to share information.

Creating a Safe Way to Report Errors Is a Key Part of the "Learning Culture"

Good information on how and why errors occur and what damage they do is essential to developing solutions. But collecting this information is hard when people fear disciplinary action, public criticism, or litigation. For this reason, researchers on health care safety suggest combining voluntary, confidential reporting systems with mandatory public ones. For example, the Institute of Medicine recommends a two-part system, with mandatory reporting mainly for errors that cause injury or death and voluntary reporting for other errors (IOM 2000). The Department of Veterans Affairs health program successfully increased reporting through another trust-building move: they worked collaboratively with stakeholders, including Congress, unions, and outside organizations, to define blameworthy acts. Only "a criminal act, an act related to substance abuse, or an intentionally unsafe act that an individual knew to be unsafe" qualified (McCarthy and Blumenthal 2006, 176).

Alternative reporting strategies are worth exploring in child welfare. Right now, child welfare agencies may have no reporting except for a very formalized procedure when a child dies. In-between reporting protocols might include some that are confidential or voluntary to capture critical information about nonfatal incidents and errors that could have dangerous consequences.

Broad Principles Lead to Practical Suggestions That Make a Difference

While the solutions that improve safety will depend on which problems analysis points to, several practical ideas do recur among successful health care settings. The first is improving communications and teamwork. Lessons from aviation and other fields suggest that errors are more likely where teams are ineffective—characterized by hierarchies that impede open communication, ambiguity about roles, and individual rather than joint training. One hospital studied by McCarthy and Blumenthal focused on improving communication during shift changes. A health care organization trained the perinatal unit in assertive and structured communication techniques so everyone would feel comfortable speaking up in urgent situations (McCarthy and Blumenthal 2006, 176–78). These ideas have obvious applications to child welfare, where fatality reviews frequently blame individual workers for not passing important information along. Reviewers should, instead, look for patterns (like deference to expertise, ambiguity about who has what information, or shift changes) that suggest broader solutions.

A second recurring approach rests on greater, yet carefully targeted, standardization and simplification. The successful health care organizations studied by the Institute of Medicine and by McCarthy and Blumenthal found that while some care-related decisions will always be complicated, others can be simplified, either by reducing the number of categories routinely considered (for example, fewer drug dosages) or by making the most likely protocol the default (say, particular follow-up medication that is almost always required after heart surgery). For example, a diabetes practice stratifies patients into three categories of risk, each with expected treatments: the large majority, who require care at prespecified levels; the second level, who have other risk factors and require additional attention; and the third level, who have developed complications and need highly individualized care (IOM 2001).

The most interesting feature of this solution from the perspective of child welfare agencies is the middle ground between standardization and individual worker discretion: the goal is not to make every service standardized or discretionary, but to make deliberate choices based on the evidence available. Also useful for child welfare is the focus on standardizing not just decisions but service availability—by giving every level-one diabetes patient a package of services determined by evidence about quality care. The diabetes protocol aims to improve not just decisions, but also the actual delivery of the right services.

How Does Research Really Help in Reform?

How much does the research on child development and social service delivery help reformers figure out what to do? Does enough evidence point to a reform vision that always works or to certain proven programs? Or must reformers improvise without much guidance from evidence?

The picture sketched here is somewhere in the middle. We know much more about successful programs than we put into practice, so there is room to get better results for children based on what research can tell us. Yet we do not know enough to define a single best vision, to choose which practice or program will work best in a given setting, or to find with certainty the right balance between important principles that conflict in a particular case.

What We Know

The research just reviewed offers strong evidence about what children need to thrive and useful, but less complete information about what parents need to provide a safe and loving home. It suggests that major approaches to reform—improving social worker skills and working conditions, engaging families, individualizing services, and developing informal and formal supports for families—all have some basis in research, though none is likely to be a panacea. It also suggests that important ideas from other fields can strengthen child welfare performance, and that evidence from many fields converges on several likely characteristics of effective interventions.

Another implication of the research reviewed here is that intervention at many different points in the child welfare system offers the opportunity to improve children's lives. While reformers have sometimes argued about whether reform should emphasize day-to-day practice or larger systemwide change, this evidence suggests that both can matter, along with reforms to strengthen the settings where children live and the services available to children and families.

Settings. The biggest influence on children's development is usually the setting they live in: their home—temporary or permanent, family or institution, loving or punitive—and their close relationships. Reformers may try to influence these settings directly by closing shelters or group homes, strengthening licensing requirements, or offering new training to kin and foster parents. Or, they may improve settings indirectly by changing social worker practice, for example by training social workers to place more children with kin and fewer in group homes.

Services. Evaluations demonstrate that well-designed and well-implemented services can positively affect children's early development, parenting and parent-child interactions, parental depression, and parental substance abuse. On the other hand, weak programs may have no effects, so reformers need to consider not just availability, but also the quality and design of services.

Assessing the performance of child welfare systems against the research evidence indicates that even the most strongly supported findings are too seldom put into practice. Research tells us loud and clear that children need stable and permanent relationships, which means that moving children multiple times and leaving them in a string of temporary settings for years will likely damage them deeply. The obstacle here is not a lack of knowledge.

The difficulty of putting what we know into practice is not limited to child welfare. Even in health care, with a more certain and widely accepted knowledge base, the share of care consistent with evidence-based standards is typically low—about 55 percent of care in one study conducted by RAND (McGlynn et al. 2003). A review conducted for the Institute of Medicine concluded that much American health care is not consistent with the best evidence (IOM 2001). Much of the rest of this book describes the obstacles to putting knowledge into practice and how reformers surmount them.

What We Don't Know

That said, there is also much that we do not know. Available research provides strong evidence about which practices are bad for children, narrows the range of promising reforms, and suggests broad principles that are likely to characterize effective programs. But the research does not tell us which practice or program will work best in a certain bureaucratic, political, and family context, nor does it suggest that a single program, approach, or vision is best everywhere. Often the research suggests principles that are partly at odds with each other, offering little guidance about how to balance them. For example, how exactly should good programs engage parents but also focus on children; or how should programs follow evidence-based practices but also respond to individual needs and strengths?

Not surprisingly, reformers in the real world, constrained by these limits on the value of research, realize that they must learn by doing, and then assessing the consequences of their actions. As later chapters show, creating a child welfare agency that can learn from experience is central to a successful turnaround.

5

The Broad Brush
Vision, Strategy, and Action

"There was a lot of change in the system even before the new staff came on board or money was spent."
—Ira Burnim, plaintiffs' attorney in Alabama

"As soon as the flex-funds hit the street, kids' status went up."
—Ivor Groves, court monitor in Alabama

"People would talk about how to fix this and that. [But there were] a million philosophies in the agency. . . . Before we go out [to talk to people about good practice], we need to determine philosophy, principles."
—Richard Anderson, deputy and then-director of Utah's child welfare agency, speaking of Utah just before the reform took hold

Looking at the "before" pictures of deeply troubled child welfare agencies in dysfunctional political settings, it is hard to imagine how to jolt them out of their historic doldrums and start up the reform engine. After all, in Washington, D.C., Alabama, and Utah, failure had persisted for years, and previous efforts at change had sputtered out, so what could spark change? Were there common themes in these very different settings, or were the approaches that finally worked completely idiosyncratic? This chapter focuses on the messy problems faced by leaders seeking to jump-start reform in each failing agency.

Several common themes mark the recollections of leaders and observers about the agencies' transition from stagnation to progress. One is the power of a vision, a philosophy, a set of cross-cutting ideas, particularly one powerful enough to cut across the different organizations that make up the child welfare system. A vision can begin to spark change even before anything else changes, as Ira Burnim argues about Alabama; conversely, the absence of a vision can hobble success, even when agency leaders have specific good ideas, a lesson Richard Anderson draws from pre-reform Utah.

A second theme is the crucial role of early action consistent with the vision. Words prime the change process, but actions are needed for sustained effect. While Burnim believes that Alabama's reform started with the articulation of the vision in the settlement agreement and Paul Vincent's presentations, Groves believes it took off with the implementation of flex-funds, the first big action exemplifying the vision. Similarly in the District, both vision and an early action were necessary to move children from group homes to family settings. The Council needed to hear about our vision to understand the reason for closing the emergency shelters; it was not a vendetta against specific providers or a blind effort to comply with the federal court's preferences. At the same time, staff and providers needed to see the action in order to take seriously the vision that children could thrive in families.

These themes are consistent with the research on the value of a clear mission and strategy for public- and private-sector leaders. For example, Mark Moore articulates the advantages of framing a strategy that includes a mission statement, its external "sources of support and legitimacy," and the "organizational and operational steps" to realize the mission (Moore 1995, 71). But applying these ideas to the challenging, chaotic world of child welfare turnarounds can be puzzling. This chapter explores these puzzles, setting out how vision, strategy, and diagnosis—articulated in words and embodied in actions—are powerful tools for leaders striving to reform troubled child welfare agencies.

Vision and Strategy as Tools for a Turnaround

The idea that a vision is a powerful tool in a failing agency may appear odd. What good is a vision when there are so many obvious problems to fix? Why not just focus on solving them, through good, proven programs such as innovative approaches to staff recruitment, foster care quality, or adoption? Besides, how could something so bland as a vision be powerful? If it were that easy, why hadn't generations of agency leaders and managers decided on a vision and succeeded already?

What Does a Vision Add to Best Practices?

Many discussions of child welfare reform by researchers and practitioners assume that fixing problems one by one must be the real way to reform, so reformers should draw on expert knowledge or best practices to solve each child welfare problem. Reformers should study best practices in staffing to figure out how to fix workforce problems, best practices in placement to match children to homes that meet their needs, and risk assessment and investigation techniques to improve the handling of child abuse and neglect complaints.

Yet, this stepwise approach is not the preferred solution of the leaders in these turnaround cases. True, the leaders draw on knowledge and experience of individual program or administrative systems. But what they put first is a broad vision, framework, and set of priorities. Why?

A Clear Vision Helps Communication, Inside and Out. Clear principles cut through the clutter of everyday experience in a way that detailed programs may not. Such clarity is especially important in child welfare because so many actors must coordinate their work to get results, including social workers, local judges, schools, health and mental health agencies, legislators, outside providers, foster and adoptive parents, and administrative units within the child welfare agency. With a clear vision, these diverse partners can understand the reform and embody it in their own work, or they can negotiate potential disagreements. But when child welfare leaders have not articulated a coherent vision, each partner invents its own principles to shape decisions and priorities. And if reform comes in piecemeal programmatic initiatives, even cooperative partners are unlikely to understand the goals well enough to offer their own ideas for moving forward.

In Alabama, observers noted Paul Vincent's repeated articulation of his vision to diverse audiences as a key feature of the reform. In Utah, the practice model tied the broad vision to each step of the reform, so all partners could understand specific changes to policy and practice in the context of the whole picture.

When partners understand the vision behind the plan, they are sometimes willing to dramatically change their roles and practices. Late in my tenure in the District, I was pleased and surprised by the Family Court judges' willingness to actively support our plans to conduct "family team" meetings when a child was being removed from his or her home. In other jurisdictions, these meetings frequently led to better results for children, but lawyers and judges had typically worried that the meetings could move decisionmaking out of the court and into a more informal setting ill-designed to protect children's and parents' legal rights. In D.C., though, the judges saw that the meetings could offer them better information and help them resolve cases more quickly and effectively.[1] The years we had spent talking about a vision focused on permanence and on engaging biological and extended family early probably helped achieve this consensus.

Principles Clarify Priorities. Reform in the context of deep and historic failure involves constant choices about priorities and ensuing trade-offs. Reforms may require resources, or time from workers or managers, or drawing on limited credibility with such outside partners as judges or foster parents. Without guidance from a clear vision to help weigh the trade-offs, leaders may never make any decisions—stymied by the risks and benefits—or make decisions randomly or in isolation, never accumulating enough impact to demonstrate progress.

Examples abound from the sites studied. When I decided to cancel a research study in kinship care because it would have increased social worker caseloads, I was choosing to put lower caseloads first, just as when I sought emergency legislation to help me staff Court Social Services cases, potentially using up credibility I might need later. Both decisions took some reflection but not a lot, because the strategic criterion was clear. Similarly, in Utah, Patterson diverted his regional directors' precious time when he instructed them to immediately answer calls from the new constituency services office, but doing so best served his overall strategy. In Alabama, Vincent understood that training everyone off-site for six weeks meant "you have to ignore procedural issues, reduce the focus on timelines." But, given his strategic mission and vision, it was the right means to the end.

Principles Better Fit Complex Systems. A cross-cutting vision and strategy are essential in complex systems. Solutions to problems in child welfare frequently cut across boundaries, as when social workers leave because judges are hostile or social workers' caseloads increase because the agency has no services to help families reunify. These problems crop up in the human resources domain but cannot be solved there and can rarely be understood correctly apart from the entire strategic context. For example, a contract official in Alabama who thought only about best practices in purchasing services might have thought that uniform statewide contracts were best for performance accountability. But in Vincent's vision, it was the wrong approach for a strategy built on individual social worker creativity and flexibility.

Are All Child Welfare Visions Equally Powerful?

Are there many child welfare visions that communicate to all stakeholders, guide leadership priorities, and help organizations work through very complicated problems—or just one or two? Research on effective practices doesn't point to a single vision but guides us to a range of sensible possibilities. If the lessons from practice bear out the research, it would mean that leaders can shape a vision from among these possibilities, much as private-sector executives redefine a company's mission to suit current capacity and the external environment. But this approach is not consistent with an alternative approach to child welfare reform: a search for the *right* vision, the one that can best drive change across the country.

Burnim argues strongly for this second point of view. He believes that Alabama's reform vision is uniquely powerful and transferable to other systems and that (in words he quotes from a colleague) knowing the answer and being unable to persuade others can feel like being a doctor: "I have a cure—I have to tell the world." As Burnim describes the vision, "It's all about how you see the clients and your aspirations for them. So the first thing in Alabama was the high aspirations that the system set. And these aspirations were legally binding."

In practice, though, the visions offered by reformers in Alabama, Utah, and the District are more consistent with the "many possibilities" view. The reform visions certainly overlap, but they also diverge. Consider the approach to improving the quality of social workers' day-to-day work: leaders in all three jurisdictions saw such improvement as central to reform, yet they articulated the vision differently and, accordingly, chose different priorities.

In Alabama, Vincent decided to change how social workers worked instead of increasing the number of social workers or reducing their caseloads. In the early phase, Vincent focused all his resources into pilot counties and the relatively small number of children they served, rather than taking statewide action. This strategic choice positioned him to achieve maximum impact on the way social workers operated in these communities and maximum leverage from other early decisions, including placing outside consultants as coaches and mandating off-site training in pilot counties. Only later did the parties to the Alabama settlement focus on statewide caseload per social worker.

Why did Vincent pick this starting point? Looking back, he and other key Alabama reformers diagnosed the state's pre-reform child welfare agency as complacent, insular, and resistant to change. Given that diagnosis, it was natural to worry that reducing caseloads would just lead to more resources being wasted on a stuck and unaccountable system, not to better results. Instead, the first step had to be to change practice. Once that happened, resources could be added. To someone with another diagnosis and strategy, the settlement agreement's expectation that reform would be phased in might have been a constraint. But to Vincent and his colleagues, the phase-in meant they could intervene powerfully enough in a few places to change expectations, get people unstuck, and demonstrate that deep and fundamental reform was possible.

In Utah, Patterson arrived after the state had hired a huge number of social workers yet still failed to perform, leading him to a diagnosis centered on the rawness of the line staff, their lack of clarity about their jobs, and the demoralization and passivity of more experienced agency staff. Building on this diagnosis, Patterson made major investments in training and practice and committed early to the gargantuan task of developing a practice model. Unlike in Alabama, Utah's leaders used internal staff to develop the model and conduct training, even when the court became frustrated at how long it was taking. This choice was a natural consequence of a different diagnosis of the problem: the Utah leaders believed that staff were beaten-down, afraid, and needed to be coaxed back into taking control and bringing their ideas and values to the table.

In the District, excessive caseloads and social workers' inability to do anything but respond to emergencies were central themes. The immediate problems were chaos and the long-term persistence of overwhelming workloads, in contrast to Alabama's rigidity and Utah's inexperienced new staff. Virtually everyone in the historically divided system agreed on the need for caseload reduction: the court monitor and plaintiffs' attorneys in the federal court, the local judges, the foster parents, and the social workers. I also thought that reducing caseloads would address a major source of demoralization, burnout, and pessimism about reform, since the long history of overwhelming caseloads, in the face of repeated promises of relief, had contributed to cynicism and a sense of powerlessness. In addition, reducing caseloads would also take away excuses allowing workers to act on their underlying passion, commitment, clinical knowledge, and values, while holding them accountable for performance. And, zeroing in on caseload reduction helped me seize a more practical opportunity:

I had resources and tools to hire social workers that had never been available to agency leaders before.

The three reform visions also overlap in their approach to the role of families, yet they differ in their emphases and priorities. In Utah the Milestone Plan expected social workers to involve families and children from the beginning. Bringing families in required social workers to be more assertive with the agency's lawyers, who preferred a more formal process that simplified taking families to court.

In Alabama, the family-focused vision meant that social workers were expected to engage families in crafting a tailored approach to keeping their children safe. The system was to shift from removing children to strengthening families so they could keep their children at home, reflecting the reformers' conclusion that the old system had removed children from their homes too easily.

In the District, our vision was that children should live in families (including kin, foster, and adoptive families) and not in shelters or group homes. This vision did not focus as much as Alabama's on whether children should be removed; rather, it emphasized the value of families whether children were at home or in care. In part, this emphasis reflected my own beliefs about the developmental research and the limits of the evidence: I was confident that children would do better in families and that the agency should improve its support of biological, kin, foster, and adoptive families so they could better nurture children, but I was not confident that we knew whether more or fewer children in the District could safely live at home. The emphasis on family settings also reflected our diagnosis that a major failure in the District's history was the assignment of even young children to shelters and group homes.

Thus, reform visions that work grow out of a diagnosis of the organization's strengths and needs, whether explicit or implicit. Within a range of reasonable possibilities, reformers define a vision that fits both their values and their circumstances.

In failing child welfare agencies, reformers pay special attention to visions that sharply contrast with past failures. In Alabama, a vision of creative and flexible practice contrasted with a history of rigidity; in Utah, a vision of well-trained and assertive social workers contrasted with a history of passive compliance; and in the District, a vision of well-supported social workers with manageable workloads contrasted with a history of chaos and caseloads out of control.

Besides showcasing contrasts, the reformers' visions also built on past values they wanted to support and maintain. In Utah, for example, using in-house talent to design the training program reflected Patterson's diagnosis that low morale had sidelined the agency's best thinkers, who needed to be encouraged and empowered. In the District, I wanted to create conditions where social workers could live up to their high quality standards, rather than become drained by an emergency-driven super-human workload.

Successful reformers also frame the vision to avoid unnecessary risks and seize opportunities, including short-term opportunities that could set the agency on track to bigger accomplishments. In Alabama, a phased-in settlement starting with small pilot counties created the opportunity to experiment with intensive off-site training that would have been far harder in a large urban office. In the District, new resources created an opportunity to show results that would matter immediately to many constituents who otherwise had differing and sometimes incompatible demands.

Marty Beyer, a consultant invited by Alabama's reformers to help design new ways of working with children and families, remembers that what helped staff most in one particularly chaotic local office was her focus on reflection before action. She would ask the social worker and supervisor handling a case to "stop the madness" and write and reflect on the needs of the child under discussion. Interrupting the mad rush to answers with even a moment of reflective diagnosis paid off in much better plans for the child and family. Successful system reformers cannot literally "stop the madness" because daily emergencies continue to bombard them. But they draw on a similar approach: allowing workable possibilities to emerge from reflective diagnosis.

A Common Theme: Vision of an Active, Assertive Agency

Besides the reformers' visions of the *content* of child welfare reform, they all defined a vision for the *role* of the child welfare agency—and these three visions were far more similar than the visions of content. I was surprised by this consistency, because I had thought that the District's unique history was the reason I spent so much time articulating the District agency's newly active role. But in all the jurisdictions, leaders and observers defined a consistent vision for the reformed agency's role and outlook: the agency should see itself as active, not passive, shaping its own future and improving results for children, rather than being the victim of external actors; the agency should be open to learning and not defensive; and the agency should take responsibility for its own failures and mistakes, rather than blaming others. Burnim's view that Alabama's reform vision was universally applicable may not be true in terms of content, but it could apply to the vision of a responsible and accountable agency.

Vincent's powerful articulation of this active, accountable, open stance is remembered by observers of the Alabama reform as one of his major contributions to change. One outside observer remembers his unwavering "we are going to do this" message, while another highlights his willingness to take responsibility and identify the problem as "us" (that is, the child welfare agency). It might seem that taking responsibility would be threatening to staff, yet insiders and outsiders valued his leadership toward a more accountable agency. Agency staff in particular found that his calm reduced their anxiety about taking responsibility for change and its risks.

Utah's early leaders saw the agency's passivity as undermining progress in the first years after the settlement and prescribed actively taking responsibility as the cure. Patterson and Anderson took ownership of the court-mandated Milestone Plan and argued that it was the right approach based on agency and community values. Patterson's early action to handle complaints internally demonstrated to agency staff that they could take responsibility for doing a good job, rather than waiting to be told they were failing. Finally, Patterson also thought that passivity colored social workers' responses to the legal system. Taking control back was an important goal of the new practice model for social workers.

In the District, I quickly concluded that the blame-ridden system with its incentives for everyone to avoid responsibility had prepared the ground for stagnation and failure. The parties to the federal litigation had already made a clear diagnosis that a strong, accountable agency was the only way to move forward, a diagnosis incorporated into the requirements of the October 2000 consent order and the April 2001 legislation. I believed strongly in this vision and used it to guide my priority choices—such as meeting the deadline for unification of abuse and neglect services under CFSA, even when many thought it impossible. I also thought, just as the Utah leadership did, that an active, accountable agency had to make the court's expectations our own, not just "comply." I reiterated this stance in testimony, all-staff memos, and speeches: our priorities were *both* required by the court *and* driven by our own vision and values.

Finding the right way to articulate this stance of responsibility is difficult when an agency has a long history of failure. The problem is how to take responsibility for the agency's failures without contributing to despair or cynicism—and how to take pride in what the agency is doing well without being defensive or dishonest about the huge remaining gaps. My use of the same words over and over in press interviews reveal this balancing act. Commenting on the good news that we had met the court's probationary period requirements, I said "This [progress] is astonishing to me" yet "there remains an "enormous amount to do."[2] A few weeks later, I used almost the same words in another *Post* interview: "I'm really glad to see the progress, but I think we have a great deal left to do."[3] To those outside the system, these answers no doubt seemed pro forma, but they reflected an effort to be honest about both our successes and our failures.

Why are these visions so much alike in the three settings, despite other differences in agency circumstances? They are all responding to the same diagnosis of why these agencies were failing: distorted systems of accountability and the associated incentives for passivity and blame. While politics certainly contributed to these problems, all the agency leaders saw the child welfare agency itself as perpetuating the cycle through the reluctance of managers, supervisors, and social workers to take responsibility for their performance. Accordingly, the reformers described here all posited a countervailing picture of a strong, accountable agency that sees openness, taking responsibility, and addressing its own mistakes as strength, not weakness.

Interestingly, as these case studies show, the federal court's oversight can promote, as well as inhibit, an agency's ability to achieve the vision of active ownership. In settings bad enough to prompt litigation, other political pressures on the agency may have already produced extreme passivity before the court's involvement. Litigation can provide some relief from such harsh or chaotic political environments and thereby help create an active and competent agency. Chapter 8 looks more closely at the role of the federal courts in the political context.

Committing to Action

What did it matter if the fog and snow meant she couldn't see the course? She learned long ago how to ski as fast as she could in blizzards and powder without benefit of sight. All that mattered, she reminded herself, was knowing where her feet were and knowing how to react when conditions got really tough.—Liz Clark, "Mancuso Storms to Skiing Gold," *Washington Post,* February 25, 2006, E1

The first part of this chapter explored the puzzle of vision—why it matters and how it works in a failing agency. This second part takes on the puzzle of action: how do leaders turn a vision into strategically chosen actions amid the chaos, perpetual emergencies, and conflict characteristic of these turnaround settings in child welfare? The tone of some research on strategy suggests that leaders calmly weigh alternatives and use good information to choose actions that embody their vision. This chapter asks what it means to act strategically in a failing child welfare system characterized by an information void, complex systems producing unintended consequences, and a history of blame and passivity, surrounded by a political minefield. For leaders in these settings, transforming strategy into action feels like deciding to take the ski-racer's irrevocable step over the edge: you are often unable to see the challenges from the top, but once you start down the slope, the challenges come at you at 90 miles an hour.

This puzzle hit home for me during my first months in the District. When I became director, I was already convinced that a clearly articulated vision and matching priorities had the power to create change. I thought that a clear vision and priorities would help me pick the right actions, and that the actions in turn would communicate the reform's values inside and outside the organization. However, I could rarely predict the consequences of an early action because of the system's complexity and multilayered failures. Nor could I predict how people would read my actions, given the painful history that had shaped their outlook. Would staff see my Friday night trip to the courthouse to persuade a judge to release a jailed social worker as a sign of commitment to my staff or a sign of not trying hard enough because I hadn't stopped it before it happened? Was it a sign of power that I influenced the court to release the worker or a sign of powerlessness that I let something so terrible happen? More generally, how do leaders use vision and strategy to drive their actions in a world of such uncertainty and chaos?

The Role of Immediate Action

Despite the information void, leaders in the turnaround sites acted early and energetically. In Alabama, Paul Vincent remembers the shock of realizing at the beginning of the reform that no one in his group of outside experts could tell him the right answer and that he might fail completely. Nonetheless, he took many early and dramatic actions: he decided to select the initial round of phase-in counties competitively, chose six winners, put all his resources into those counties, invented a new approach to the work by using outside consultants as coaches, quickly commissioned a new training program, required all staff in the pilot counties to go through it, and got the money for flex-funds. Similarly, in the District, we acted aggressively in the first year despite an information void. We closed three emergency shelters, hired a new senior team, reorganized the agency to take on wholly new responsibilities, tried a half-dozen strategies to reduce social worker caseloads, co-located 40 lawyers in the child welfare agency, and met 15 of the 20 performance measures, among other sweeping changes.

In Utah, the reform team came in after several years of action that had not yielded results. So it might seem that a time for gathering and analyzing information would be required. Nonetheless, the new team quickly completed the mandated Milestone Plan—a "massive overhaul of the child welfare system"[4]—developed a practice model that linked the plan to social workers' day-to-day activities, and revised its approach to controversial cases.

Interestingly, this high level of activity in the first months through the early years is consistent with what a classic study says senior-level private-sector managers do when they take on big new jobs (Gabarro 1985). Typically these managers take about two to two-and-a-half years to fully take charge of their new assignment, but they do not study first and act later. Instead, they act and then step back three times, in waves that alternate rapid action with reflection and changing course. Almost a third of the personnel and organizational changes that managers made during the whole two-to-three-year "taking charge" period happened in the first six months, with another similar burst in months 12 through 18. A sub-group of managers in the study was charged with turning around a failing organization. Their initial period of intensive action took the same three to six months as their non-turnaround counterparts, but their later action waves peaked earlier.

Interestingly, these turnaround managers "knew they would have to redo later some of the changes they were making in the taking-hold stage":

> In one case, the new general manager reported he knew from experience (this was his third turnaround) that it would take five to six months to design and implement a cost system that was sophisticated enough to provide all the information he needed on which products were losing money and why. He concluded that he simply did

not have the time to do it perfectly and opted instead for a system that would give him, as quickly as possible, a better vision of the problems. (Gabarro 1985, 119)

In the public and private sectors, reformers act early and aggressively, even when there is a great deal they do not know, and even when (or especially when) basic systems like personnel and information are in disarray.

Why act early rather than waiting for better information and a clearer plan? First, action is necessary to learn in a complex organization: action ultimately dispels the fog and confusion. To figure out how to reduce social worker caseloads in the District, we had to start trying out some solutions. We could not start out through planning (though we tried, unsuccessfully), because no one understood the causes, never mind how they interacted, clearly enough to figure out a plan. For example, at the beginning, no one understood how the graduation cycle of master's in social work programs interacted with our recruitment cycle. After a failed recruiting effort, we understood that our greatest appeal was to new graduates, so we had to beef up our spring recruiting to bring in enough hires to carry us through the year.

Why couldn't we plan for spring graduations from the beginning? Basically, the hiring process was too complicated to understand without trying it, and since the agency had never had sustained support for recruitment, no one there had tried it. Without experience, we did not understand the obstacles, or how to fix them, or how to put solutions together into an effective plan. To counter this blindness, we had to start trying solutions. When a proposed solution failed, we figured out why to come up with new solutions. When a solution succeeded, we confirmed our initial hunches about possible causes and learned which changes could and could not be implemented. Each attempt was a learning experience that enabled us to figure out what worked and why, or why not.

Alabama's reforms were most explicitly built on learning by doing in the phase-in counties, following Paul Vincent's discovery that the experts were unable to tell him what to do. One person who worked for him remembers how deliberately he fostered learning from action: when Vincent was told of a failure, he'd say, "Let's go back and make some new mistakes." The idea, of course, was that mistakes are educational, that acknowledging them honestly is healthy, and that they continue to be educational as long as you always make different ones.

Donald Schon's famous book *The Reflective Practitioner: How Professionals Think in Action* argues that learning through action rather than theoretical reflection is characteristic of many professionals, not just public managers. Writing about an architect confronting a messy site problem, he captures exactly the mix of intended and unintended consequences, and the ways successes and failures both contribute to learning, that are so characteristic of the child welfare stories:

> In the designer's conversation with the materials of his design, he can never make a move that has only the effects intended for it. His materials are constantly talking back to him, causing him to apprehend unanticipated problems and potentials. As he appreciates such new and unexpected phenomena, he also evaluates the moves that have created them. (Schon 1983, 100–101)

Thus, the "unanticipated problems and opportunities" that we found in trying to reduce caseloads amounted to the system talking back to us, teaching us lessons about what to try next, and allowing us to better evaluate our previous moves.

What distinguishes this kind of learning in action from simply flying blind—from hurtling down a path, heedless of possible wrong turns? Schon suggests that openness to being proved wrong is the essential ingredient of learning—the materials have to be able to "talk back" and reveal that your original idea was a failure. Taking an action and then interpreting every possible response as a sign that you were right in the first place is the opposite of learning. Again, this idea resonates with the experience of the child welfare reformers, with their focus on openness, accountability, and non-defensiveness.

Second, acting rather than just speaking is crucial to communicating a strategy and vision. Without the actions, staff and observers in a failing agency will quickly disbelieve the words; their long history of disappointment and broken promises has likely bred cynicism. In Alabama, Groves reports that once the state got the flex-funds into workers' hands, nonbelievers were convinced by seeing the state back the vision with money. In the District, the union initially did not believe we were serious about hiring more social workers, despite what I thought were aggressive recruitment steps. Instead, it feared that my hidden agenda was to outsource the agency until large classes of new workers finally demonstrated that the actions, and the results, were genuine.

This lesson is not limited to child welfare or to the public sector. John Kotter argues that short-term wins sustain motivation in private-sector transformations as well, and the failure to develop them is a prime reason for failure:

> Real transformation takes time. . . . Most people won't go on the long march unless they see compelling evidence within six to eighteen months that the jour-

ney is producing expected results. Without short-term wins, too many employees give up or actively join the resistance. . . . In a successful transformation, managers actively look for ways to obtain clear performance improvements [in this period]. (Kotter 1996, 11)

To achieve these wins, leaders operating in the fog of uncertainty characteristic of the child welfare sites need to be even more aggressive in taking early actions than leaders in easier situations. With little initial information to guide their guesses on the likely success of various initiatives, leaders need to take many actions so the small proportion that succeeds early will be enough to generate progress and momentum.

During my early months in the District, I thought the court had too many expectations; I would probably have said that we should be judged on two or three measures, not 15 of 20. But in retrospect, I suspect that having such an array of expectations was helpful. With less pressure, I might have tried fewer things—and since my track record in predicting what would be easy to solve and what would be hard looks weak in retrospect, I could have tried the hardest steps first and failed on most of them. With fewer early successes, it would have been even harder to build momentum in the agency and among political office-holders and constituents.

Seizing Opportunities for Strategic Action

To promote learning and communicate effectively, actions need to be strategic—to fit the leader's vision and priorities for change. This may seem obvious, especially when it is applied to the actions leaders themselves initiate. But leaders must also spend time on activities they do not initiate: responses to tragedies and emergencies, participation in ongoing bureaucratic and political processes (for instance, the budget, the contracting cycle, monitoring reviews by federal, state, or local auditors), obligations to staff and outside partners, and efforts to resolve long-festering problems not specifically part of the reform. Can leaders fit these responsive rather than entrepreneurial actions into their strategic vision?

Both the case studies and the management literature suggest that they must or they will fail. Mintzberg's classic description of the manager's job finds that "the manager has to spend so much time discharging obligations that if he were to view them as just that, he would leave no mark on the organization." Therefore, "the effective manager turns his obligations to his own advantage" by using actions he or she does not initiate to move the agenda forward and send signals about vision and priorities (Mintzberg 1975, 60–61).

Patterson's decision in Utah to create the internal ombudsman's office arose not from a big plan but from his realization that responding to outside auditors and reviewers was draining valuable staff time away from vision, solutions, and operations. Patterson and his deputy, Anderson, were forced into this strategic action when "just coping" with the time drain no longer worked and the practice model was getting short shrift. Creating and empowering the internal office was a gamble, but one that paid off and sent strong messages about the efficacy of the strategy.

An example in the District came when I had to decide how to carry out an annoying but important bureaucratic task: ensuring that agency social workers and supervisors who had previously been employed by the federal court receivership would be transferred to the District's civil service system. I decided to ask the mayor and the council to make a few small changes to the civil service law so the transfer was as invisible to staff as possible. I made this decision because of my strategic focus on social worker caseloads, which led me to reject the idea of holding competitions for all the jobs—legally required under a narrow interpretation of the law but, in my view, a nightmare for reform. If we had to reopen hundreds of jobs to competition in our first weeks as an independent agency, I thought it would cripple our human resources office, set back recruitment, torpedo morale, and leave us unable to cover cases for months. The mayor and the Council agreed, but, as with all strategic calls, not everyone did: some social workers argued that by failing to require supervisors to compete, I was condoning widespread incompetence.

The Consequences of Action: Choice and Conflict

By definition, strategic action is not neutral and always has a downside, since it emphasizes some goals and values over others. An action with no downside would not be a choice between plausible alternatives, so it would offer no hints about the leader's priorities or vision. Accordingly, all the examples we have seen come with downsides, whether Paul Vincent's choice to select pilots competitively even though that left some counties with deep problems unassisted or my choice to forgo an early opportunity to assess competence to avoid turnover and rising caseloads.

In all the reform jurisdictions, strategic actions also entailed conflict. This should not be surprising, since in these turnaround settings, reformers are upending entrenched patterns of failure that involve many stakeholders. Not surprisingly, conflict arises from many sources: differing interests among stakeholders, differing professional outlooks, differing visions about child welfare, and differing perspectives about roles and role changes. Agency reformers may want a new, more accountable and more active child welfare agency to become a leader in the system, but partners may prefer the previous, more passive version of the agency, which gave them more leeway.

I have told several District stories of conflict chosen or accepted because important issues were at stake. In refusing to accede to Maryland's ultimatum—to reduce foster care rates or face the return of District foster children from Maryland homes—we were staking out a battle over our top strategic priorities. Complying with the demand to reduce rates, in my view, would have put children in harm's way, placed us in direct conflict with the federal court, devastated morale among foster parents, reversed our progress in moving children from congregate settings to families, and undermined the conception of an active and accountable child welfare agency. When we reassigned social workers from non-case-carrying assignments and eliminated duplication between private- and public-sector social workers, I regretted the ensuing conflict with the union but thought it was unavoidable because we had to bring caseloads down. Similarly, when we confronted the judges over their choice to offer loaned staff an opportunity to return to the court earlier than we had agreed, I thought it was better than losing critical staff and seeing caseloads rise and morale plummet.

Every conflict entails some risk. A leader may lose an important substantive battle, damage a relationship that is key to future success, or be misunderstood in the heat of battle. In the most damaging cases, conflict snowballs and puts the whole strategy at risk. So successful leaders pick their battles carefully, looking for ways to resolve as many differences as possible through negotiation. In both the District and Alabama, we sought constructive ways to resolve the collision between reforms to enable children to live in family settings and the vision, professional pride, and financial interests of the group and residential care providers on whom the public agency depends. Paul Vincent reports that in Alabama, encouraging providers to diversify and apply their strong convictions about what's good for children to home-based rather than residential services resolved the conflict for some, leaving only "a smaller subset" opposing the reforms (Vincent 2006, 7).

A side benefit of conflict, though, is that it communicates a leader's strategy with particular vividness. Conflict grabs people's attention and underlines that a leader cares about something—lower caseloads, children's opportunity to live in a family, a strong and independent agency—enough to take risks for it. Thus, leaders communicate vision through the battles they pick even if those battles end in only partial successes.

Deeply troubled agencies, then, can begin their turnaround with a vision and strategy grounded in a diagnosis of what has gone wrong and what is worth saving. Effective leaders communicate the vision through both words and action, moving fast through a fog of uncertainty to learn by doing and to pick just a few, necessary battles. The next chapter further develops three issues touched on throughout this discussion: learning, information, and accountability.

6

Information, Learning, and Performance Management as Keys to the Turnaround

"Unless you have the numbers and are telling people regularly where you are and where you are going, you can't get it done."
—Linda Gibbs, former chief of staff, New York City Administration for Children's Services

"You get what you measure. [Once the Quality Services Review was created] people knew there would be accountability in each county. That can alter practice itself. It's a powerful reinforcer of everything else. . . . It closes the loop."
—Paul Vincent, former child welfare head in Alabama

"The most important event in child welfare is when a social worker meets with a family. You can manage that event by training, data, and then getting outcomes."
—Richard Anderson, former child welfare head in Utah

Before the reforms, none of the troubled child welfare agencies in the study sites knew how to use data for decisionmaking, tracking the simplest aspects of their caseloads, or setting and monitoring performance standards for counties or individuals. Ivor Groves, Alabama's court monitor, said staff and county offices "performed as they performed," because without data, "who knew?" how to judge them. In the District's years as a "data-free zone," there were always reasons even the most basic caseload data could not be accurately counted. Social workers spent substantial time entering information into a sophisticated automated system that had worked in other states, but stakeholders viewed what came out as useless. In Utah, the lawsuit was supposed to transform a laissez-faire system into one that could effectively track compliance on hundreds of indicators, but that didn't happen in the first years.

Yet, using information to guide action was central to all the reforms. Every reformer saw better information systems, both quantitative and qualitative, and better use of information as key ways to upgrade or revamp child welfare services. Gathering and analyzing information, setting measurable targets, tracking progress, giving individuals and units feedback on their performance, and reviewing individual cases in detail were all at the heart of reform.

Even with a growing emphasis on performance management in the public sector, including such specific innovations as Compstat in New York City's Police Department or CitiStat in Baltimore city government,[1] it seems remarkable that agencies this troubled learned how to measure and track performance and base decisions on the findings. How did reformers get started in environments that for years had resisted information? How did they succeed when so many others before them had failed?

Answering these questions fully requires two chapters. The first lays out the reformers' approaches to collecting and analyzing information, strengthening information systems, setting and measuring performance targets, and encouraging learning and curiosity within the agency. The second examines the expectations of key players outside the agency— elected officials, the federal courts, and the media—and how their approaches to holding the agency accountable supported or hindered information use.

Year 2 in the District: Championing the Value of Information

In the District, the first direct benefit that social workers saw from better information systems came when CFSA's computer experts collaborated with the Family Court so social workers could know when and where they had court hearings. Every night, the court downloaded up-to-the-minute information about scheduled hearings into CFSA's system, and every morning, social workers walked in the door to find updated reports on their computers showing court obligations and deadlines, including rooms and times. Simply knowing when a hearing was rescheduled or moved made social workers' jobs easier. In fact, social work staff invented a new agency award for responsiveness to honor the information systems office. The new automated interface with the Family Court also improved CFSA's credibility with the judges: now the agency could give them useful information they couldn't get from their own system, convincing them the agency was getting its act together.

Pitfalls Along the Way

Yet without careful attention to the context, even reliable measures can take an agency in the wrong direction, as we realized when the percentage of timely case plans dropped sharply in fall 2002. We suspected that social workers had met the probationary period targets with a one-time blitz of case plan completions, not by fitting plan updates into their regular work schedules. It was now six months after that blitz, so a large number of plans, due every six months or sooner, were suddenly out of date. Clearly, a blitz was not the way to meet our real underlying goals, because hurried plans would be unlikely to offer a thoughtful blueprint for children's futures. The setback also reawakened some staff's cynicism about all our measured accomplishments and their fear that all could turn out to be a fiction. We addressed both concerns by redoing the planning process and gradually catching up to, and then exceeding, the agency's prior levels of performance.

The Implementation Plan: Immediate Expectations, New Information Needs

As reform proceeded, we needed new information to meet the court's emerging expectations and fulfill our own plans. In May 2003, almost two years into the reform, we completed negotiations with the plaintiffs and court monitor on the next round of targets for the agency—specifically, an implementation plan, a four-year blueprint for progress. The first deadline would arrive in less than two months, when we were scheduled to meet public commitments to some 20 tough performance requirements.

To get there, the management team restructured its regular meetings to focus on results and met every week until we had met our first deadlines. Senior staff with accountability for a particular priority would start the discussion with a progress report summarizing the data, the lessons learned, and the problems awaiting fixes. I hoped this format would put responsible managers enough on the spot to push performance higher, but not so much it would revive the old agency habits of spreading blame and hiding bad news.

Using Data to Untangle New Problems

Our new performance expectations included boosting the percentage of licensed foster families. That meant collecting data from the units that licensed and trained foster parents, which had not been part of our information push before. This request led to a rerun of arguments from the early days of the reform about whether the data were accurate—in this case, data that showed many foster parents were unlicensed. And, just as I had concluded earlier that agency managers didn't seek accurate information partly because they were afraid of what the data would show, I realized that behind the social workers' mistrust lurked fear that a licensing review was just asking for trouble. If the home could not be licensed (perhaps because a foster parent had a criminal record), yet a child had lived there happily for a long time, where would that child go? But we could not address these fears because we had no information about why foster parents were not licensed, or whether their licensure problems were fixable (by, say, updating a foster parent's training or correcting a physical defect in the house).

So we set out to find the information. The obstacles were familiar, and we had learned a lot since the early months about how to overcome them. The senior team asked the information systems director to make the automated data good enough so we could start every meeting with a review of performance—whether corrections required collecting new data or using existing data that had been overlooked. To do this the information systems team interviewed three or four units with roles in the licensing process to find out what they did, what information they tracked, and how it showed up in the automated system. The interviews turned up surprises: for example, we discovered that the adoption unit kept separate licensing information for foster parents who planned to adopt, unbeknownst to the other units.

As soon as we had the newly compiled data in front of us, we made an important discovery. Much of our problem came from lapsed licenses, meaning that foster parents and the social workers responsible for overseeing their licensing could not keep up with the frequent deadlines for redoing paperwork and fingerprinting. So we added staff to relicensing, created automated reports on upcoming relicensing deadlines, and simplified our rules to make it easier to stay licensed. We still had plenty of work to do to meet our target, but at least we had come up with a partial solution that had none of the bad side effects staff had feared.

Measuring Performance at the Contracted Agencies

CFSA delivered some services through contracted nonprofit social services agencies. Many of these providers had distinguished reputations and had served as havens for talented social workers fleeing CFSA during its most troubled years. Although these agencies generally believed that they provided much higher quality social work than CFSA, when we expanded our performance data to include them, the results showed the opposite. These partners cried foul, citing technical problems that continually hampered their connections to CFSA's computer system and insisting that cleaning up the data would take time away from caring for children.

We couldn't ignore their serious concerns or the worrisome evidence of poor performance on basic child welfare indicators. When CFSA's information systems director commissioned a quick-turnaround study, it became clear once again that an all-or-nothing mindset wouldn't solve the problem. Part of the problem was purely technical: connection glitches and the providers' outdated hardware were exacerbated by spotty staff training in using the data system and scant access to hands-on help with problem-solving. At the same time, there did seem to be real performance problems at some contracted agencies.

We moved ahead on all fronts at once. The information systems team enlisted provider staff and leaders to develop joint plans for fixing the technology problems and assigned CFSA technical staff to work on site with the providers. We also directed CFSA staff monitoring the contracted agencies to stay focused on the core performance measures, and I met with provider agency executive directors to discuss the measures myself. The directors of large agencies with low scores generally appreciated the direct conversation, and some even reported that the automated information enabled them to diagnose and fix performance weaknesses that they had previously suspected.

As the reform moved into its second and then third year, use of the automated data system expanded greatly within CFSA. Managers and supervisors at all levels now used reports tailored to their needs, and the court monitor started assessing our performance using automated data, rather than manual samples. Staff attitudes toward data and measurement changed radically. One longtime social work manager was so impressed by the now-measurable performance improvements and by the information systems team's responsiveness to social workers' perspectives that he wanted to measure everything we were doing through the automated system.

Most of us, though, saw the need to use information besides the automated data to gauge progress toward the more subtle improvements that we were now aiming for—such as higher-quality plans that involved family input, and services that matched their needs. So in fall 2003, two years into the reform, we conducted our first quality services review, a variant of the assessment tool that Alabama had invented early in its reform. In our QSR, outside experts were paired with CFSA staff to examine a small number of cases through structured interviews with the social worker, the parent, the child, and others. In the review I participated in, I met TJ, whose courage I found very moving:

> TJ is a young woman of 14 who entered foster care at the age of 7 as a result of an uncle's sexual abuse of her and her siblings. (She testified against him, and he received a lengthy prison sentence.) Because there was not confidence that TJ's mother would protect the children, all three siblings were removed. The mother has since relinquished her parental rights, and the plan for TJ is adoption.
>
> TJ and her younger brother have lived with one foster parent for their whole time in care. During this time, the foster parent has approached the point of adopting them three times and each time withdrawn her commitment. The last time this happened was just the week before our case review. We talked to many people including the foster parent herself about the reasons for this ambivalence: fear about TJ's increasingly challenging behavior, the potential financial disadvantage of adoption, and mixed signals from one judge, who reportedly said to the foster parent that it doesn't matter whether she adopts so long as she continues to care for the children.
>
> As TJ becomes a teenager, the foster parent worries about TJ's safety from sexual activity and assault. Although TJ is in therapy, her recent experiences suggest the powerful impact of her past traumas. The foster parent describes TJ as very aggressive in meeting boys; last spring, TJ met a boy on the subway who talked her into skipping school and coming to his house. He called some of his friends and she was raped by the group of boys. The police have been unable to locate the house or boy as TJ cannot remember exactly where she was.[2]

This review renewed my belief in the importance of our work for families and children, and my admiration of CFSA's social workers and foster parents who persisted in such difficult work. Yet it also helped me see how doing many things right was not enough, when a few critical things were wrong. The agency had many pieces in place for TJ: her foster parent advocated passionately for her, her social worker saw her weekly, the judge and the guardian *ad litem* had been on her side for years. Yet her situation remained dangerous and unsettled. Her team did not have a shared plan for how to protect her from sexual violence; they did not interpret the violence as the consequence of her abuse, but as a problem of her own aggressiveness as she moved into her teens. They also did not have a plan for how she could grow up in a permanent home. As a result, the review made the abstract ideal of higher-quality practice much more real to me. When the expert reviewers criticized "real confusion within the system. . . .around adoption practice and time frames" that "may potentially harm [children's] security and well-being," I had just seen what this meant to TJ, who had hope of a permanent home raised and dashed three times.

Performance Management Matters, Even in Chaotic Turnarounds

The child welfare agencies in Alabama, Utah, and Washington, D.C., were deeply troubled, with a history of failure and no history of using information. In New York City (a reform experience that I also draw on in this chapter), local offices did not even have computers in 1996. That year, Mayor Rudy Giuliani created the Administration for Children's Services after a tragic child death and charged Nicholas Scoppetta, its first commissioner, with reforming the child welfare system. Scoppetta remembers that local offices he visited were keeping case files and records entirely by hand, on paper.

Yet, all the reform leaders report lessons consistent with broader research about the value of performance management. Collecting, tracking, and analyzing information about performance, keyed to the agency's goals, boosts performance in all the sites studied.

Measures Motivate Performance

A panel of experts on public-sector performance management convened by the Kennedy School of Government concludes that: "Performance measures motivate. Since people want to do their best, even in the absence of a direct link to rewards, the simple act of generating feedback in the form of performance measures can improve results" (Executive Session 2001, ii). Child welfare agencies' experience confirms this finding. In Alabama, the QSR created a feedback loop so counties could see how they were doing and were spurred to strive for performance keyed to the vision for practice reform. In the District, the dramatic improvement in the number of social worker visits to children that occurred once we started measuring, but before we brought down caseloads, is another example. In addition, involvement in qualitative reviews like the QSR helps recharge people's sense of how the work of the agency really helps children and families. As Ken Patterson reported, "when the auditors in the office of compliance . . . started to talk to families and workers, they became advocates for family-centered practice."

Measures Clarify Work Priorities and Responsibilities

In the words of the Kennedy School experts' report, "Setting performance goals and monitoring progress towards them communicates your priorities" (Executive Session 2001, ii). Similarly, assigning measures to specific managers, teams, supervisory units, or workers clarifies whose job it is to achieve the expected level of performance—one simple definition of accountability. That is one reason Baltimore's mayor created CitiStat, an approach to performance management based on regular data-focused meetings between the mayor and department heads. According to Robert Behn, "in the city's bureaucracy, no individual is responsible for any specific result (or non-result). The organization itself is supposed to be responsible. . . . If the leaders of an organization—any organization—want to establish responsibility for particular results, they need to find a way to establish personal responsibility" (Behn 2006, 2).

Clarifying job priorities and naming responsible parties were central to achieving results in the study sites. In the District, this was another reason that the measures drove change during the first year of reform, when the agency had to meet tough performance standards under probation before we were able to make other systemic improvements, such as hiring more social workers. In retrospect, the early measures imposed needed clarity, focus, and structure, a lesson we applied later when we used measurement to clarify the muddy organizational structure that impeded foster care licensing.

In Utah's and Alabama's statewide reforms, county-level information had to be collected to clarify priorities and responsibilities for county directors. In Alabama, when counties decided they were ready to demonstrate that their quality of service had reached the standard required by the court order, they asked for a QSR review and met to present data and offer stakeholders a chance to comment on county performance. Reforms moved Alabama from a place where counties had no standards to a place where expectations were crystal clear, so counties knew when they were ready to pass the exam.

Measures Promote Learning about Problems and Solutions

Shelley Metzenbaum finds that "measurement's greatest power comes from its ability to illuminate problems and promising solutions" (2007, 7). Both kinds of illumination are central to turning around child welfare agencies.

Because these agencies are so complex, systematic data collection is necessary to get a grip on what the problems are and begin to solve them. In the District, when we started regularly tracking cases and their assignment to social workers, we discovered managers who were not good at distributing caseloads, and agency practices that allowed some cases to be assigned twice (once to a public agency and once to a social worker in a contracted organization). When we tracked foster parent licensing, we learned that the problem was not just getting parents licensed, but also keeping them licensed. In fact, no simple diagnosis of a problem was ever exactly right in the District. Measuring performance over time and trying to assess the effects (or lack thereof) of various solutions was essential to understanding the agency's workings and the causes of failure.

Measurement suggests solutions by identifying the successful moments, teams, programs, or counties so the rest of the organization can learn from them. As Metzenbaum writes, "measurement can . . . point to promising interventions and confirm their effectiveness" (2007, 7). Atul Gawande gives an example from medicine in his book *Better,* where a focus on "positive deviance"—getting people to try things and highlighting the successes—finally cracked one of the toughest and most dangerous hospital problems, health care professionals transmitting infections from patient to patient:

> The team made sure to publicize the ideas and the small victories on the hospital web site and in newsletters. The team also carried out detailed surveillance—taking nasal cultures from every hospital patient upon admission and upon discharge. They posted the monthly results unit by unit. One year into the experiment—and after years without widespread progress—the entire hospital saw its [drug-resistant] wound infection rates drop to zero. (Gawande 2007, 26–27)

The power of positive deviance coupled with measurement is evident across the study sites. In Alabama, measurable success in the first wave of counties gave the new approach momentum and staying power. In the District, as we tracked the declining number of children in the three temporary shelters and learned that many were able to live with kin, we realized the value of working with kin who had wanted to take children in, but who had been ignored by the agency. We applied the lesson in other efforts to reduce the number of children in group settings. Once we had unit-by-unit measurements of such basics as case plan completion and visits to children, we asked stronger performers to share their strategies.

Improving External Credibility and Public Debate

Performance measurement can also contribute to an agency's external standing. Robert Behn notes that "one of the basic reasons that any organization measures its own performance is to promote its reputation for competence" (2001, 119). The Kennedy School's panel of experts argues that the benefits go beyond the organization itself, to strengthen democracy: "By setting clear goals and reporting concrete progress, agency leaders facilitate better informed deliberation among the public and its representatives" (Executive Session 2001, ii).

In the District, the first credibility gains were with the local courts and the federal court, but the District Council, the contracted provider agencies, and other partners all noticed the improved tracking and information flow. In Alabama, careful data collection and analysis helped sustain the reform, even when one governor and his commissioner opposed it and blamed the reform's failings for several tragic child deaths. The data helped overturn those accusations, according to some I interviewed: "When someone wants to show that you're harming kids and families and you have QA results that show you're not . . . it makes a huge difference."

Using Performance Measurement in a Child Welfare Turnaround

The why of performance management is much the same in the troubled child welfare sites as in the broader group of public organizations studied by researchers. But what about the how? To what extent do agency leaders use the same techniques to implement performance measurement as in other, less troubled settings? And, to what degree are the challenges and therefore, the solutions, unique?

Link Information Collection to Goals and Strategy

Equally evident in the broader research and in the child welfare turnaround sites is the most important technique of all: the tight link between performance measures and the agency's core goals. Forgetting this basic premise is the first error of Robert Behn's "Seven Big Errors of PerformanceStat":

> Public managers need to start with a clear purpose: "What results are we trying to produce?" "What would better performance look like?" "How might we know if we have made some improvements?" Only after the members of the leadership team have agreed to some common answers to these questions can they adapt the PerformanceStat strategy to help them achieve these—now very explicit—purposes. (Behn 2008, 3)

All the child welfare turnaround sites studied demonstrate the centrality of this link. Perhaps most dramatic is Utah, where the initial attempt to measure performance on hundreds of criteria failed, at least partly, because it wasn't tethered to any coherent philosophy or set of goals. Efforts to enforce the measures frightened workers rather than motivating them. So even with reduced caseloads, the measures did not budge. In Robin Arnold-Williams' words, "If the workers don't understand what the job is, all the money in the world won't buy you performance." After developing the Milestone Plan and the practice model to communicate goals and demonstrate how social workers' jobs furthered them, Ken Patterson created a new measurement strategy that aligned better to the new goals. He adapted Alabama's QSR strategy to Utah's needs, introducing intensive qualitative review to more directly measure what the Milestone Plan and practice model committed the agency to do.

In the District, we linked our measures to core goals in two ways: they were directly required by the federal court and they were central to our seven priority goals. Since few social workers and judges believed that their work could be quantified, overcoming their resistance required early measures with obvious links to goals and values widely shared in the agency. Increasing visits to children, reducing the backlog of uninvestigated abuse and neglect reports, reducing the number of young children in congregate care, and increasing the number of finalized adoptions all fit that bill and effectively motivated performance.

In Alabama, the team invented the QSR precisely because they had no measurement tool aligned with the settlement goals, which were expressed in hard-to-quantify principles about high-quality practice and desirable outcomes for children and families. Building on work from developmental disabilities and other fields, Vincent, Groves, and others designed a measurement tool that provided a rigorous qualitative assessment keyed to these principles.

Use Information—Personally, Actively, Publicly

In the intense environment of an agency amid reform, it may seem odd that an agency head or senior staff should be poring over numbers to see whether they add up. But all the reformers interviewed reported spending time personally improving data systems or reports, and reviewing, analyzing, collecting, and talking about data. Paul Vincent and Ken Patterson devoted considerable personal time to the design of the original QSR in Alabama and its adaptation in Utah. Linda Gibbs, Commissioner Scoppetta's first chief of staff in New York City, remembers early discussions with outside data experts about how to interpret data. John Mattingly, the current commissioner of children's services in New York City, conducts ChildStat meetings every Thursday morning with managers from two zones of the city, going over data and reviewing a randomly selected case in depth. In the District, I spent a great deal of time on information: planning with the CIO and the program team how to measure what we needed, reading multiple drafts of our regular data reports, writing constant notes to senior staff about what did or did not make sense in the reports, suggesting next steps that might make the data better or more useful, participating in a QSR review, and talking in meetings and one on one with senior staff about emerging performance patterns and ways to improve them.

When I first tried to understand why all these leaders invested so much personally in performance measurement, I wondered if it was about the particular background of the reformers. Were we all just data people by our previous experience? Or was it that the involvement of federal courts in Washington, D.C., Alabama, and Utah put performance measurement front and center in the settlement agreements? Or was it that the child welfare field had reached a watershed, when the quantity and quality of information both increased dramatically and opened up new possibilities?

While all these explanations may have some truth, it turns out that leaders' personal involvement in data review may be a more general lesson: it is a key ingredient in all the most celebrated performance management successes. For example, consider Robert Behn writing about the lessons of Baltimore's CitiStat:

> If a mayor is to convince the city's agency directors and managers to take the CitiStat process seriously, he or she has to attend—and actively participate—in many of the meetings. . . . Moreover, the mayor needs to know the data—or, at least some of the data. . . . Otherwise, everyone will quickly comprehend that the mayor doesn't really understand these targets, let alone care about them. (Behn 2007b, 10)

Atul Gawande's stories of major improvements in health care also frequently center on leaders obsessed with measurement, even in the most difficult possible settings. For example, innovations in battlefield medicine in Iraq arise from personal passion about collecting and understanding data:

> At the 31st CSH [Combat Support Hospital], three senior physicians took charge of collecting the data; they input more than seventy-five different pieces of information on every casualty—all so they could later analyze the patterns. . . . Doctors don't have time, I am tempted to say. But then I remember those surgeons in Baghdad in the dark hours at their PCs. Knowing their results was so important to them that they skipped sleep to gather the data. (Gawande 2007, 64)

Our site studies suggest that this lesson applies doubly in turnaround settings. Where there have never been data, or never a passion for using data to learn and improve, leaders need to overcome cynicism and model their approach to reform by visibly demonstrating their willingness to commit their own time to wrestling honestly with information.

Balance Challenge and Support

As we have seen, performance improves when measurement motivates, clarifies priorities and responsibilities, and prompts learning about the problem or its solutions. Conversely, do not expect improvement if measurement prompts fear and its train of dysfunctional behaviors: unkept promises, action-postponing debates about the numbers' accuracy, the hiding of key information, and the shifting of blame. But since this second set of behaviors is all too familiar in failing agencies, how can performance measurement avoid triggering them?

Researchers writing about performance measurement in other, more functional agencies propose the same broad approach as the reformers in the study sites: find the right balance of challenging staff and supporting them. Writing about how states and cities should implement CitiStat projects, Behn recommends fine-tuning the structure of meetings to create "a balance between identifying inadequate performance and motivating the desire to improve performance" and between "appearing too forgiving [and] coming off as too harsh" (2007a, 9 and 12). In the District, I planned the results-driven management team meetings to strike a balance that seemed right for our history. To short-circuit the technique of shifting blame in order to divert attention, I set a rule that no one could cite a problem in a colleague's area as an explanation for bad results without having mentioned it to him or her before the meeting.

Whatever the tone inside the meetings, actions outside are likely to send an even louder signal. Will staff be punished for not meeting targets, even if underlying problems that hinder them are not solved? Will there be no consequences for anyone? Or is there a middle ground? Leaders need to think carefully about how they blend or sequence accountability and support, and about whether, when, and how to use measurement in evaluating performance. This is especially true in troubled agencies that have not offered their social workers, supervisors, and managers any basic supports for high performance. In the turnaround sites, reformers didn't choose between helping staff and holding them accountable, but instead saw the two strategies as intertwined.

In Utah and the District, a punishment-only approach had been tried, and it did not work. The more Utah's administrators punished workers for failing to meet hundreds of standards after the settlement, the more demoralization led to more failures. Peter Senge in *The Fifth Discipline* identifies this problem as a common feature of complex systems: in some systems, the harder you push, the more resistance you get (Senge 1990). Senge says that pushing harder is foolhardy and recommends backing off, but our case studies suggest that creative leaders may find opportunities to do both. Through words and actions, leaders may be able to ease up on a specific measure, while pushing harder on the underlying goal—zigging or zagging in the short run to stay the long-run course.

Finding a both/and strategy that works is not easy, though. In a long-troubled agency, providing the supports that social workers and supervisors need can take far longer than reformers have, before they must demonstrate performance improvements. Leaders may worry that responding to demands for support downplays accountability, signaling that excuses for not performing are acceptable. Inside and outside observers can see a mixed approach as not tough enough or too tough, depending on their line of vision at a given moment. When we discussed performance with District contract providers while also helping them improve their technology, the providers thought we were making unfair demands. At the same time, some of our senior staff thought we were not tough enough, offering too much flexibility and undercutting high expectations for our own staff. Nonetheless, since both groups had some truth on their side, the approach that worked was to keep moving down both paths, gather information to better define the specific problems and support needed (as our CIO did by hiring a consultant to assess the agency's technology problems), and refuse to give up on either support or accountability.

It may seem especially hard to find a both/and approach to accountability in judging the performance of individuals—either they are accountable for performance or they aren't. But in fact, there are many ways of paying attention to measures but not making them the whole story. One possibility, recommended in certain circumstances by Metzenbaum (2007), is to hold subordinates accountable for managing strategically toward goals, but not for meeting the exact numerical targets. Another variation is to phase in accountability over time, as supports become available and as leaders learn what it will really take to achieve the targets. As Jonathan Walters puts it, "data on performance should not be used to beat people up—at least initially" (2007, 28). A third approach, which I used in the District, is to use different strategies at different levels of the agency. Given that the court and the public would judge us on accomplishments, not just effort, I thought that senior staff had to be accountable for delivering on the measurements, not just trying hard and strategically. My approach differed with the agency's intermediate and lower-ranking staff, where constraints were far greater and authority far less. For those employees, we needed to get such supports as technology, training, and reduced caseloads in place before tying individual performance assessments closely to specific measures.

Finally, a crucial, yet too-often ignored, accountability strategy for balancing challenge and support is positive recognition for high-quality performance. As Linda Gibbs argues about New York's turnaround, "The most important accountability is acknowledgment of accomplishment—not negative but positive accountability." In Alabama, the celebrations as counties reported meeting the court's standards exemplify the power of measurable success to transform the resistance to information into an embrace of accountability.

One key application of positive accountability is the opportunity for promotion. Promoting strong performers sends a strong message to the organization that measured performance matters to career prospects, without being punitive. Linking promotion to performance has a double impact on agency-wide performance, because in addition to sending signals, it places the most promising and entrepreneurial employees in positions with greater organizational scope and power.

Build Trust among Line Workers and Supervisors

To make performance measures usable in the District, we needed social workers and supervisors to value and trust the data, so they would care enough to enter it accurately. This step is not frequently noted in researchers' reports on the broader range of less troubled agencies, but it was crucial given the District's history. Unlike the military doctors staying up at night to enter every last fact, CFSA's exhausted and overstressed social workers and supervisors saw entering data about their cases as burdensome and, given their professional training, demeaning. They had little confidence in information from the computer system, did not believe these data could ever help them do their jobs better, and did not count on the information systems staff to support them. The CIO who pushed forward the reforms, reporting to his peers in other states, said that when he arrived, "a large portion of the caseworkers believed that using [the automated] system reduced their status to data entry clerks. As a result, much data was missing, making information from the system unreliable."[3]

Past demands that social workers enter data, and threats to punish those who did not, had all failed, but new strategies eventually produced results, and shifted perceptions about the role of the automated system from anxiety to comfort and even enthusiasm. These strategies included the daily court updates and long-requested revisions in how the system dealt with case plans. They also included the creation of a new change control committee, created and co-chaired by the program and information systems directors, which gave social workers a voice in setting priorities for possible computer system changes. Social workers soon saw results for children that were traceable to better measurement and tracking, such as reductions in the number of young children in group homes. And social workers' continued involvement in reconciling automated with manual data gave them the chance to watch information quality improve. Finally, the information systems team took pains to adapt reports to supervisors' and workers' needs. All these strategies provided the incentive for better data entry, more trust in the system, and, in turn, data quality.

Start with the Information You Have— and Invest in High-Quality Data

After providing an ambitious list of suggestions for what environmental agencies should measure, Shelley Metzenbaum concludes, "Of course, no agency can measure everything at once. Don't worry about it. Just get started and get better" (Metzenbaum 2007, 12). This general advice was put to a difficult test in the initially data-poor turnaround sites, but all heeded it in some way—usually, pushed by the court. In the District, the automated system was initially so unreliable that the court monitor based her assessments on time-consuming manual reviews of case files. But we needed frequent, timely reports to manage effectively, and since these could not be developed manually, we had to jump in and use automated reports before we fully trusted them. We did the best we could, reconciling them with manual data until we could achieve consistency.

The second part of Metzenbaum's message, "get better," has even more relevance in the sites studied. The most striking message from the sites is that performance measurement in a child welfare agency requires investing serious time in developing solid quantitative and qualitative data. Although performance management gurus' advice to "start where you are" rings true, all the site reformers had to move quickly beyond that starting point, substantially improving their performance data.

Leaders in all three sites spent long hours developing and instituting rigorous qualitative measurement systems to supplement the quantitative data their administrative systems were producing. This strategy makes sense, given that reform plans at all three study sites required not only more frequent and timely social worker actions, but also high-quality ones.

In the District, Utah, and New York City, major improvements in the quantitative systems were also crucial. In New York City, John Mattingly, who observed the initial reforms as an outside expert, counts better data among the key achievements of the early reform period: "For the first time, the city had a system with electronic monitoring, knew where every case was, knew what was done or not done at 7 days or 30 days or 60 days." In Utah, the agreement to end the litigation specifically notes that "developing and maintaining a well-functioning information system" was fundamental to the reform's success.[4] As noted earlier, the District had made its major financial investment in an automated system during the receivership years, but when the reforms began, the data from it were still largely unused and unusable. Improving the data required an enormous investment of time. Luckily, we did not have to request budget resources because the money to pay for the technical programming work was already set aside in CFSA's base budget.[5]

This major emphasis on large, labor-intensive, and therefore inherently expensive improvements in information collection differs from the picture researchers paint of other agencies, where great performance benefit can be gleaned from existing information systems. But reading between the lines of other accounts suggests that considerable technological improvement may be necessary in other performance management success stories as well. For example, one summary of the Compstat breakthrough in the New York Police Department points to a critical investment in personal computers in the precincts, which made it easier to gather and analyze timely data (Smith 2001, 463). Researchers studying Baltimore's CitiStat also mention the development of 311 phone systems, which make more consistent data collection possible by directing all requests for city service to one phone number (Behn 2007b; Walters 2007).

Manage the Trade-offs and Unintended Consequences

The Kennedy School's expert panel emphasizes that managers should "listen carefully, learn, and adjust" to arguments about why measures cannot work, and then go ahead anyway (Executive Session 2001, 14). While evidence from the studied sites also argues for charging ahead, it illustrates the importance of being aware of likely problems and designing an approach to forestall or manage them. Some of the most likely sticking points in measuring child welfare performance are these three:

- Measuring quantity or timeliness only (for example, timely investigations or number of case plans) may mean short-shrifting quality.
- If the number of measures is too small, or the group of measures poorly chosen, important goals may be left out. In the District, we could measure many features of children's cases when they were in foster care but could not measure families' progress when children were at home. This disparity risked diverting our attention from our goal of high-quality community services.
- Important subgroups like very young children, older youth, or African American children may still suffer, even though aggregate numbers are improving. Using the wrong measures may even worsen these groups' situation and outcomes, if, for example, a measure of improving adoption rates encourages working first with the children who have the best chance of adoption.

The sites studied used several strategies to manage these risks. First, nesting performance management in other leadership strategies, including the effective articulation of goals and the development of policies and program models to carry out the goals, contributes to higher performance and safeguards against distortion. In Utah, the practice model was created in part so social workers would understand how a visit or a case planning meeting contributed to the agency's goals, making workers more likely to achieve quality as well as quantity. Second, the development of new qualitative assessments in all the sites provided new ways to directly measure the quality of work and the outcomes for children. These new assessments countered, to some degree, the distorted incentives toward quantity. Third, leaders need to keep abreast of unintended consequences and fix any that emerge, as we did in the District when we discovered the sharp decrease in timely case plans. Finally, leaders can choose a portfolio of measures to balance the flaws of any single measure, and emphasize different measures at different points in the reform. Early in my tenure, I was not very worried about the quality of visits because the starting point was that most children never saw a social worker. Later, though, we needed to pay more attention to the content of these visits.

Involve Stakeholders and Aim for Transparency

In a system with as many outside stakeholders and partners as child welfare, all the reformers saw opening up the performance management process as a way to strengthen support and achieve shared goals. Alabama brought outside stakeholders into its data collection and analysis by inviting them to join the county quality assurance committees that reviewed cases and gave feedback. In court monitor Groves' words, this strategy "created a political base of support for reform and developed people who were knowledgeable. [It] opened up the black box [and] put in more sunshine." Utah's agreement to end its court order relied strongly on the agency's commitment to share a great deal of data with state and regional quality improvement committees consisting of outside stakeholders, and with a panel of state legislators.

Persevere

Putting all these strategies together in troubled agencies takes time and perseverance. Serious improvement requires that major building blocks for the information system be put in place, and that social workers, managers, and information technology staff build the skills to collect and analyze data and to improve performance. Honing these skills takes repetition, coaching, and a message that stays consistent over time. Along the way, unintended consequences need to be identified and fixed, and data quality needs to get better in more parts of the system, so performance improvements can move forward. For each phase, new data may need to be collected or automated, old data improved, and manual data most likely must be repeatedly reconciled to the new automated system. Data improvement, in the words of the architect of CFSA's information systems reform, is "a long-term project that requires continuous effort."[6] Finally, beyond all these practical reasons, persistent commitment to performance measurement builds trust, sending a message, both outside and inside the agency, that expectations will be held steady for a time and that leaders do not intend to repeat past patterns of plans unfulfilled and ideas abandoned because of changing priorities from above.

Conclusion

To turn troubled child welfare agencies with no curiosity about information and no expectations for performance into agencies highly focused on measuring, learning, and improving, reformers used many performance management strategies common to effective public and private organizations. To succeed in these floundering organizations, however, leaders and reformers also had to do more, persevere longer, and intervene on more fronts at once. Specifics may differ by setting, but the reformers typically had to address organizational culture and goal clarity while improving the technical capacity of the information system; build trust and data quality concurrently; and improve social workers' understanding of their jobs, with and through a better understanding of the data. The sheer number of approaches and practices that break with the past is the key lesson here.

Beyond these site-tested conclusions, though, there is more to the story. The shadow of legislators, the press, and the courts has been looming over the discussion: the explanation for past failures and for present turnarounds has a great deal to do with the political context. The next chapter turns to the external context for accountability.

7

Accountability and the Politics of Performance Improvement

"Political neglect, budget neglect, indifference."
—Andy Hornsby, on his first impression of the department

"We felt we were doing work the way we had always done it. We were the welfare agency, always beleaguered, not enough resources . . . doing the best we can. In this state, the legislature won't give you what you need or funding till the federal lawsuits happen."
—Long-term Alabama child welfare official, explaining why the pre-reform failure had persisted for so long

"The history in New York was that there would be a tragedy, the mayor would fire the commissioner, nothing changes—of course nothing changes."
—Nick Scoppetta, on the reasons for many years of child welfare failure

To improve performance, staff and leaders in an agency have to believe that they can, and should, take action. But before reform, the prevalent view among staff at the three sites was that all action was futile, or even punishable, and that the best they could do was lie low, avoid responsibility, and live with the way things are. Even if staff were partly at fault for this beleaguered and defensive state of mind, all the leaders believe that the pre-reform political environment deserves much of the blame. None of the leaders believe they could have engineered the changes that they did without corresponding and supportive changes in the external political environment.

Perhaps surprisingly, the studied sites suggest two different external environments that engender passivity and discourage responsibility and constructive action. In one environment, there is no outside interest in the agency, as we saw in Alabama and Utah before the lawsuit. In the other, firings are frequent, top officials turn over regularly, and social workers, supervisors, and middle managers fear having their names attached to a decision that could show up in the newspaper, as in pre-reform New York City, the District, and Utah immediately after the law-suit. Interestingly, the consequences of these two failed accountability environments look similar.

This chapter examines these external environments, especially the actions and outlook of the oversight institutions that can tell the child welfare agency what to do, visibly blame or praise its actions, or provide or withhold crucial resources. Child welfare agencies cannot reform in a vacuum. Instead, they desperately need support, both political and prac-tical. So this chapter asks two questions: What changed in the outside world to make the reformers' jobs possible? And, what did the reformers do to shape that change?

Year 2 in the District: Political Attention to an Evolving Reform

In May 2003, the plaintiffs, the District, and the federal court announced the completion of the implementation plan (IP), our joint map of the road to reform. The IP organized our work inside the agency and offered us a chance to advance the agenda externally by briefing our diverse part-ners and overseers on specific provisions, the District's broader vision, and our partners' roles in achieving both. The announcement, as reported in the *Washington Post,* offered a sense of hope and progress:

> "This is a landmark agreement because it represents a joint commitment," said Judith Meltzer, court-appointed monitor. . . . "The plan is endorsed by the plain-tiffs, the city and the court. There has been a lot of acrimony in the past 10 years, and this sets out a program everybody has bought into."[1]

Having a completed IP also helped the court monitor, the plaintiffs' attorneys, the mayor's office, and me explain to the District Council just how the path to reform meshed with the agency's budget needs. The Council was frustrated that the increase in CFSA's budget was not just a one- or two-year investment. Council members knew that plenty of problems remained, but they wanted to move on, to cross CFSA off the budget to-do list. The IP made explicit the remaining steps to success and showed, through innumerable examples, that reform was far from over. For example, even if CFSA staff visited half the children every month, a tenfold increase from before reform, we were still far from the eventual biweekly visitation requirement.

The Congressional Reaction to Reform

The good news announcement was especially welcome because just a month earlier, the U.S. Senate Appropriations Subcommittee on the District of Columbia had held an unexpectedly hostile hearing on the progress of child welfare reform. The tone of the hearing surprised me since I was proud of the agency's progress on the federal court's performance standards. But Congress had directed the General Accounting Office (GAO) to measure performance independent of the court's standards. As the *Washington Post* reported:

> Congressional lawmakers expressed growing frustration and impatience with the District's child protection agency and called the findings of a recent review of its performance disturbing.
>
> Though the review by the General Accounting Office noted some progress, the investigative arm of Congress concluded that nearly two years after the Child and Family Services Agency returned to city control, it continues to be plagued by a series of problems, including a failure by social workers to frequently visit children or help them visit their parents while they are in foster care.
>
> "The question is, what has changed in these past two years?" said Sen. Mike DeWine (R-Ohio), chairman of the Senate Appropriations subcommittee on the District. "The preliminary GAO findings would suggest that very little has, in fact, changed."
>
> . . . . The chief of the agency asserted that changes have been made and that more are coming. . . . She pointed to accomplishments that include a reduction in the backlog of abuse and neglect investigations and an increase in finalized adoptions. But she told the Senators that turning around a big urban foster care system takes five to 10 years, citing similar efforts in New York, New Orleans, and Cleveland.
>
> DeWine and Landrieu noted that for a child, even a few months is too long to wait.[2]

GAO, charged with finding a different focal point from the court's assessment, had studied how our automated information system dealt with data from old case files, files that went back to before responsibility for abuse and neglect cases was unified under CFSA in 2001. It found (in the *Washington Post*'s words) that "critical information was missing from the agency's computer system in 70 percent of active foster cases because records had not been transferred from paper files to the new system." In a Catch-22, GAO criticized the new system because the old one had not included important information—a major reason for developing a new system in the first place. Thinking back to the hearing, I may have been so frustrated by criticism that I saw as uninformed and so worried that the senators would urge us to abandon our successful information systems improvements that I may not have responded respectfully enough to their concerns.

Surprisingly, after the hearing the subcommittee committed to a major appropriation to advance child welfare reform in the District and defined the appropriation's purposes to fit the IP and our reform plan. That meant the alternative ideas floated in the hearing were out, such as earmarking resources for a GAO proposal to manually enter data from old files into our information system. In came funding for moving to a web-based system, our information systems priority.

I still do not understand what happened. Perhaps the hostile hearing was designed to support extra Senate appropriations by documenting problems serious enough to justify them. Possibly, the hearing intended to create a record without being as harsh as it became, and my responses raised the senators' hackles. Possibly, the initial instructions to GAO to assess performance in a new way reflected the Senate's worry that the federal court, not Congress, was getting credit for improvement. Whatever the reasons, the results of the hearing were ultimately good.

Budgets, Revenues, and Federal Audits

My first year, however difficult in other ways, had been a fiscal honeymoon. Everyone in the District, including the office of the chief financial officer and the District Council, felt proud that their commitment to the agency had brought it back from receivership. By fall 2002, though, new revenue projections suggested that the District budget for the upcoming year needed to be cut below the budget adopted by the Council. In the resulting "gap-filling" exercise, I found myself constantly needing help and intervention from the mayor's office to fix cuts that would have torpedoed our plans. Each time, the mayor, the special counsel for receivership, and the city administrator came through. But I was always on edge, fearing either that a cut would slip in unnoticed if I wasn't in the room for the budget deal or that I would exhaust everyone's patience with the constant alarms. With the demanding expectations from the court settlement, either problem could have derailed us.

At the same time, the revenue side of the budget caused problems. Child welfare agencies rely on the federal government to reimburse a portion of the money appropriated in the state budget. Getting that money reimbursed requires carefully tracking eligibility for the federal programs. Unfortunately, the federal government's review of CFSA's Medicaid reimbursement claims concluded that some money would have to be paid back because of inadequate records. We came up with a partial fix when our information technology team figured out how to gather the needed information from the automated system, so social workers would not have to add more documentation to the files. While this saved future claims, our fiscal staff had to reduce substantially the amount the federal government owed us from past Medicaid claims. That meant a shortfall in federal revenues that we had promised the District.

This bad news came amid a blizzard of federal revenue issues in several District agencies that claimed reimbursement through Medicaid. Hindering solutions was a high level of mistrust and disagreement among the agencies involved, pitting those that relied on federal Medicaid revenues against those responsible for monitoring and predicting the federal claims. While the issues involved were very technical, participants always feared the discussions would end up in the press—with the agencies reliant on Medicaid described as either leaving federal money on the table or cheating the federal government. To everyone's relief, the city administrator, who was trusted by all parties, took on the federal revenue issue personally, convening the agencies biweekly to sort out the problems.

Social Worker Hiring and Personnel Oversight

The IP's tight deadlines for reducing social worker caseloads and increasing hiring were within sight by the May 2003 announcement. March had been a breakthrough month, with caseloads finally coming down to 24 per worker on average, and no social worker with over 50 cases. Just six months earlier, 18 social workers had caseloads that high.

But I worried about whether we would be able to maintain the success and meet the IP target of 300 social workers by September 30, 2003. To do so, we would have to solve a problem that had haunted us in 2002: ensuring that the new graduates hired in the spring and summer promptly passed the District's licensing test. We had permission under the District's personnel rules to hire unlicensed graduates with master's degrees in social work in trainee positions, but they had to receive their licenses within 90 days or face losing their jobs. Unfortunately, many trainees hired in 2002 had failed the test that fall, leaving us with fewer case-carrying workers than expected.

Some staff thought we should cut our losses politically and stop hiring unlicensed trainees, fearing that terminating them in 90 days if they failed their licensing exam would make us vulnerable to Council criticism. But I thought this would be a mistake. We had the legal authority and a strong reason for using it. We did not want to lose hiring momentum by turning

down recent graduates who could be excellent social workers. Top graduates with many job offers could consider the District too much trouble if we
required licensing up front, since few other jurisdictions required it at all.

In the end, we designed a more focused strategy for the spring 2003
recruiting. We encouraged but did not require candidates to take the
licensing test before applying, gave a salary bonus to social workers
already licensed on hiring, and made sure unlicensed trainees understood
how hard they needed to study for the test. The new strategy worked, and
caseloads dropped within months to court-required levels, for the first
time. At the end of September 2003, we had 309 social workers and an
average caseload of 20.

Accountability: What Promotes Success and What Guarantees Failure?

It is easy to see how an atmosphere of indifference could lead to persistent failure. With no interest, support, guidance, or monitoring from
elected officials, staff lack the motivation, the resources, and the capacity to transform weak systems.

It may be a little harder to see why harsh environments lock in agency
failure—as they did in New York City and the District before the reforms
and in Utah right after reform. After all, many would argue that visibility and more public outcry are the only ways to produce change. But
in fact, criticism, blame, and rapid turnover of leaders lead to the same
paralysis, stalemate, and failure as indifference. The blame may be greater,
but the change in performance is just as small.

As Robert Behn concludes, accountability in the public sector is generally one-sided. When it is particularly aggressive, it can push those held
accountable to be too cautious.

> The people being held accountable know. . . . what being held accountable means
> to them—to them personally. They recognize that, if someone is holding them
> accountable, two things can happen: When they do something good, nothing hap-
> pens. But when they screw up, all hell can break loose. . . . Accountability means
> punishment. (Behn 2001, 3)

We have seen innumerable examples of this dynamic in the sites
studied. In Utah, the aggressive accountability right after the lawsuit led
clinical experts to stay out of sight. In New York, Commissioner Scoppetta
pointed out that when a "gotcha" world leads to excessive turnover, no

one delivers reform. In the District, the pre-reform practice was to avoid acting or at least to avoid responsibility for acting, usually by blaming others.

Most likely, the link between harsh accountability and passivity that stymies reform is even closer in child welfare settings than in other public organizations. What can go wrong is not just a bad audit or a budget deficit but potentially a child's death. Such a tragedy can be personally and professionally devastating for anyone involved in the case, so the incentive to be cautious and to spread blame is even greater. In addition, the harsh environment stymies collaboration among partners, each of whom thinks deflecting blame to others is necessary for self-preservation. Yet change in the child welfare system depends so much on collaboration among numerous internal and external stakeholders that undercutting collaboration makes positive change impossible. Thus, harsh and random accountability in child welfare freezes a failing system in place.

The Role of the Federal Court

What, then, does it take to change these distorted political environments, whether indifferent or harsh? In all three sites, the federal court was instrumental. Because of the limits of case study research, this does not prove that the court is necessary to success in child welfare, but it certainly suggests questions about how and why the court succeeded in reversing three histories of failure.

How the Federal Court Made a Difference

To answer these questions about the court's success, I compared the periods in each case study when reform moved forward with the periods when it did not. I examined the participants' perspectives on how the court contributed to change and tested the conclusions against the insights of the New York City interviewees, whose reform experience was not driven by the court. Even though most states have or have recently had court involvement in child welfare reforms,[3] my goal was to identify techniques with reach beyond the courts. In particular, I looked for lessons that elected officials could adopt to turn around failed settings without court involvement.

Comparing the periods of effective court-driven transformation with the periods of dysfunction, I found five such lessons. First, the courts created moments of opportunity: deadlines that focused the attention of all parties and, using both carrots and sticks, shocked them out of their old, failed methods of interacting. In Utah and the District, it took more than one try to achieve such a moment. Second, the parties to the court litigation bought into a vision of reform that was largely shared by the agency, the plaintiffs, and the court. Again, in some settings, second and third tries were needed. Third, the court had a relatively long-run time frame, consistent with the reform's multiyear timetable, even though it demanded some early results to show progress. Fourth, the court operated in good faith as an accountability holder: the standards it used in judging performance were clear, and it had the capacity to regularly examine detailed measures of performance and recognize successes achieved. Finally, the court had the power to influence or coerce other important stakeholders in the agency's environment, so the agency was not completely at the mercy of forces pulling it in opposing directions.[4]

Moment of Opportunity. It is hard to change historically unproductive relationships between outside stakeholders and agency staff—and it is especially hard for one party to change if the others do not. The three site examples suggest that a tragedy or crisis alone is not enough to galvanize change, but that a crisis combined with new structures, agreements, and expectations can be.

In the District, the moment of opportunity offered by the consent order that laid out the agency's return to District control brought previously warring stakeholders together. The consent order created the structure, consolidating authority at CFSA, reducing fragmentation, and setting clear performance targets. The agency's return from receivership created excitement and a sense of a fresh start. Why hadn't the settlement almost a decade earlier provided this critical moment? A partial answer is that it did not create the structure to support change: observers cited the continued fragmentation of authority, which sabotaged every director's and receiver's efforts.

In Alabama, the settlement agreement created the moment. It built on the fundamental change in outlook state officials had experienced when the legal discovery process revealed the damage created by past failures. Litigation undercut the agency's complacency and set the stage for the accountable, responsible stance that Vincent sought as staff acknowledged the damage done to children. Externally, the litigation and settlement grabbed the attention of state officials who, as James Tucker points out, had missed several earlier opportunities for movement:

> [Before the litigation,] the governor said he was concerned, the juvenile judges pushed their concern, there was a decent report with recommendations—and it comes back and nothing happens. The governor doesn't act, the legislature doesn't act. Only after that is the lawsuit filed. It's a 50-year pattern of public policy in Alabama.

Vision Aligned with the Agency. Where the agency and the external authorities, or various powerful external authorities, cannot agree on the right framework for accountability, paralysis is the result, at least temporarily. In Utah, even with all the court's power, social workers could not figure out the vision behind the hundreds of requirements in the settlement agreement before the Milestone Plan clarified it. Commissioner Nachman's tenure in Alabama also yielded no progress because she and the governor had a vision diametrically opposed to the court's. For court-mandated reforms to succeed, the agency's internal and external game plans have to be approximately aligned.

During periods of success at all three sites, the agency and executive branch leaders helped develop the agreements' substance. In the District, the mayor's office took a central role in developing the framework for the probationary period, since the agency leadership team had not yet been recruited. The next stage of negotiations, over the implementation plan, involved both the agency and the mayor's office. In Utah, agency officials considered the negotiation of the original settlement as chiefly the work of the lawyers; by contrast, they had the lead in developing the Milestone Plan, which they could then energize staff to implement.

During their successful periods, the agencies also worked closely with the chief elected official. Cabinet secretaries who were close to the governors in Alabama and Utah were strongly involved. In the District, the special counsel was a highly effective liaison between the agency and the mayor.

Some Alabama reformers think the articulation of broad principles in the Alabama agreement (rather than specific quantifiable requirements) was essential to aligning the visions. In the District, though, a more prescriptive court settlement was an effective foundation for moving forward. Other documents such as the IP helped all parties see how the requirements tied to a shared vision.

Finally, as we have seen, leaders in all three sites took ownership of the court's plan as their own vision, once they had sufficient input. Instead of describing the settlement or consent decree as instructions imposed from outside, they emphasized a shared vision for performance improvement, using shared, mutually trusted measures and guideposts.

Long-Term Time Frame. Despite the U.S. Senate's and the District Council's frustration that reform would not be completed in a year or two, the evidence from all the sites and other public and private organizations is that turning around a large agency with a history of failure takes years. As Commissioner Scoppetta points out, "time to develop and implement reform" is crucial for turnarounds because most failing agencies have multiple failing systems. In New York, computer systems and civil service had to be fixed before the organization could improve performance. Short-run improvements are crucial as well, since reforms will sputter and die without a great sense of urgency to meet deadlines in the first months and years. But performance improvement won't get from 0 to 50, let alone to 100, without multiple building blocks in place.

Given that reality, the court's sense of time can be much more conducive to reform than that of elected officials, especially legislators. As Ivor Groves points out, "Lawsuits provide continuity." He explains:

> In Alabama, there have been six or seven commissioners, three directors of child welfare, four governors. Through all that, there has been one set of expectations. I have been monitor the whole time, the arbiter of expectations. [This is important because] changes don't happen as fast as people think.

In New York, according to Scoppetta, Mayor Giuliani's long service as mayor led to the same effect: Scoppetta's predecessors had averaged two years to his six.

Good Faith Measurement of Progress. The court's value in reform is also in keeping the vision steady. That way, performance expectations and accountability are not set to moving targets. In sharp contrast, elected officials may feel the need to move targets for many reasons. Maybe the membership or leadership of relevant committees has changed, maybe the agency's performance has become part of a larger debate such as a budget crunch or an opportunity to add resources. Maybe officials are hearing from a changing group of constituents, or perhaps a scandal or tragedy has riveted attention on just one aspect of performance.

Holding at least one set of expectations steady makes a focus on performance and accountability possible for large service systems that have to experiment, measure success or failure, and then learn and improve over time.

An external stakeholder is also more likely to encourage honest performance measurement and genuine efforts at improvement when it has the capacity to assess performance accurately, or at least to recognize accurate rather than inaccurate assessment. In litigation that includes a court monitor who works with the judge and the parties, the court is unusually well-staffed and well-equipped for this role; elected executive branch officials may also be well-staffed, but elected legislative branch officials typically are not. A common feature of the three sites was a highly regarded, trusted court monitor whose track record and child welfare expertise made contributions to solving tough problems possible.

Perhaps most important for breaking the cycle of blame and failure is the courts' recognition of interim successes, not just failures. In failing agencies, the belief that accountability means blame for failure and no reward for success is burned into staff's memory. The courts in these sites broke with that paradigm by recognizing the District's success in meeting first the probationary period standards and later the IP expectations, by celebrating the achievement of the settlement practice standards by Alabama counties, and by helping to design a new assessment to capture Utah's child-welfare agency successes more accurately.

As part of this good faith accountability, the courts also assessed performance differently than the usual accountability holders. The courts looked in at regular intervals or when the agencies said they were ready (as in Alabama's counties) rather than calling for overnight change following a crisis. While the courts in the three jurisdictions were not immune to crisis-driven demands for investigation or information, they were better able to place crises in the context of the agency's full performance, drawn from a longer history of more complete assessments.

Enough Power to Influence External Partners. No matter how good the measures and the process, accountability suffers when multiple powerful overseers pull in different directions, especially if the failing child welfare agency is too weak to tug them back into line. Thus, a good accountability holder needs enough power to coerce or cajole others into supporting a single reform plan.

This power was critical in the District, with its fragmented authority held by the District Council, Congress, multiple agencies, and a historically strong local court, along with the frequent movement of client families across a three-state metropolitan area. The federal court began consolidating authority when it required that the mayor and the Council pass legislation creating a stronger, more unified agency. This restructuring addressed fragmentation within District government, but that was just part of the problem. Beyond District government, the federal court had no formal control, but it often wielded influence, in part because other participants wanted to keep the agency in District hands. In addition, both the court monitor and the plaintiffs' attorneys communicated their expectations through testimony, statements to the press, or direct actions. When I had my painful hearing before the Senate, the court monitor was on the panel as well—no doubt a factor in the eventual positive outcome. And when Maryland issued its ultimatum on removing D.C. children from Maryland foster homes, plaintiffs filed for an injunction with the court, which directed the two jurisdictions to resume negotiations.

In New York, some I interviewed thought that court intervention was less crucial because Mayor Giuliani had the statutory and personal political wherewithal to impose a single standard of accountability on the various stakeholders without court action. As Commissioner Scoppetta put it, "In D.C., you didn't have the clout."

Without a strong political figure or a skillful court monitor, the agency risks failing everyone's expectations because they are inconsistent with each other. Imagine the outcome for CFSA's reform plan had the Senate insisted that we delay our information systems improvements while we entered data from thousands of manual case files, or had we respected the Council's desire to cross the agency off the budget to-do list, or had we removed a thousand children from Maryland foster homes. One explanation interviewees offered for the difficulties of the receivership (before the consent order that returned control to the District) was that the receiver did not have enough power over other D.C. government agencies or the local judges to force joint action.

Critics of the Court Role in Institutional Reform

How do these findings from the study sites relate to the broad debate on the role of federal courts in institutional reform? Sandler and Schoenbrod, in *Democracy by Decree,* argue that court involvement is undemocratic, especially when the judge relies on experts who put together a consent order, a key element of the reforms in these sites:

> The constitutional and statutory powers of elected officials are eroded in favor of a negotiating process between plaintiffs' attorneys, various court-appointed functionaries, and lower-echelon officials. This group, which we call the *controlling group,* works behind closed doors to draft and administer the complicated decrees. (Sandler and Schoenbrod 2003, 7)

The researchers also argue that the long-term perspective, which worked so well in the three sites, is part of what makes courts undemocratic: under democratic procedures, legislatures ought to be entitled to change predecessors' policies. They find the budget consequences of court involvement particularly undemocratic, because in their view agencies conspire with litigators to force resource appropriations.

But the child welfare sites suggest that in assessing whether the courts are more or less democratic than the alternatives, better or worse at enforcing the will of the people, it is important to consider the alternatives honestly, and to remember Winston Churchill's insight that very flawed systems (including democracy itself) can still be the best there is. In all three settings, the courts became involved only after the other accountability holders had failed over long periods. Elected officials had failed to abide by democratic laws, and the lack of transparency that Sandler and Schoenbrod blame on the courts had been endemic for years along with agency failure.

In the District, the interaction of Congress—in which the District has no vote—with a harsh media climate, the District Council, and, for many years, a weak mayor surely resulted in a less democratic process than having the federal courts enforce a law legitimately enacted by the city's elected council. In Alabama, the state legislature resisted Governor James's efforts to undercut the settlement. Several years into the process, they apparently believed the settlement agreement supported their goals as elected officials. And everywhere, openness seems to have increased considerably after litigation, with a flow of performance data measured against standards.

Besides arguing that court oversight is undemocratic, Sandler and Schoenbrod also claim that the decrees do not work: "States and cities cannot be run effectively through court decrees that are as thick as phone books" (2003, 9). Not only do the three sites' experiences invalidate this claim, but they also suggest that little else can work in certain deeply dysfunctional settings, except perhaps a mayor in a uniquely strong political situation.

Nonetheless, practicing managers would certainly agree that there are plenty of examples where badly implemented or excessive court involvement can undermine good management. Cumbersome procedures can empower lawyers over content experts, impose poorly thought-out requirements, favor short-term demands driven by plaintiffs' attorneys with no understanding of trade-offs over reform's long-term needs, and undercut successful sequencing of reform through over-broad expectations that overwhelm the agency. Leaders in New York and Utah gave examples of all these problems. The lesson from the study sites is not that the courts cannot make mistakes, as do other agency overseers, but that they have an unmatched capacity to make reform possible even in failing agencies. Nonetheless, as I indicate briefly below and more fully in chapter 10, the ideal path would be reform by way of an improved political climate, without the courts, because a great deal of damage to children occurs while a situation deteriorates to the point where the courts step in.

The Role of the Media

The path to child welfare reform is deeply affected by the intensity of media and public attention to children's deaths, which are likely to occur with some frequency even in higher-quality large systems. Chapter 4 examined this topic from the perspective of research on safety improvement. Here, the focus is on ways to keep reform on track under high-intensity media scrutiny. Is it possible to keep systems from being paralyzed by the fear of media attention? And how can reform leaders maximize the chance that media attention will drive good changes?

One important insight from the study sites is that the consequences of media attention to child welfare, both good and bad, do not derive only, or even primarily, from individual stories. Rather, patterns developed over time shape the behavior of various partners as they try to manage the mere possibility of media coverage. In a historically harsh environment, where every media story prompts a rush to blame by elected officials and potentially leads to firings or other personnel actions, stakeholders naturally try to avoid responsibility. Stakeholders may also use the media to advance their agendas, shift blame to others, and stop change that they see as counter to their interests—a frequent pattern in the District. In this setting, many events can trip a cycle of media coverage, followed by blame, legislative oversight, and then more media coverage of the oversight, in which key people leave, and reform strategies change with the winds. Robert Behn analyzes this dynamic in a way that rings true for many child welfare leaders:

> Any party . . . can reduce the amount of blame assigned to it by being the first to blame the others. . . . In today's accountability-holding business, the rewards go to those who speak with supreme confidence, to those who blame others, to those who point the finger of blame first. (Behn 2001, 144)

Coverage of individual tragedies can intensify the vicious cycle of blame, passivity, and leader turnover. Because the individual case receiving publicity can be so emotionally powerful, even if not representative, the coverage can prompt the wrong policy and program decisions. Media coverage focused on individual social workers can breed fear and an expectation of scapegoating, taking a stiff toll on morale and hindering recruitment. Social workers may become more concerned with covering their tracks than high-quality practice. As we have seen, child welfare practitioners also fear that a death from abuse in a biological family will lead to agency practices that are too quick to remove children from their homes. By bringing a flood of children into foster care, such a cycle damages not only the subgroup of children who are removed unnecessarily, but also those cases that are overlooked or short-changed by overwhelmed social workers.

On the positive side, coverage of a shocking individual case can galvanize public energy and resources, and potentially contribute to changes in the child welfare agency or the judiciary (including changes in leadership and in statute) that could contribute to reform. Shock and sadness also can strengthen the broader community's responses to troubled families and children, making citizens more willing to report abuse and neglect, to come forward as foster or adoptive parents, or to support stressed parents.

In this complicated context, what strategies and circumstances support the positive effects and minimize the negative ones?

Strong Agency Relationships with Other External Partners

The most important part of a child welfare agency's media strategy is not about the media. To prevent the damage that occurs when stakeholders use the press's bullhorn to sidestep negotiations, stop changes in the system, or shift blame, or when stories ricochet from the newspaper to hearings, with stakeholders scurrying to get out of the way, child welfare leadership must build strong relationships with outside partners and stakeholders.

In the District, the Superior Court judges and I agreed not to negotiate with each other through the press but to work together directly. We struck this deal because of our shared interests: our joint commitment to children, the court's need for me to be on its side with Congress, my need for judges to help implement the federal court's orders. Once we made the deal, we kept it, and very quickly saw the benefits. To change the relationship with Maryland so it did not involve an ultimatum delivered through the newspapers, we had to resist the ultimatum and demonstrate that the strategy would not work. Only then could we work together more effectively, under the eye of the federal court.

For other accountability holders (such as the District Council and Congress) and other stakeholders (such as providers and community organizations), the key was to talk to them directly whenever a story seemed likely. Meanwhile, our regular newsletter to partners became meatier and more credible as our information systems got better. As we built stronger relationships and a more reliable system of calls the night before a potentially divisive article was published, we felt more comfortable that they would talk to us directly, rather than indirectly airing their concerns through the press or formal oversight channels.

Modest Expectations

It is also helpful for child welfare leaders to have reasonable expectations of what kinds of media coverage are compatible with reform. For a leadership team working night and day on change, it can be tempting to imagine newspaper stories that validate that hard work and report on important success—like the editorials in the *Birmingham News* that provided strong, evidence-based support for the reforms, even in the face of tragedy. But such steady media support is rare. It is hard to distinguish success from failure in the early months. Naturally skeptical, reporters are also anxious about being co-opted. Clashes about confidentiality and release of information are likely. And in an agency that has failed for many years, each success will probably be offset by many failures. A more realistic goal is coverage that is not so terrible as to be destabilizing—coverage that doesn't destroy political support, partnerships, or staff desire to stay and work hard.

This more achievable goal is all an agency needs to have a chance at reform; however, it is emotionally unsatisfying and hard to accept. Early in my first year, I complained to a friend with communications expertise that I was spending far too much time and energy talking to the *Washington Post*, and the result was just moving coverage from terrible to moderately bad. He said that achieving "not terrible" press was central to continued reform and that "good press" would be lucky, but not essential.

Strong Internal Communications

Especially since staff will have to do without pats on the back from the media, they need to hear praise from the reform's leaders. This is no easy task. Internal staff need and deserve direct communication from the agency's leaders. At a minimum, they should not learn about the agency's plans from the newspaper. While this sounds easy to fix, it can be hard in a culture where everyone has always staked out their views by talking to the press, not to each other. Like many other self-reinforcing cycles in these distrustful cultures, tight internal control of information and outside leaks reinforce each other. The more managers and political leaders hold information close and trust no one, the more staff who feel powerless go outside with whatever scant information they have, reinforcing the distrust and the next cycle of misguided gossip. The only way for leaders to break the cycle is to share information liberally and regularly with staff, so there are fewer secrets and a broader understanding of the agency's status and plans.

More difficult is communicating when tragedies occur, since staff may want reassurance that they will be supported at a time when leaders do not know whether an individual social worker, supervisor, or manager acted appropriately. Perhaps the only useful advice is to keep in mind the multiple competing values: fairness, which requires not taking a formal position until information is available; non-defensiveness and openness to learning, which require seeking information to understand whether the agency, including top management, could have done things better; commitment to staff, which requires avoiding unnecessary secrecy and giving social workers emotional support; and compassion and a sense of duty to children and families, who are the reason for the agency's work. In weathering difficult situations, I know that I made many mistakes in internal communications, particularly in underestimating the impact of tragedies on social workers and members of the senior team. Once again, the response only has to be good enough to keep reform moving ahead, not perfect.

Internal communication about success is not straightforward either in these harsh environments. Media and external partners' cynicism inevitably affects staff reactions. When the *Washington Post* described our on-time unification of abuse and neglect services as organizational chaos, our efforts to celebrate success probably rang hollow to many staff. They understandably believed the newspaper more than a leadership team of just three months' tenure. Once again, persistence and modest expectations of the boost staff will feel from any single success are the only solutions.

External Validation and the Court

Even if expectations are modest, an agency's momentum and long-term success demand some external media validation, enough to keep staff and partners hopeful and involved. The court played a key role in making positive coverage possible, at least in the District. Every time we met major court requirements, the press covered it. Given how hard it is to tell, especially early on, whether there has been positive change, journalists needed outside experts, and the court monitor and the plaintiffs' attorneys were knowledgeable and credible.

Consequently, the court helped make media coverage more attuned to results over time and less random. Whatever happened in between milestones, we could expect coverage of our success or failure in accomplishing predictable and agreed-to targets at regular intervals. The court's first report, which found that we had met the probationary period criteria, was particularly important because it was early confirmation that the District had done what many had thought impossible: bringing the agency back from receivership and turning around its performance.

Do Administrative Oversight Agencies Inevitably Stop Reform?

"What creates great difficulty in the profession of the commander of armies is the necessity of feeding so many men and animals. If he allows himself to be guided by the commissaries he will never stir, and all his expeditions will fail."
—Napoleon, quoted in Tilman (2003, 437)

Unlike Napoleon, child welfare reformers do not face the necessity of developing supply lines to feed staff. They do, however, desperately need support from budget, personnel, contracting, and other administrative agencies.

They need help and authority from these agencies to recruit and retain (or terminate) social workers; change job titles, qualifications, bonuses, and incentives; create funding mechanisms that allow social workers to purchase what a family needs; shift budgeted resources to where they are most needed; end contracts, start new ones, and redefine performance for contractors; or refine information systems. Before the reforms, the administrative agencies frequently failed to meet these needs, whether because of rigidity, incompetence, alternative priorities, or all of the above.

As a result, administrative agencies in the pre-reform sites often reinforced the passivity of failing child welfare agencies, providing yet another reason for child welfare staff to give up on performance improvement. In Alabama, a long-time child welfare staffer remembered how he came back from graduate school "rejuvenated, excited, thinking [he] had discovered new things" only to be quickly defeated by the rigid contracting system, which did not allow for individualized services: "I wanted to expand service options, so families could be served at home . . . to shape services around the families, not what the mental health counselor was offering . . . But there was no mechanism and no funding."

Reformers stalled by rigid administrative systems can face a choice between giving in to them and bypassing them. Neither option is appealing. Giving in can stall crucial steps of the reform, while bypassing failed systems risks retribution from oversight and investigative agencies, whose job is to punish violations of personnel, contracting, or fiscal practices. In the District, given its history of blame, even special authority to bypass the regular system was not always enough to allay staff fears of retribution. As Marc Zegans summarizes American political accountability, "rule-obsessed organizations turn the timid into cowards and the bold into outlaws" (1997, 115).

News coverage of the earliest months of reform in Alabama illustrates this dilemma. Using consultants to improve practice was a lodestone of the reforms because the agency lacked the skills required to transform the counties' work. But Alabama's administrative oversight agency criticized Paul Vincent and Andy Hornsby, fearing that this strategy circumvented personnel rules:

> Lawyers and outside consultants have received more than half of the money spent so far to revamp Alabama's services for abused and neglected children. . . . Some officials already have sounded alarms about the escalation of such contracts in state government. . . ."It's all over the place," said state Finance Director Jim White, acknowledging he knows little about the overhaul at human resources.

"Why do we have state departments and personnel? I think that departments have to carry out their responsibilities . . . If they're not able to do that, then we need to get the personnel who are capable."[5]

In the end, criticisms like these did not derail the Alabama reformers; nor did the rules about social work trainees or battles about federal revenues derail our efforts in the District; nor did civil service obstacles derail reform in New York City. In all the settings, the reformers were able to win some battles, often by finding a way to hold the administrative agencies accountable for their role in reform. The most obvious route was organizational and statutory change to bring some troublesome administrative functions under the child welfare agency. In New York and the District, failed administrative agencies outside the child welfare director's control were identified as a priority problem. In both cases, reformers' strategy of elevating and strengthening the child welfare agency, increasing its authority, and holding it accountable extended to administrative functions. Through D.C.'s CFSA Establishment Act, all parties agreed to give CFSA its own contracting and personnel authority, previously handled by centralized oversight agencies.

Another widely used approach to holding administrative agencies accountable was a partnership between the agency and someone close to the chief elected official, who was responsible for ensuring that those administrative systems outside agency control delivered the essential supports for reform. In the District, I knew that I could count on colleagues in the mayor's office to convey that child welfare reform was the mayor's priority so all parties should work something out to protect budgets or avoid a public blow-up over revenue. In Alabama, several people interviewed credited the cabinet secretary, Andy Hornsby, with providing cover and support for reform. Because he was close to the governor and had the authority to move money within the cabinet agency, Hornsby was able to solve such administrative issues as inappropriate hiring caps. To avoid the caps, he told the governor that he would stay within his budget and "if I overspend, fire me."

Elected Officials

Strong relationships between agency heads and elected chief executives or those close to them also help leaders weather politically difficult times and give agency staff clarity about their duties and priorities. These relationships matter so much that in the one site example where they seriously broke down, the reform nearly ground to a halt. In Alabama, after the new governor, Fob James, appointed a commissioner who would oppose reform and challenged the settlement in court, agency staffers struggled to figure out how to behave ethically and effectively:

> It was a very difficult time. Paul [Vincent] had retired. It was very difficult because we were bound legally to implement the consent decree but felt we were not supposed to be doing that. Trying to stay the course and also be a public servant and government employee was hard. . . . [It] required a tremendous sense of balance.
> —Long-time Alabama child welfare official

In the end, the federal courts dismissed the governor's appeal, and the commissioner resigned amid votes of no confidence from the state legislature and county directors.

Legislators were less involved than elected chief executives. I didn't interview any legislators or their staffs for this book, but the site stories and my experience suggest the challenges they face if they want to contribute to sustained reform. Frequently, legislators have little staff support and little time to absorb information themselves. They feel pressure to check any one priority off the list so they can move on to a competing one. Steady behind-the-scenes support may get them no political reward; instead, they may have to demonstrate publicly that they are fending off a crisis. Or, they may need to take credit for their own reform plan, rather than buying into a broader one already in place.

In Utah, however, the legislature seems to have been more involved than in the other two sites. It created a standing committee on child welfare (the Child Welfare Legislative Oversight Panel) so members could get in-depth knowledge. The exit agreement from the federal court settlement specifically included the panel's role and required the child welfare agency to keep the panel fully informed of performance and caseload data.[6] This model helped the legislature overcome staffing and information challenges, and its success in Utah suggests that agency reformers might consider engaging legislators on reform.

State and Local Judges

Far more than other public human services agencies, child welfare agencies interact with and are overseen by state and local judges. These judges hear individual children's cases and make crucial decisions, like when and whether a child can go home or whether to terminate parental rights. In addition, because of their close-up view of all parts of the child welfare system, judges may be early and forceful advocates of reform legislation and more resources.

Judges' stature in the community and day-to-day experience of the child welfare agency can work either for or against reform. Where a long, painful history has led them to view the agency as incompetent and untrustworthy, that view will carry weight with the media and elected officials. Ivor Groves interviewed Alabama judges before reform, to get their perspective on child welfare, and was told: "Those people don't return phone calls, don't keep kids safe, we don't work together." One big success of reform, Groves said, was getting judges and child welfare staff to work together. Even if judges are supportive of the agency, if they do not buy into the specifics of the reform, it is less likely to happen, as when District judges' initial skepticism about adoption held them back from encouraging foster parents to adopt.

As with other powerful partners, judges need to be on the same wavelength as the agency for reform to succeed over the long haul; otherwise an agency struggling to emerge from failure will be pulled in too many different directions. Even if a painful history sometimes works against such partnerships, a shared commitment to the day-to-day work with children can be a powerful connection, and so can the power of achieving success together. In the District, once the two institutions took practical steps together, such early successes as increased adoption rates and more reliable court scheduling reinforced the bond and cemented the cooperative relationships.

The Budget Process and Its Results

Before the reforms, two features of the budget process stood out in these sites: low resources and an opaque process, never informed by discussion about what level of activity or performance the resources were meant to support. The two features are likely related, because the public might not have accepted such low funding levels if the process had been transparent and the consequences had been openly discussed. In all three studied sites, changes in both features contributed to the reforms and to the agency's increased effectiveness.

Why did the pre-reform agencies live with such low funding levels, if their performance was thereby hobbled? In an indifferent accountability environment like Alabama's, it is easier to understand how budgets were enacted with no attention to consequences. The governor and the legislature did not ask because they had other priorities. Agency heads did not volunteer information because they had no expectations of a positive result and because upsetting the existing rules was not their job. Their job was making do with what they had no matter how inadequate or, in the words of one interviewee, "doing the best we can."

But why would the same be true in harsh political environments? In those cases, isn't there an incentive for people to say what they need, since they can cast blame for failure later when they don't receive it? Yet, in the District before reform, CFSA officials typically failed to raise budget issues, and the agency's budget was persistently inadequate. One reason, besides the District's history of fiscal stress, is that agencies with a long history of failure have little credibility, so it is easy to blame them and dismiss their requests for resources. Further undercutting child welfare agencies' credibility is that they often have trouble spending the money they said they needed during periods of failure: for instance, they cannot recruit social workers even though they need them. Also, estimating child welfare budgets is hard because predictions of federal revenue and of the number of children who will need help are often wrong.

A battle between Governor James's appointed commissioner and the leadership of Jefferson County (Birmingham) over the amount of money Birmingham needed illustrates the dynamics of shifting budgetary blame to an agency with little credibility. According to the state, Jefferson County had irresponsibly allowed a deficit of more than $1 million to develop, partly because it used flexible funds for inessentials:

> "There has been gross financial overspending and lack of accountability resulting in a $1.2 million shortfall in Jefferson County," the statement [by the Alabama Department of Human Resources] said. . . . The funds in question are "flexible funding" dollars, which are used at each county's discretion. . . . Mrs. Nachman has questioned the prices Jefferson County has paid for items such as prom dresses, musical instruments, and cab fare with the flexible funds.[7]

But according to the county, with the Birmingham newspaper's backing, the deficit stemmed from an increase in the number of children coming into care as the backlog of overdue investigations was addressed and workers grew more cautious in response to tragedies. The state's insistence on moving children from foster homes into more expensive settings and the county taking on state costs for certain children in residential facilities also added to the deficit. The *Birmingham News* suspected that the state's allegations amounted to a "witch hunt" targeting the county.[8]

Without a supportive watchdog like the *Birmingham News* editorial board, the tactic of shifting blame often succeeds because true culpability is hard to assess when it is so difficult to estimate child welfare agency budgets.

Several factors dramatically changed the budget process in the study sites, even though the "gotcha" aspect never went away completely. Most directly, court expectations shone a brighter light on the assumptions used to estimate the budgets and created expectations about results that influenced the budget debate. For example, if the settlement committed to decrease social worker caseloads or improve the timeliness of investigations, dollars to accomplish those goals should be in the budget. There could be (and often was) considerable debate about what resources were needed to achieve the goals, but the debate was now framed by results, not by history or the statewide need for cuts. The court involvement also raised the visibility of agency requests and the level of public scrutiny and involvement in the process. The *Birmingham News* would surely not have weighed in on a routine dispute between state and county directors had it not been for the overall reform. In addition, when the court monitors feared the process had gone wrong, they sometimes found a way to weigh in either publicly or behind the scenes on the importance of staff and monetary resources to achieve compliance.

But the change was not solely about the federal court's direct involvement. The personal commitment of the chief elected officials changed the climate substantially by holding budget officials partially accountable for this shared reform strategy. Further, as the agencies improved their data capacity, they became far stronger players and harder to dismiss as not credible.

Although the process was not steady and all three sites found it difficult to maintain the budget commitment throughout the reform period, resources did increase in all the study sites, along with changes in the budget process. In Alabama, a reporter estimated the increase as threefold.[9] In the District, while the budget process was filled with cliffhanger moments, the mayor's commitment, the clear reform plan, the court order, and our own increased data capacity did lead to funding increases and a bigger role for the agency in the process.

But if these improvements and budget increases were generally tied to federal court orders, what lessons are there for leaders seeking to catalyze reform without litigation? One potential model is the Utah exit agreement, which includes a more open and data-driven budget process agreed to by all parties, once the court is no longer involved. It calls for the agency to share data, including quantitative and qualitative performance measures and caseload information, with state legislators and other community stakeholders, as part of its "good faith efforts to ensure that sufficient resources are made available to sustain the reforms."[10]

Is Money the Key to Reform?

Child welfare researchers frequently debate whether reform requires more resources. It might not if reform produces substantial offsetting savings (for example, children go home more quickly when the agency hires more social workers to work with their families) or if many resources being used counterproductively can be switched to better uses. Because the study sites were so underfunded before reform, they cannot answer the resource question from a national perspective. However, they illustrate the breadth of investments that reform demands, suggesting at least that in previously neglected agencies, improving performance requires investments in many aspects of operations. Major resource expansions in the sites included more social workers to reduce caseloads and eliminate backlogs; investments in social worker training, salaries, and incentives to improve qualifications; higher payment rates for foster and group homes to support higher quality expectations; additional services for children and families; increases in adoption subsidies associated with more children adopted; increases in guardianship subsidies associated with more children in subsidized guardianship; and more agency lawyers, guardians *ad litem*, and other legal supports.

Reformers often hope that such increases will be offset as better practice allows more children to stay at home rather than move to foster care, or live in foster families rather than in group homes and residential treatment programs. While this idea of offsetting savings is intuitively appealing, it would take a detailed analysis of each jurisdiction to judge whether it has actually happened. Such an analysis would have to include estimates of what would have happened without reform, which is especially hard in child welfare because so many poorly understood factors influence the number of children in care. For example, in Alabama, the number of children in care decreased early in the reforms but has since gone up for reasons that may include the methamphetamine epidemic and changes in practice, according to the court filings. In the District, several trends countered each other during my years there: children moved from informal, unpaid care into paid foster care with relatives (a program plus, but at a cost), children moved more quickly to adoption (a cost in adoption subsidy offset by a savings in foster care), and children moved to subsidized guardianship faster (a potential net cost to the District, since subsidized guardianship was locally funded while the federal government shared foster care costs). Thus, no easy answers emerge from the sites.

Conclusion

These cases offer glimpses into strategies that work to create a better political environment for performance improvement. Although the federal court was key from the beginning, reformers in all three sites attracted other supporters along the way, some tightly aligned and deeply informed about the performance goals and measures, others more casually informed and intermittently supportive. In the District, the most involved group included the local judges, the federal court, and the mayor's office; in Alabama, for some periods, the *Birmingham News* editorial page tracked performance closely; in Utah, the standing committee of legislators was more involved than legislators elsewhere. Everywhere, the elected chief executive was a crucial partner for the agency during successful periods of reform.

Reform leaders had to pay close attention to building and nurturing the team of partners and gently herding them in one direction, more or less aligned with the shared reform vision and its execution. The leaders "publicly engage all the partners," in James Tucker's definition of strong leadership, make their case about the vision and performance expectations, and then look for partners who are most invested and can sign on most fully. In turn, these partners sign on, deciding to focus on performance improvement and problem-solving rather than public blame. Finally, either the reformers or their partners use their power to keep the coalition stable by creating consequences, when stakeholders get out of line and revert from problem-solving to blame.

This approach to creating a healthier political environment may seem precarious, but the sites studied suggest it can work long enough to transform agency performance and attitudes. Once far enough along, this transformation may be sturdy enough to weather some political conflict, hostility, or chaos without reinstating the agency's passive, information-free outlook. If the agency has developed extensive information sharing and quality assurance capacity during the good times, it may be better able to weather later periods of political crisis, media blame, or battles among external partners. With credible information and partners ready to speak up in its defense, the blame coming an agency's way may be more short-lived and less intense.

Adding these external steps to the internal ones explored in the last chapter nearly completes the puzzle of how to create a climate of learning, performance measurement, and performance improvement in child welfare agencies long crippled by passivity and failure. Still missing is a personal sense of the reformers' experience. The next chapter takes up the story there.

8

Leadership

"It's that first step of moving a bureaucracy that is really hard. Figuring out how the systems get so bad and how to get them to be better. . . . About this question of why some places work and others don't, I asked [a colleague with wide experience], and she said 'leadership'."
> —Interview with nationally expert plaintiffs' attorney

"The leadership provided by Paul Vincent day to day—competent, unpretentious, undefensive—was extraordinary."
> —An outside view of the Alabama reform from James Tucker, Alabama Disability Advocacy Program

"Paul's leadership was critical. . . . He helped make it not so scary—to see him not be threatened [helped others]."
> —An inside view of the Alabama reform from a long-time Alabama child welfare agency staffer

Inside and outside these child welfare reforms, observers say the same thing about what it takes to transform a system: leadership. An enormous academic, professional, and popular literature discusses what leadership means and how to get enough to achieve societal goals. This chapter explores what leaders who turn around child welfare agencies do, what they should do, and why common leadership myths may be misleading.

Year 2 in the District: The Experience of Leading Change

In December 2002, 18 months into my tenure, I reflected, as I often did for the New Year. In a memo I still have, I wrote down the reasons I felt so tired and burned out:

- "always having disasters that I fear could wreck the agency—waking up at 4 a.m.
- sense of personal responsibility for failures

- anger of so many people, built up over the years
- internal squabbling, bitterness, power struggle
- need to build every system from scratch/no confidence in any
- sense that it's impossible ever to celebrate success for more than a nanosecond—anger from internal or external sources always sabotages
- districtwide gaps in systems/supports
- bureaucratic battles"

Struggles within the management team were painful, leading me to doubt my skill as a supervisor and coach, a quality I had long considered my greatest strength. My constant personal involvement in fiscal, revenue, and budget analysis and problem-solving was exhausting. I was waking up in the middle of the night worrying not only about children but also about the possibility of a fiscal failure so dramatic it would undermine the reform's credibility. I worried about a possible federal government finding that the District owed large amounts of money, serious overspending because costs were not predicted accurately, or a damaging battle with the District Council over spending levels.

I also wrote down more than a dozen items I thought we had done right in the previous year, including clarity about mission and plan; accountability regarding performance measures; FACES, our information system; a good start on social worker recruitment; and tremendous skills brought by many members of the management team. Even in December, I could see that the agency's performance on basic measures, like visiting children, continued to improve.

Yet battles among the senior team had been getting worse for several months. A year earlier, after working through what it would take to achieve our ambitious reform goals, the team had committed to measurable targets keyed to the federal court's expectations, to common values that contrasted sharply with the agency's historical culture, and to specific behaviors intended to make those values real. We had pledged to hold each other accountable and be open and nondefensive. But by fall 2002, many team members worried that we had failed to live by these values. At a November retreat, where I had hoped we could use our achievements as a springboard to recommit to the values and start changing behavior, the rift deepened. Contentious issues, such as what role to give outside consultants in exploring our failures, prompted anger and tears.

Still, I kept plugging ahead, given the urgent deadlines for improvement. The consultants, whose role had been so contentious, turned in a thoughtful report that praised progress to date as "heroic" yet sharpened my picture of the damage the senior staff's internal divisions would do to the next stage of our work. The report was intended to help us understand our broad problems with placement: why children ended up in inappropriate settings and why they moved around so much while in care. The reviewers found that these problems could not be solved without changing "a core set of values and norms." Agency staff at all levels needed to switch from managing crises to supporting children's longer-term needs for permanent families and had to get out from under "a culture of restrictive placement . . . a tendency toward over-diagnosis, heavy use of therapeutic foster care and residential treatment."[1] If these findings were right, and I thought they were, then it was time to start the intensive work of changing values and practices. I feared that a senior team deeply divided in its approaches to sharing information and empowering others in the agency could not do that work.

As we delved deeper into the placement problem, management team friction came to a head. Because so many parts of the system—contracting, licensing, social worker investigations, foster parent recruitment—contributed to placing children in high-quality settings, many members of the senior team had to work together. Early in summer 2003, to try to fix one part of the placement conundrum, I convened the managers involved in licensing more foster parents. But these mid-level managers reported to senior staff who were on poor terms, and the managers felt stymied because they were hearing from above that compromise would be disloyal. I could see that our team was recreating the old culture of blame and stalemate, and I knew we could not let it go on.

Some agency staff left for other opportunities, and the team remained relatively stable from then on. Looking back, I wondered why it had taken so long to arrive at a smoothly functioning team, despite all the evidence that we needed to change. One reason was my concern that we could not afford disruptions when so much was riding on every moment's performance. I was also uncertain about how much the team's difficulty reflected my own leadership failures and whether those problems would change if I did. In the end, though, the relief was enormous. Having shared values and ending the battles boosted performance, the team's energy level, and the sheer joy of the work.

Ten Rules for Agency Reformers and Child Welfare Leaders

Looking back on the roller-coaster ride of agency leadership to write this book, I found myself eager to figure out what was unique and what was similar to the two other turnaround sites and to the findings of management experts. To me, the knowledge, skills, and temperament needed to lead a deeply troubled agency in a turbulent environment often seemed distinct from the content knowledge so often highlighted in child welfare research. I wondered how others studying such settings had thought about these disparate dimensions. I also wondered how best to convey my experiences of the huge gulf between intellectually grasping the steps to reform and putting those ideas into practice. In the messy life of an agency leader, how do plans for reform translate into day-to-day action? These 10 rules for agency leaders summarize what I learned from my own experience, the sites, and the research of others.

Use Priority Goals and Results to Guide Everything You Do

Even though the private-sector management literature and the experience of the studied sites consistently demonstrate that vision and goals should guide an agency's early actions, leaders find this rule enormously hard to put into practice. When bombarded with demands from those above, outside, and below, it can often seem far easier to give in and just do what is asked. After all, the demands are not wrong, they are just not priorities. But as Ken Patterson and Richard Anderson found when they had to create a new internal complaint unit to avoid having their time consumed by multiple reporting requirements, doing things that are not a priority contributes to failure, not reform. Possibly, in small or simple situations, ignoring the rule of priorities and trying to do everything might work. But in a turnaround situation, acceding to every demand overwhelms a leader's capacity, spreads talent and energy too thin, and distracts from a clear message about what is most important.

Instead, successful leaders use core priorities to drive nearly every day-to-day decision: scheduling; matching staff to assignments; setting recruitment priorities; and shaping speeches, resource allocation, organizational and political calls, and judgments about which fights to take on and which to leave alone. One way to do this, according to Henry Mintzberg's classic article "The Manager's Job," is to modify demands from others so they fit the priorities. He finds that successful managers handle demands by linking routine assignments to an underlying purpose: "A speech is a chance to lobby for a cause; a meeting is a chance to reorganize a weak department" (Mintzberg 1975, 61). Successful leaders also impose their own priorities on a stream of demands by understanding everything the day presents as a *choice* rather than a given, recognizing that every scheduling decision, meeting agenda, or staff assignment can be recast several different ways. So when taking on a new initiative that moves a key priority forward, even if the expected approach would be to assign it to someone with free time, another option might be to assign it to the most entrepreneurial, talented, or powerful member of the senior team, even if other assignments get bumped.

Stay with Commitments Until You Deliver on Them— or Until You Explicitly Change Your Mind

Changing a culture without accountability into one imbued with it is not a matter of systems alone; it is a matter of personal modeling. All eyes are inevitably on the leader and the management team to see if they make and keep clear, explicit commitments—a good definition of accountability. Thus, CFSA's senior team adopted and desperately wanted to live up to the value of "Do what you say you will do," because it was the exact opposite of the agency's history, where grand ideas had come and gone not just without results but without acknowledgment that the plan had been modified or had failed.

But keeping commitments is difficult, especially for leaders entering dysfunctional agencies where everything is harder than it looks. Jolie Pillsbury, a longtime organizational development consultant, has observed public- and private-sector leaders struggle with these dilemmas. She proposes an "accountability continuum" that illustrates the many steps people typically traverse on the way to "owning" and realizing their own commitments: blame, excuses, and "wait and hope" responses, for example.[2]

To blast through these responses and successfully make and keep commitments, leaders and their teams need organizational skills, persistence, discipline, and integrity. Organizational skills matter because a basic requirement for keeping commitments is not losing track of them—a difficult task in a chaotic and emergency-driven agency. Making fewer commitments and confining them to agency priorities can help. But an agency head and senior staff still need the skills to track multiple demands, a weakness of many human services leaders, according to an expert coach.[3]

Persistence matters because keeping commitments in a deeply troubled agency is likely to take far more time than originally planned, as each successive system problem is peeled back and solved. Staying with it pays dividends, as people come to understand you are not easily discouraged and are in it for the long haul.

Discipline and integrity matter because new leaders, trying to achieve ambitious results in a fog of uncertainty and complexity, will always make commitments that they find out later cannot be met. It takes discipline and integrity to acknowledge the failure explicitly and make modifications, rather than pretending that the initial commitment never existed. Over time, honesty pays off in credibility, trust, and commitment from partners and staff. In the District, it was important for our partners to realize that if we agreed to something and then found we couldn't do it, we would come back to them with an explanation and a plan, rather than "wait and hope" that they would not find out.

Constantly Gather and Analyze Information about Your Results and Goals

In all the successful sites, the leaders saw the active and constant use of qualitative and quantitative data as central to reform. Chapter 6 described the many techniques the reformers used to create new information systems and convince people to use them in agencies that had traditionally been data-free or laissez-faire.

But the most striking lesson for leaders is how much personal involvement that change demanded: each reformer personally and actively sought and used information from the data systems. The key lesson is to exhibit curiosity and a drive to use information yourself, and to build around you a curious, data-driven organization. Without the example of top leaders consistently tracking information and evidence, it is too easy for staff to slip back into a sense that they are doing the best they can in a tough situation and lose track of performance. Losing track even for a little while makes it far too easy to miss the warning signs of potentially dangerous problems.

The other lesson for leaders is to identify people who can translate leaders' curiosity into an effective technical system and communicate needs and solutions between technical and program people. No matter how much technical expertise in information systems an organization has, it will fail if no one can put that expertise at the service of program staff and program goals. The District's expensive and highly skilled information systems contractors were not able to help with reform until I hired a CIO who could connect them to the rest of the agency.[4]

Build a Team That Uses Information to Learn by Avoiding Blame and Welcoming Conflict

I experienced in the District child welfare agency both the stress of an organizational culture not conducive to thoughtful conflict and the satisfaction of a culture capable of accommodating it. The contrast between CFSA's senior management team in my first year and in my last was stark, and so was the contrast in my experience with District government colleagues before and after the city administrator took charge of the cross-cutting Medicaid problems. Without a culture that accepts different views and comfortably manages conflict, individuals can experience great stress as they bear the brunt of others' fury or personal attacks. Problems often go unsolved because staff are afraid to raise them or to provide helpful information if it might anger someone else; groups accept unsatisfactory solutions perceived as "fair" just to avoid a dispute; and data are not collected because no one really wants to know. When issue-focused conflict and divergent views are unwelcome, even the best performance data will not be used effectively to improve results.

Because high-decibel personal battles are so unpleasant, agency directors sometimes mistakenly try to avoid conflict or to paper over it, only to cut off learning. Especially amid reform and rapid change, where every bit of information could be vital to choosing or fine-tuning strategies, leaders must strive to open discussion to all viewpoints, and then resolve issues based on all the available knowledge, without prematurely cutting off discussion.

Comfort with conflict is hard for many groups. Private- and public-sector organizations frequently respond to conflict with either silence or "political" solutions, such as splitting the difference, that seem fair but avoid addressing the substance of the underlying dispute. In contrast, successful organizations bring conflict into the open and address it directly. John Kotter summarizes what he thinks is required for organizations to handle rapid change, requirements that are as applicable to child welfare agencies in the throes of turnaround as to businesses facing a changing market:

> Systems will need to be created to provide honest and unvarnished news, especially about performance. . . . To both create these systems and use their output effectively, corporate cultures in the twenty-first century will have to value candid discussions far more than they do today. Norms associated with political politeness . . . and with killing-the-messenger-of-bad-news will have to change. (Kotter 1996, 163)

How does a leader get there? Probably, it will take many approaches over time, particularly in an organization accustomed to avoiding conflict over years of failure. Personal openness by a top leader, who models a positive response to disagreement, is one approach widely represented in the case studies. But often this won't be enough. Chris Argyris notes that if senior staff become experts in "bypass and coverup," then a leader's candor can lead to "disruptive actions" (Argyris 1993, 102). Still, disruptive actions can be a step toward a solution, forcing everyone involved to recognize the need for a change in team membership or approach. In addition, many people find it helpful to use an outside consultant to help a team increase its ability to address conflicts.[5] As with so many other reform strategies, team members' experience over time is crucial as well. They will need to see that when they question the leader's perspective, provide unexpected information, or point out a failure, the leader continues to support rather than undermine or blame them.

Manage the Team's Stress Levels so Members Can Maintain a Culture of Learning

As I discovered in the District, a harsh environment can make a culture of learning and inquiry hard to maintain. When staff members expect intense and unforgiving public scrutiny, it takes unusual courage and trust to share your vulnerabilities with colleagues and unusual self-control not to use shared information against colleagues.

Yet a too-lenient environment also sabotages learning, as in pre-reform Alabama, where everyone accepted the constraints unquestioningly and assumed that poor performance was to be expected, or pre-reform Utah, where counties "performed as they performed" without data or expectations. Such "complacency" is the prime factor John Kotter sees sabotaging change in private-sector organizations (Kotter 1996). Avoiding both extremes requires leaders, in Ronald Heifetz's words, to stay on "the razor's edge," keeping the stress level high enough so people know they need to change but controlled enough so they don't break down, individually or as a team (1994, 106):

> People cannot learn new ways when they are overwhelmed. But eliminating the stress altogether eliminates the impetus for adaptive work. The strategic task is to maintain a level of tension that motivates people.

Elsewhere, Heifetz offers "the pressure cooker analogy" for the leader's job: "keep the heat up without blowing up the vessel" (1994, 128).

How does a leader do this? One approach is to model the right balance of urgency and calm during a crisis, as observers say Paul Vincent did. I witnessed an example in a New York state agency (not a child welfare agency) that had endured several months of criticism in the press and the state legislature for its work supporting a controversial gubernatorial priority. When I met with the staff on behalf of the governor's office and thanked them for their high-quality work under difficult circumstances, I was astonished to hear virtually every member of the senior team tell me the experience had been exhilarating. Everyone had been at the top of their game, working unbelievably hard but learning constantly. I asked how that could be given the harsh public attention, and they all commented on their commissioner's perspective: "When your boss is calm, you're calm."

Leaders also manage the team's stress by striking a balance between protecting others from anger and criticism and exposing them to it. For example, leaders handle meetings alone with angry stakeholders or invite them in to address the team. Leaders also manage stress by choosing which of the team's challenges or failures to push at any moment and which to leave for later ("pacing and sequencing," in Heifetz's words [1994, 109]). When the agency's bosses—the mayor or governor, the legislature, the federal court—exert great influence over deadlines, leaders manage stress partly by negotiating with those outside groups to create a plan that achieves the right balance.

Build a Top-Flight Senior Team with Diverse Strengths, and Deal Directly and Promptly with Any Failures

Agency heads or their elected bosses may not see the need for a high-powered team. Elected officials may feel they've done what they need to by appointing a new leader, and agency leaders, even if they believe in a team, may begrudge the time it takes to recruit and develop it. Both agency heads and elected officials may think one person can do it all because of their own experience in an easier setting, because they believe in the myth of the single great leader, or because bureaucratic or funding constraints make the idea of recruiting a team seem utopian.

Yet the case studies and research on rapid change in public- and private-sector organizations demonstrate the role of a strong and diverse team; one person cannot do this work alone. In all the sites, the leaders built teams that brought insiders and outsiders together. Outsiders, like Ken Patterson and me, recruited strong insiders, while a (partial) insider like Paul Vincent used outside consultants to bring in new perspectives. All the agency leaders also built teams with colleagues and bosses who represented the governor's office or mayor's office, as their help was needed for political, budget, and cross-agency support. In the private sector, John Kotter notes the special importance of a team in high-change settings: "In a slow-moving world, all an organization needs is a good executive in charge. . . . In a fast-moving world, teamwork is enormously helpful almost all the time" (1996, 163).

Agency leaders seeking to put this idea into practice may encounter immediate practical constraints, such as civil service rules, political expectations, or difficulty recruiting. To overcome them, leaders must first see management recruiting and team development as a reform priority, worth the investment of time and perhaps political capital. Specific solutions will no doubt vary by situation; leaders in the sites used creative techniques (foundation support for recruitment, consultants, fellowship programs) to improve their access to talent. Where civil service or political constraints pose a challenge, an agency's history of failure may offer leverage for changing past practices. For instance, a new leader who comes in to reform a troubled agency after a tragedy may be in a strong position to make independent hiring decisions, even if past practice has been to hire candidates based on political connections.

Besides devoting sufficient time to building a team, a successful reform leader also needs to be comfortable bringing in talent that complements his or her own strengths and compensates for weaknesses. Some leaders have trouble recruiting the right team because they are comfortable only with people whose strengths and weaknesses mirror their own, threatened by strength in others, or unable to see their own strengths and weaknesses. Ideally, at least one trusted colleague can provide feedback to help a leader see past any blind spots.

Further, a group that looks perfect on paper may not work well under pressure. Constantly developing and sustaining an effective team is essential, even if it means unpleasant conversations with team members when their skills, experience, or values no longer are in sync with organization needs. Most of us have trouble confronting a colleague's or senior staff member's failure, particularly when the evidence is ambiguous or when a colleague is not at fault but is a poor fit for the team or the job. Many leaders try coaching or rearranging roles and job descriptions, hoping that the peer pressure from others or improved team dynamics will work. If none of those strategies work, however, successful change depends on direct action to replace individual members to preserve the team's integrity and effectiveness.

Diagnose How the Political World Affects the Agency's Internal Capacity and How the Agency's Internal Strengths and Weaknesses Affect the Outside Climate

Perhaps the biggest missing element in the conventional picture of child welfare leadership is the need for sophisticated political skills in the service of reform. In particular, successful leaders need to analyze, understand, and act to change the longstanding links between external failure—political accountability that is either punitive or laissez-faire—and internal failures. These cycles are not limited to child welfare or to the public sector, but they are strikingly prevalent in the failing agencies discussed here.

To succeed, a leader needs first to understand and then to break the cycle. Different settings have different traditions for how the cycle will play out and the roles for the players—the press, elected officials, outside constituencies, other government agencies. Successful leaders need to grasp those intuitively or through conscious reflection to design ways to break out. When Robin Arnold-Williams familiarized the governor and key legislators with the practice model, she relied on her knowledge of how the negative cycle had played out in Utah. She anticipated that if elected officials understood and approved the agency's approach in advance, they would not back off from the reform if a tragedy occurred. In the District, community leaders helped me understand what I should look out for in the media and political environment that shaped our cycles. The lesson began when I was introduced at the mayor's press conference and the speaker asked others there to break the tradition of over-hyping and then destroying leaders.

Once they understand the cycle, leaders sometimes choose to break it with a response that is distinctly unexpected, such as taking responsibility where defensiveness is expected, or fighting back when passivity is expected. For example, when Maryland demanded that we either reduce payments to foster parents or remove children from Maryland homes, we refused to comply with either option—unexpected, but backed up by the court's choice to hold a hearing and require the two jurisdictions to negotiate.

Draw External Partners into Your Vision, While Also Seeking to Understand Their Complex Goals and Motives

We have seen already that well-defined priority goals and results helped each leader draw in external partners. But having the right goals and results did not bring partners to the door automatically: agency leaders also needed to reach out to their partners. This is a stark change from past practice in some failed agencies, either because agency directors have never reached out directly to stakeholders or because communication has traditionally focused on problems or failures, not goals.

After reform, leaders reached out directly. Alabama observers remember Paul Vincent's explicit choice to take the vision to all the stakeholder groups as a key factor in the reform. My regular one-on-one conversations with the presiding judge of the Family Court, addressing broad goals and particular problems, consciously departed from a history of very little direct communication.

At the same time, it would be unrealistic to think that the goals of external partners, however committed, are identical to those of the agency leader. So child welfare leaders need to do more than communicate their own vision; they need a nuanced understanding of their outside partners' goals, beliefs, and interests. Reformers need to take partners' perspectives into account realistically and acknowledge that partners' views are held in good faith. If reformers see their own motives as noble but everyone else's as self-serving, they risk misunderstanding what others really care about, as well as provoking lasting anger. Both realism and respect matter when it comes to assessing partners' perspectives and motivations.

When I first started to work with the local judges, for example, it was important for me to understand realistically how congressional interest in reforming the District's family court system set the stage for our collaboration. The judges needed me as a partner more than they had needed previous child welfare agency directors, because I testified before Congress on behalf of the mayor about what the court reform should look like and because I had worked with some congressional members in my earlier jobs. I could help the judges where appropriate and where our goals overlapped—for example, by including in my testimony information about the resources the judges needed to achieve change. But not being cynical about the judges' motivations for collaboration also mattered. It would have been deeply insulting for me to assume the judges were working with the agency only to satisfy Congress, when in fact they had spent many more years than I had on the front lines of child and family issues.

Know Yourself, and Learn from Successes and Failures

Whether a leader's big strategic choices are noticed, innumerable daily interactions, style, tone, and mood always are. These choices and interactions can drive or sabotage positive change, model the leader's values and organizational goals or contradict them, intentionally calm or energize people or unintentionally bestir or demoralize them, welcome divergent views or shut them out. While perhaps some born leaders get everything right by instinct, most of us cannot get there without observing our own behavior and its effects on others, to learn and do better. A 20-year study of Harvard Business School graduates shows that, even for a group that started out highly educated, "lifelong learning"—the ability to learn about and strengthen one's own leadership capacity—explained much of their lifetime success (Kotter 1996).

For leaders in the child welfare turnarounds, self-awareness is crucial. First, it is especially important for a leader to model learning, calm, nondefensiveness, and other desirable values in an agency making the first steps toward a new culture, because few other models are available. If some of these values don't come naturally, then a leader has to figure out how to behave better than naturally. Second, a leader has to figure out how to consistently model these behaviors even when under considerable emotional pressure. Third, turnarounds are by definition fast-moving, and the strategic situation and demands on the leader can change rapidly. An aggressive style that works for challenging failed processes may backfire in the next stage of reform, when the key challenge is encouraging staff to come up with long-suppressed ideas for achieving change. David Nadler analyzed the experience of private-sector CEOs brought in to make major changes in an organization and found that most had to face a "Act II" for which their skills were not suited. When that happened, they either found themselves forced out or worked to remake themselves, groom a successor, or readjust their role. According to Nadler, "all but the first require a power of observation, a propensity for introspection, and a strain of humility that are, in truth, quite rare" (2007, 68).

Why is this combination of self-observation, introspection, and humility so rare? In part, the problem is that without practice and feedback, it is easy not to notice one's own style; it comes naturally and feels like a fact of life. In part, though, the problem is that we want to believe the best of ourselves. We often fool ourselves into believing we are more patient or better listeners than others would say (Wilson 2002). Honestly considering evidence that we are not doing well at something important is extremely painful. A Cornell University project asking human services staff to identify "what was effective and ineffective in helping them to identify and change their own unhelpful behaviors" prompted a considerable number of people to say they would prefer not to answer the question. Comments included the following: "For a long time I was too brittle to even acknowledge the things in myself that I needed to change or to accept feedback from others" and "Why would I ever tell anyone the answer to a question like that?" (Cornell University 2005).

What techniques do self-aware leaders use to improve? According to the case studies and the evidence of larger studies, approaches include these four:

- *Regular reflection.* Kotter describes this as "regular assessment of successes and failures, especially the latter" (1996, 183).
- *Use of honest feedback.* As leaders move up, they may have to work harder to ensure honesty, but it is worth the effort.
- *Long-term perspective.* Kotter suggests that the successful leaders in the Harvard Business School Study have experienced the long-term benefits of learning from negative feedback and even from failures, which helps them overcome the "short-term pain" that comes from honesty (1996, 183).
- *Conscious attention to managing stress.* Part of self-awareness is knowing what it takes to be at one's best. A leader may respond angrily to criticism at the end of a bad day, but see the truth in it

the next morning. John Gardner reports, after talking with many leaders, that the list of renewal techniques is long but usually involves "retreat or solitude" as well as "do[ing] something nonverbal" (1990, 132–33).

Trust Your Own Judgment about the Best Route to Reform, and Take the Risks Necessary to Get There

In the end, after appropriate listening and reflection, the leaders in the reform sites had to trust their own judgment. They were charting new territory, and no one else could give them the definitive answers. But trusting your own judgment in an uncertain situation means that you could be wrong. For instance, I now believe I was wrong to delay dealing with the senior team's personnel issues, and right when I finally worked with the team to address them. But it could have turned out that I was wrong the second time—I could have miscalculated whether we could do without the lost expertise, and torpedoed the reform.

As many similar decisions in the case studies illustrate, leaders who are driving reform have to take risks; totally safe options don't lead to dramatic change. How do leaders take those risks and last long enough to have an effect? The short answer seems to be that they identify and develop a lot of options, not just one status quo option and one risky and self-destructive alternative. Like an expert skier compared with a novice, leaders who are good at taking risks can see routes for getting through terrain that looks impossibly fraught with peril to someone else. According to Kathleen Reardon's study of managers in the private sector,

> Faced with having to take a risk, most people make only one attempt: They ring the doorbell, and if a response is not forthcoming, they give up and go away. Those who accomplish their primary and secondary goals try knocking at the back door, tapping at a window, or even returning a second time. . . . People who take bold risks and succeed are versatile thinkers; they ready themselves with alternative routes. (2007, 63)

What does it take to invent multiple options between the safe but unproductive and the unacceptably risky? One helpful resource to find new routes is an extensive network of partners: leveraging the support of one external partner or stakeholder to reach another, or to influence internal change. Another resource is negotiating skill in the leadership team. People with a nuanced understanding of the perspectives of stakeholders may be able to invent unexpected ways to address their underlying interests and break out of dilemmas. Also helpful is access to multiple perspectives that will increase the chance of escaping old ruts and finding new choices. A "kitchen cabinet" of outside experts can serve this purpose.

But perhaps the most unexpected suggestion from the case studies is that leaders, at least in these tough turnaround situations, have other job options in mind so they can think with less fear and constraint about risks. In Alabama, Andy Hornsby kept his federal civil service slot when he became secretary of human resources, using the Intergovernmental Personnel Act mechanism to make his assignment to Alabama possible. In Utah, Ken Patterson took the job feeling that the risks were acceptable because he had been in a foundation-sponsored fellowship program with national visibility, which would help him land another job if necessary. Similarly, I had reflected on my options before accepting, deciding that if the job ended badly, I could find another.

Since this finding surprised me, I asked two colleagues who have been coaching high-level human service agency officials for decades for their sense of how broadly applicable it is. Both colleagues agree strongly, believing that leaders frequently constrain their effectiveness and creativity because of fear. They have observed that top agency officials often misjudge the likelihood that risks will pay off, overestimating risk and underestimating the benefits of action, thus limiting their effectiveness. One wrote:

> This is a huge issue in my experience. I've seen many commissioners unwilling to risk the wrath of elected officials by asking for very legitimate staffing requests, etc. I have found that when they have a Plan B for themselves, they are much more likely to take those risks.[6]

Myths

This picture of leadership in child welfare turnarounds belies three persistent myths: that leaders are fundamentally different from managers, that successful leadership in child welfare primarily requires in-depth subject matter knowledge, and that successful leadership is a joyous experience (while unsuccessful leadership means low morale, high conflict, and angry stakeholders).

The first myth is that leaders differ fundamentally from managers. Leaders offer inspiration and vision, while managers make the trains run on time and the budgets come in on target. For example:

Managers and leaders are two very different types of people. Managers' goals arise out of necessities rather than desires; they excel at diffusing conflicts between individuals or departments, placating all sides while ensuring that an organization's day-to-day business gets done. Leaders, on the other hand, adopt personal, active attitudes towards goals. They look for the potential opportunities and rewards that lie around the corner, inspiring subordinates and firing up the creative process with their own energy. Their relationships with employees and coworkers are intense, and their working environment is often, consequently chaotic. (Zaleznik 1998, 61)

By contrast, in the child welfare turnarounds studied here, the successful leader must bring some part of both temperaments and both skill sets. One reason is that in agencies with a long history of demoralizing failure, the leader has to demonstrate vision embodied in action—a vision that can (to mix metaphors) make the trains run on time. Staff and outside observers have typically become cynical after years of watching visions disconnected from action and results, and will not take the vision seriously without the accompanying action. According to Nick Scoppetta, his number one lesson was that "management *was* reform."

Also blurring the traditional distinction between leaders and managers is the central role of information systems and careful attention to data in these turnaround stories. Conventional wisdom would have the manager construct information systems, but in these agencies, creating a passion for information is crucial to the leader's vision and personally modeled by the agency heads. Building the information system is not routine but, rather, creative, entrepreneurial (including Alabama's invention of a whole new way to gather data), and tightly linked to the mission.

John Kotter's study of private-sector organizations reaches somewhat similar conclusions about the need to pair strong management and strong leadership when major change is the goal. In his view, organizational transformations must deliver early results to keep supporters on board and motivated, and delivering these results requires strong, active management (1996).

The reverse idea, that agency heads could be managers with no leadership capacity, is born of a perception that people who work in public agencies ought to "just implement" the will of elected officials. In other words, their job is to take straightforward and easily defined actions to carry out a legislated vision. But, as the case studies illustrate, this perception is nothing like the reality of the work that appointed agency heads in turnaround settings have to do. These directors constantly exercise leadership in framing a vision, inspiring staff and external constituencies, stimulating and modeling creativity and openness, sharpening some conflicts while resolving others, and ratcheting the level of tension up or down to sustain the commitment to change. Agency heads have to be leaders to achieve the performance that the public expects of them. To be sure, effective leadership by appointed executives must rest on a sophisticated understanding of the role of elected executives, elected legislatures, and the statutory framework that guides agency action. But that understanding undergirds rather than precludes a creative and assertive leadership role.

One final version of the myth, unique to the public sector, is that top-level appointees should be purely leaders while civil service employees are purely managers. In settings like the case study turnarounds, dividing leadership from management this way delivers misleading messages. It suggests to appointees that they can accomplish results through "leadership" alone—meaning vision disconnected from day-to-day operations—and leave management to others. It also suggests to mid-level managers that they should be satisfied with keeping routine processes operating at their current level, even if that is not the best way to serve the agency's purpose. Managers who buy into this thinking—whether school principals or mid-level child welfare administrators—become part of the system that frustrates them, and they may fail to develop the change-oriented skills that would prepare them for agency leadership later in their careers.

The second myth is that a child welfare agency can be led only by someone with deep substantive knowledge of the field. To some degree, this myth is a reaction against the idea that no knowledge of the field is necessary and an aggressive "outsider" can knock sense into a failed government agency. In the turnaround settings, neither extreme held. The successful agency heads had backgrounds that were close to child welfare: Paul Vincent had spent years in human services but not specifically in child welfare; I had a Ph.D. in public policy and a career in child and family policy; and Ken Patterson had perhaps the most traditional child welfare background, though he had spent a year in a national fellowship intended to broaden his experience. In New York City, Nick Scoppetta was a lawyer and prosecutor who had spent years on the board of a private child welfare agency, was familiar with the system as a former foster child, and had served in several roles in city government. The background of these leaders fits the research on the development of senior managers and leaders, which suggests that substantive experience matters but breadth helps too. Managers who take on major new assignments are more likely to succeed, and succeed more quickly, if they have experience in the same industry (Gabarro 1985, 123), but spanning different worlds also contributes to success:

> Contemporary social organization is rich in boundaries. Professions spawn sub-professions, each with its own arcane knowledge. . . . Young leaders . . . should be introduced soon to the boundary-crossing experience. They should learn to find their way into an unfamiliar organizational culture, to honor that culture's sensitivities, and to develop empathy for its values and assumptions. (Gardner 1990, 175)

The third myth—that successful leadership is a joyous experience, while unsuccessful leadership means low morale, high conflict, and angry stakeholders—has not typically been supported by research but is alive in leaders' expectations. Leaders often suspect that if their day-to-day experience is painful and difficult, they must be failing. My successor told me that the most useful advice I gave her was that I felt like a total failure about three times a week; this advice kept her going on the days she felt the same way. One reason it is important to explode this myth is to encourage talented leaders to persevere until success comes into view. Even more important, identifying personal pain and stress as a part of leadership makes it clear that leaders must develop effective habits and skills despite pain, rather than waiting for it to disappear. As Heifetz writes, introducing a chapter filled with practical suggestions for these habits and skills:

> Shouldering the pains and uncertainties of an institution particularly in times of distress comes with the job of authority. It can only be avoided at the institution's peril . . . To lead and yet sustain the personal stresses that come with leading requires inner discipline. (Heifetz 1994, 252)

In the failed agencies described in these case studies, a new leader bent on a turnaround will find staff and outside partners directing at him the fury they have built up toward the agency after years of betrayal, incompetence, and blame. A honeymoon period may help for a while, but such a period of grace is fragile and often short-lived. Further, one source of pain that I had not anticipated was feeling responsible for a whole host of day-to-day failures, with their terrible effects on children. No matter how much progress the agency is making, its failures will continue to damage some children and families for years. And, of course, many cases involve public and press criticism, which is often wrong about what could have been done and unrealistic about the possible pace of reform but completely right about the damage done.

Add to this mix the process of change itself, with the turmoil and conflict it can create. Typically, a leader disappoints some people because change seems too slow, and angers others because it moves too fast, or because it threatens the one aspect of the old system that worked for them. Morale can easily worsen under conditions of rapid change before it improves. Change also requires internal and external battles that take a toll on all but the most combative personalities. As John Gardner writes: "Defeat can be costly. . . . All leaders carry bruises, balanced or not by the bruises that they have given others" (1990, 133–34).

At the same time, turning around a troubled agency yields tremendous joy. A team that works together under tough circumstances builds close and lasting friendships. Leaders, their teams, and staff throughout the agency experience the excitement of working at top capacity, doing what people said could not be done, and inventing new ways of working. They can see real progress on a mission they hold dear, sometimes for the first time after years of feeling burnt-out and disconnected. Nonetheless, while each child welfare leader remembered tremendously rewarding aspects of the experience, a leader should be prepared for many days when the pain and stress far outweigh the satisfaction.

Conclusion

For researchers and policy experts, leadership's role in improving results might seem almost beside the point. Focusing on leadership can seem a distraction from making the policy and budget case for sufficient investments in proven policies. And surely emphasizing leadership guarantees that results will be fragile, since extraordinary leaders will leave their jobs, and the success will evaporate. As these experts see it, good policy and sufficient funding will lead to good results, with or without good leaders, just like the progress in disease control that came with widespread childhood immunization.

But the case studies argue for *both* stronger leadership and stronger policy, not for a trade-off between them. Effective leaders can make a difference to the lives of thousands within the current system, hardly a marginal result. By demonstrating that positive change can happen, they have already made the case for resources, and in some cases for policy reform, in their jurisdictions. More leadership successes can form the backbone of a case for national change. Further, the need for strong leaders will not go away if we get better policies and funding, because large, complex organizations do not achieve high performance on automatic pilot.

But strong leadership alone will not deliver the results children deserve. As long as national policy toward troubled families is muddled, underfunded, inconsistent with research on what works, and characterized by complex and hard-to-maneuver funding streams, we will not achieve the reform required to meet national goals. Strong leaders would be able to do far more for children with more sensible policy and funding arrangements at their disposal. Sustained reform requires change at both levels.

In examining what it takes to bring change to the front lines of child welfare, the next chapter runs head-on into this challenge. The chapter identifies some improvements that can arise from local leadership, along with a bigger policy context that demands federal change.

9

Taking Reform to the Front Lines

"Alabama started its reforms with the values and belief system—training, reinforcement, voice of leadership. . . . That was key to keeping [the reform] alive. If all [the reformers] had done was change policy, it could have been changed again—but they started with values and beliefs."
—Jerry Milner, former child welfare reform leader in Alabama

"You can teach people all day, but if the infrastructure doesn't work to support it, it won't change what they do."
—Jerry Milner, Alabama

"The [foster] family expressed confidence in their ability to meet the target child's needs both now and in the future, between the efforts and abilities of the grandmother, the great-aunt, and the target child's uncle and his wife. The target child has a sense of stability and security that is evident."
—Case #15 of the District's fall 2003 review (CSSP 2004b, 10)

Earlier chapters have described the big-picture strategies that produced turnarounds in the sites: vision and early action, learning and performance management, effective political accountability, and leadership. Social workers, foster families, and service providers have been at the edge of these stories. But this chapter, which looks at lessons about taking reform to the front lines, places them at the center.

Sometimes, the front lines in child welfare refers to the social workers who investigate and manage cases. But here I give the phrase a wider meaning, building on research about who can directly influence a child's or family's experience. In addition to social workers, the settings children live in and the people who care for them directly can strongly influence their development. So too can the workers who provide other direct services to children and their parents: nurses in a clinic, mental health therapists, parent training teachers, schoolteachers, and caregivers in an early childhood program.

This chapter looks at reform on the front lines in all three studied sites. It draws lessons from the sites' successes, as well as from the persistent gaps where important benefits for children remain elusive. Those gaps feed into the final chapter's recommendations for federal policy changes to make reform on the front lines easier and more far-reaching.

Two Steps Forward, One Step Back: The District, Years 2 and 3

In June 2003, I summarized for our senior staff retreat what we had achieved and what we still had to do. We had many accomplishments that mattered to children, from ending children's stays in the building, to closing the emergency shelters, to improving social worker caseloads and basic case management practices. Yet we were just beginning to tackle the fundamental changes that lead to more permanent placements and just beginning a path to stronger family engagement and community links. After two years, we had not yet achieved consistent quality and put the worst outcomes behind us. Given these gaps, we agreed that during the next six months, we had to dig far deeper to genuinely achieve permanent families for children, engage families and communities, and achieve consistently high quality.

The quality services review that fall illustrated the same themes: important accomplishments yet widespread weaknesses. For example, reviewers complimented a new drug court program that offered parents intensive substance abuse services in a "therapeutic, stable environment" without being separated from their children, who stayed in the same facility. In the case reviewed, the mother saw the program as "a time of healing and renewing" (CSSP 2004b, 12). Yet in the same case, reviewers criticized the social worker for failing to look beyond the immediate future:

> The mother is scheduled to graduate from the treatment center in December and will need to have housing and employment in place before then in order to keep the case plan on schedule. There were no specific or identifiable alternatives should she be unable to secure both. . . . There were no contingency plans . . . for relapse or unsuccessful completion of the program. (CSSP 2004b, 16)

Typical problems in the cases reviewed were failures in health and mental health care, too few substance-abuse services to meet the need, and a "lack of clarity and purposefulness in setting permanency goals and time frames" (CSSP 2004b, 16). Among the positives were foster and kin caregivers who offered children good homes. CFSA social workers were actively involved in all but one case, which reviewers noted as "a significant improvement from past practice" (CSSP 2004b, 11).

Achieving Permanent Families for Children

Even after our first-year increase in completed adoptions, an enormous gap remained. Although more than 1,000 children living in temporary foster care officially had a case plan calling for adoption—meaning the court and the agency had decided they could not go home—300-some children were actually adopted. For children whose relatives wanted to give them permanent homes, one route to closing the gap was subsidized permanent guardianship. Although the federal government did not then share the cost of subsidized guardianships, a generous District law provided local funding. However, when I arrived as director, not a single guardianship had been finalized.

Why the slow start? One reason, as the QSR reviewers and others observed, was that some CFSA staff, judges, and lawyers did not believe a permanent home was achievable for children in foster care, and they accepted temporary stability in a foster family as the best obtainable outcome. As a result, kin might have received mixed signals about whether it even mattered for the child to have a permanent home, or whether they should just continue day by day as foster parents. Also, lawyers for children's relatives and Family Court judges were skeptical of the District Council's commitment to guardianship funding. Staff at CFSA were not used to promoting a policy option, so they waited for relatives to come to them.

To get moving, we asked all the involved parties—judges, lawyers, and kin foster parents—to identify their concerns; we then gave briefings and developed informational materials. Once we started to actively recruit, provide information, and track the number of guardianships each month, we eventually succeeded. In the year ending September 30, 2003, the District finalized 102 subsidized guardianships of children from foster care.

But we had to fix our adoption process too. It was broken for many reasons, including the mixed feelings of judges and social workers that led to mixed signals to children and potential adoptive parents. Breakdowns also arose from the sheer complexity of the adoption process: failures of information and tracking, technical aspects of adoption—subsidy policy, licensing requirements, and interstate adoption—and staff workloads, particularly those of lawyers who were responsible for terminating parental rights.

We tried many strategies. One was to develop new adoption policy, a requirement of the implementation plan that had initially prompted my skepticism, since I had seen a lot of policy in my federal years that was too abstract to be useful. But once we realized that policy should be specific enough to help workers link their day-to-day jobs to the vision, we began to see how adoption policy could help. Our first hint was when the team charged with drafting the adoption policy recommended that it should cover only the work of adoption specialists—the social workers assigned to a child once a judge had specified the goal of adoption, often very late in the child's time in care. Our management team realized that we had a chance for a breakthrough if we overruled that suggestion and expanded the policy to show the whole staff how adoption fit into their jobs. We guessed that the sharp dividing line between the work of the adoption unit and that of other social workers was a barrier to changing the culture about permanent homes. We also realized that much of the delay typically came before the adoption specialist was assigned, and much of the sound social work that would speed adoption had to happen before then. For example, if a social worker built a strong relationship with a foster family, they might feel more comfortable coming forward to adopt.

Once we decided to make the policy both practical and broad, we uncovered other barriers and set about solving them. The working group asked us to define a social worker's responsibility if she thought a judge was not acting in the best interests of the child—for example, by delaying action on the agency's adoption recommendation. The senior team agreed that the policy should articulate the agency's expectations about when a social worker should elevate such disagreements to her supervisor or consult our lawyers about asking the judge to reconsider. A policy spelled out in advance would avoid second-guessing the social worker afterwards for being too aggressive or too passive.

Family Engagement: Facilitated Family Team Meetings

The consultants CFSA hired to advise us about placements recommended that before any child was removed from a home or placed in a new setting, we should hold a facilitated family team meeting (FFTM) that brought together the social workers involved in the decision, the extended family, and others with a strong tie to the child or family. Experience in other jurisdictions suggested that such meetings would engage families, dramatically improve the quality of placement decisions, reduce moves within the system, and help everyone reach an understanding of the child's plan.

Our senior team found this ambitious idea controversial: some thought it too difficult for us to implement successfully amid so many other initiatives. But I approved it because bringing everyone together to make such high-stakes decisions made sense and would increase the information available to staff. I also believed that taking on a few big challenges would help us transform our practices. We were spread too thin to effectively coordinate our changes in training, policy, supervision, and clinical oversight unless we could weave these threads together through a high-impact initiative; FFTMs seemed perfect.

By the time I left, the steps for implementing FFTMs were laid out but not yet taken. We had worked with the judges to revise the District's statutes to build in time for the meetings, making the District's legislative framework unique among states (Edwards and Tinworth 2005). Eighteen months later, the early evaluation reported that the innovation was promising. A magistrate judge thought the initiative had led to "more parents coming to the initial hearing who are willing to work with the agency and . . . less defensive about what's happening to them and their family." A family team meeting coordinator saw direct benefits to children from seeing so many people assembled to talk about their future: "[The process] gives children hope that people want them to be with their family members" (Edwards and Tinworth 2005, 4).

Changing Practice across Organizational Boundaries

Besides the judges, many other partners were important to improving the quality of results for children. The seven Healthy Families/Thriving Communities Collaboratives, located in the District's high-poverty neighborhoods, were the most important partners in our goal of linking families to their communities. All the collaboratives played multiple roles; some saw themselves mainly as direct service providers and others as support organizations to a network of other providers. As community-based organizations, they responded to their neighborhoods' diverse needs, such as gang-related violence or housing gentrification. As CFSA's "community arm," they provided services to families in support of the agency's child welfare mission. As networks of providers, they helped local organizations coordinate and build their capacity. All were funded through a sole-source CFSA contract, though several also raised money from other sources.

CFSA's new management team and the leadership of the collaboratives conducted a joint retreat early in the reform to share goals and discuss ways of accomplishing them together. Afterwards we were all optimistic about reenergizing the partnership. Sadly, though, we never completely fulfilled that initial sense of promise. CFSA did not effectively translate our shared goals into specific expectations or contracting procedures, and our persistent administrative difficulties with timely payment took a day-to-day toll on the relationship. The complexity of building a new partnership that would meet our joint goals and fit the District's contracting and payment systems defeated us, at least for the moment. We were simply stretched too thin.

The District's lawyers were another crucial partner, because they represented social workers' views in court about the best decisions for individual children. Unfortunately, in my last months as director, I found myself once again negotiating their relationship with CFSA. The legislation creating CFSA stated that the District's lawyers were to work in an "attorney-client relationship" with the agency, a structure intended to end the earlier practice of attorneys contradicting social workers at trial. With social workers and attorneys planning for children together, front-line practice and results for children were expected to improve. In the reform's early months, we had agreed on and implemented an organizational structure to make this happen, one of my earliest accomplishments for the federal court.

But turnover on the District's top team challenged this agreement. The corporation counsel who had negotiated the agreement was appointed to a judgeship in 2003. His replacement disagreed with the structure, believing that the lawyers needed more independence so they could rein in CFSA mistakes. I had a very different view, believing that divided authority had led to stalemate and damage to children, while a strong and accountable agency was the best way to achieve success. As I explained my views, I realized how different the reform project looked to those of us on board when the agency first came back from court receivership, compared with those entering now. To me, having lawyers check on social workers was a reprise of the District's old, failed strategy of fragmenting authority and promoting blame. But to someone just entering the debate, my perspective, which I considered a commitment to dramatic change, could look like defending the (recent) status quo. When I left the agency, discussions about how to best mesh the roles of lawyers and social workers were still continuing.

Services to Children and Families

To achieve child welfare goals including child well-being and prompt movement to permanent homes, the IP required us to improve access to some services that were the province of other agencies, such as health, mental health, and substance abuse treatment. All along, we had been discussing these requirements with the mayor's office and budget staff; once the IP was done, we briefed colleagues in the other agencies and asked for their help. Despite everyone's goodwill, progress was slow.

Take mental health. The District's mental health agency was returning from court-ordered receivership just as CFSA was. It too was a work in progress, beginning with virtually no community-based services for children and families. The director was eager to figure out how to meet the challenge. An opportunity came when the Senate asked us to identify specific federal appropriations that the District needed to improve child welfare; CFSA and the mental health agency jointly asked for funds to improve mental health services to children in foster care.

Even with the money, progress was tough. For one thing, since our special appropriation was temporary, we needed to develop services that could be funded by Medicaid after the special appropriation ended. But Medicaid as implemented in the District had intricate claiming and payment rules that made it difficult to support the right programs. Other obstacles were limited staff time and expertise in both agencies; a tendency for the mental health referral staff to screen out CFSA children, even when the higher-ups in both agencies had tried to change the policy; and the failure of CFSA social workers to make referrals, in part because they assumed the screening out would continue. As we tried to shift money to the mental health agency's new programs and away from our old contracts, some observers thought we forfeited services that were good for children without successfully replacing them.

Health care was another tangled puzzle. As we tried to meet the IP deadline for an improvement plan, we found the complexity of the task overwhelming. The ideal system would provide emergency testing and services to children (including forensic testing, to determine whether abuse took place), assess children's health and developmental needs as soon as they came into care, make sure children got the services they needed while in care, link smoothly to their physician in the community before and after, and fit into the District's financing and provider system for Medicaid, while also filling Medicaid's gaps in services. Once we knew what we needed, we had to design a contract that fit the District's procurement rules and avoid paying for services that Medicaid should have covered. When I left in spring 2004, we were still working on our solution.

When I posed some of these challenges to our national advisory panel, just after completing the health care assessment in December 2003, one expert surprised me by saying it was almost impossible to link the complex health care system to the complex child welfare system, no matter how much goodwill and collaborative spirit went into trying. His advice was to pick a narrower goal, such as making the child's health care accessible to foster parents while the child lives with them.

Probably our clearest success in developing new services was a small pilot substance abuse program for mothers with young children, operated and designed by the Family Court. The program targeted mothers facing first-time neglect charges. We enthusiastically put up the funding for the program, which permitted the child to live with the mother during her inpatient treatment. However, by the time I left, we did not yet have a large-scale partnership with the District's substance abuse agency.

Lessons from Success

When a social worker talks to a mother and father about the plan for their child, when a nurse responds to a child's health crisis or a substance abuse counselor works with a parent, and when a grandparent or foster parent sits down to dinner with the children they are caring for, we are on the front lines of child welfare. From the research, we know that all these interactions can affect children's development and family stability, for good or ill. While the studied sites took somewhat different approaches to strengthening these interactions, several common lessons emerged.

Include Caregivers, Service Providers, and Social Workers

In much ordinary conversation and media coverage of child welfare, the agency social worker is front and center. Yet, as we have seen, social workers are far from all-powerful when it comes to affecting children's lives and development. They can't substitute for a loving family or a terrific early childhood educator, although they can certainly help or hurt a child's chances of connecting with either of those. The sites illustrate that front-line reform that truly affects children will need to improve all three dimensions: social worker practice, settings where children live, and services.

Sometimes, reform starts with more than one of these dimensions in mind; sometimes, it starts with one and expands to address the others. In Alabama, reformers saw a clear connection between social worker practice and reforms in settings and services. They believed that, before the reform, social workers consistently chose restrictive, long-distance placements for children over home or nearby family foster care. Without in-between service options, social workers removed children who could have stayed home if their families had received a little help. So Alabama's early reforms focused both on retraining workers and on crafting new services, individualized to meet the needs of each family and child. A summary of the reform's early years describes how new social worker practices and new services were linked:

> As the R.C. reform was implemented, county DHR workers and providers together learned to design services and supports unique to each family and child, crafted collaboratively by the worker, the family and often an extensive network of provider partners. Sometimes the team put together a mix of existing services, including some from outside the traditional system. (Bazelon Center for Mental Health Law 1998, 61)

Among many examples of these new services were

- "coaches for children with emotional problems to help them improve their self-confidence and develop success in . . . normal social activities" and
- "home-based substance abuse treatment for parents to help them recognize how the abuse causes them to neglect or maltreat their child . . . and helping them get involved in outpatient or inpatient treatment" (Bazelon Center 1998, 62).

Change can also begin with improved services or settings and then spread to practice. The District's substance abuse program for mothers and children blended an improvement in setting—children living with their mothers—with high-intensity services to the parent. Social workers had to be willing to refer families, and as the QSR pointed out, they had to help parents plan for continued success after the program ended. But even with minimal practice changes, the setting was likely much better for children than prior arrangements. Another potential improvement in setting, the District's guardianship legislation, stalled for a couple of years until social work practice caught up with the legislation and social workers (and judges and lawyers) began encouraging kin to take part.

Our earliest successes for D.C. children came from changing settings: moving children from emergency shelters and group homes into foster and kin families. Many of our strategies to achieve this goal did not involve social workers at all, as when we closed emergency shelters, reduced the number of congregate care slots purchased for young children, paid higher rates to foster parents willing to take in children at night, and simplified interstate licensing for kin who wanted to care for children. And while we made some initial efforts to change social worker practice (for example, we required more levels of approval to place young children in group settings), the first successes made it easier to change practice later on. Once social workers saw kin come forward to care for children who had been in the emergency shelters, they were more confident kin might be available for other children in congregate care.

Where should front-line reform start? It can start with practice, settings, or services, or with all three at once. Wherever it starts, the effective reformer is almost certain to circle back to the others quickly to take advantage of positive links or forestall negative ones. Reformers may choose to start by trying to remove the biggest roadblock to children's well-being or by seizing low-hanging fruit. Both helped determine the focus on case practice in Alabama and on shelters and other unacceptable settings for children in the District.

Change Culture and Values to Change Practice

In one way or another, all the sites demonstrate the powerful connection between the underlying culture and values of social workers and the specifics of day-to-day practice in child welfare. Culture is not merely an abstraction, a theory untethered to the real world. Rather, it shapes the decisions that hundreds of individual social workers make in uncertain and difficult situations.

When decisions driven by these values conflict with the reform strategies, reform will slow despite changes in organizational operations or structure. Thus, the District Council can appropriate resources for subsidized guardianship, but social workers who don't believe in it won't recruit families, and the money will go unspent. And a social worker imbued with the District's emergency-driven culture will miss the need to look ahead to a mother's graduation date from inpatient drug treatment, anticipating neither her need for housing if she succeeds nor her need for a back-up plan if she drops out. In Alabama, on the other hand, the problem with the culture was not so much an attachment to emergencies as harsh judgments of poor families and an assumption they couldn't change, summarized by James Tucker as "cultural judgments translated not into official policy or procedure but into practice . . . . which has a bad impact on poor families."

Yet the sites illustrate how sustained efforts can change a deeply embedded culture. Directly addressing the values and culture is one approach. In Alabama, the reform leaders articulated new values, provided intensive off-site training to all, instituted one-on-one coaching from outside consultants, and coached and trained supervisors and local managers along with line workers. In Utah, the right mix included training, the Milestone Plan (which articulated the new culture and values), and the practice model (which translated it into the daily work of each social worker). As Jerry Milner argues, once values truly change, the reform is solidly anchored: Commissioner Nachman could urge social workers to place more children in foster care, but with their new perspective, they simply didn't see the need as often as they had before.

Another culture-changing strategy we have seen before is measurement, which sends a strong signal about values, and its close partner, demonstrating success. Measurement alone jump-started change in the sites, as the QSRs and performance measures based on administrative data communicated the new values. When measurement identified successes, it had a redoubled effect by countering the old culture's message that change is not possible. For example, by reaching 100 guardianships, we sent the message that extended families were prepared to make a lifetime commitment to children. And the strategy of changing the culture through success, first small and then larger wins, went far beyond measurement. Most dramatically, Alabama's strategy of achieving success in the pilot counties convinced skeptics that the new culture could deliver very different results for children than the old one did and could do so countywide.

Finally, one other widespread culture-bending strategy is to create new decisionmaking and information-gathering procedures, usually team-based, that provide a structure for bringing the new values to bear.

By bringing transparency, more information, and an explicit focus on values to decisions that might otherwise be made by caseworkers in isolation, these approaches speed change when unspoken assumptions are a mainstay of the old culture. In Alabama, Marty Beyer saw her work as a coach in part as creating a structured way for caseworker and supervisor to reflect together systematically about the child's and parents' needs. In the District, I hoped the facilitated family team meetings would serve this purpose. In our policy meetings, too, bringing a team together to articulate the key choices and decisions unearthed deeply embedded assumptions so we could directly counter them—like the assumption that adoption should only be planned for after a judge had formally changed a child's plan.

If the sites offer hope that changing culture is possible, they also suggest that it takes a great deal of time. The QSR report assessing District cases after our first two years indicated only the very beginning of an impact. And after early successes in the pilot counties, Alabama took years to remodel the culture in the largest urban area and then statewide. John Kotter, reflecting on the private-sector change experience, argues that speed is a counterproductive goal for culture change and that for lasting effect, "cultural change comes last, not first":

> Culture changes only after you have successfully altered people's actions, after the new behavior produces some group benefit for a period of time, and after people see the connection between the new actions and the performance improvement. (Kotter 1996, 155–56)

While certain attitudes and behaviors may change early, truly "anchoring change in a culture" requires demonstrated results, repeated articulation of the new principles and practices, turnover of people attached to the old values, and careful attention to succession and promotion of people who hold the new values. An emphasis on the long term is certainly consistent with experience in the study sites.

Social Workers Need Skills, Detailed Expectations, and More Supportive Administrative Systems

Changing values and beliefs is not enough to enable front-line workers and caregivers to achieve better results. Social workers and others on the front lines usually need highly specific skills to make their work serve the desired new values. In the many child welfare reforms that seek to change culture so workers are more open to engaging birth families (including those in Alabama and Utah), new skills are needed to relate to parents while still keeping the child safe. Marty Beyer sought to teach Alabama workers and supervisors the skill of building a bond with parents that is grounded in the child's safety. She notes that when child welfare staff lack these skills, they either blame the child's behavior or address the family's needs (say, a new roof) as a substitute for the child's needs (parents who don't yell at or hit him). John Mattingly in New York sees a related skill challenge: workers who don't know how to raise a child's safety directly while engaging with a parent. His ChildStat case presentations are one of many strategies for building these skills at all levels of the child welfare agency. Clearly, it is possible to combine a deep belief in parents' capacity to change with a rock-bottom commitment to children's safety, but it takes sophisticated skills to get there.

Besides skills, workers need clear expectations, so they are not constantly guessing what the new culture means in their daily work. Utah illustrates most dramatically the effort to work through the desired values step by step, giving workers guidance through the practice model on turning the values into action. Clear expectations can also help align the perspectives of the many different people involved in complex child welfare processes, such as social workers from different parts of the agency, judges, and lawyers. This was a goal D.C. tried to achieve in our adoption policy, by clearly signaling the expectations across organizational boundaries.

Implementing a new culture and new practices typically requires supportive administrative systems. As Jerry Milner points out, if training leads social workers to engage families and identify needs but the system prevents them from funding services to meet those needs, nothing will change. In Alabama, a central problem was the rigid state contract system that would not allow counties to shape new services to meet family needs—a problem solved by using flex-funds and hiring county resource developers. In the District, the difficulty of ending children's stays in the CFSA building illustrated a similar point. Until we made services more available for families in crisis and recruited foster families for emergency placements, no one social worker, no matter how skilled and principled, could be sure that a child on her caseload would not end up there.

Reducing Caseloads Is Crucial, but not Sufficient

In both the District and some Alabama jurisdictions, particularly Birmingham, high caseloads before reform had immediate and obvious effects: children who were never even visited, investigations left to languish for weeks or months, piles of cases assigned to no one, and even the most conscientious social workers coping with emergencies full time. Less obvious, though, is how high caseloads damage the service delivery culture even after the caseloads are lowered.

First, coping with impossible demands can erode a sense of accountability for quality or results. As we have seen, long-time social workers remember Alabama's old system as one in which scarcity made it acceptable to do whatever you could, however little or much that was. In Birmingham, local officials told the *Birmingham News* that they simply postponed investigating neglect reports when caseloads were too high for social workers to get to them.[1]

High caseloads in the District also contributed to an exclusive focus on emergencies at the expense of the child's continuing or future needs. The QSR identified countless ways that this emergency focus continued to distort social work decisions even once caseloads came down. Social workers and supervisors who have learned one way of operating in chaos do not automatically know how to shift gears when caseloads come down, nor do they necessarily notice that they are operating in an emergency mode. A worker who has for years juggled so many cases that she could only respond to emergencies must now learn how to plan ahead, to look for transition points and trouble spots, and to work with the people who care about the child to plan for a permanent family.

Treating Social Workers Fairly Improves the Agency Culture, While Scapegoating Drags It Backwards

How social workers are treated in the case of a mistake or a tragedy can strongly affect agency culture. The evidence is scanty, since it is not possible to replay a particular incident and see how it would turn out with different leadership responses. But the site experiences suggest that when workers are punished by termination, suspension, or public shame, and when the punishment is not linked to a pattern of inadequate performance but instead to a single high-visibility event, all their likely responses undercut the effort to inculcate a new culture. On the other hand, when leaders clarify expectations, seek to link personnel actions to fair and clear standards, and take responsibility for explaining the complicated systems issues to the press and public even at the cost of coming under criticism themselves, reform is more likely to proceed.

In the District, based on what I saw in my early months, social workers' responses to the history of turmoil and public finger-pointing included cynicism about the values and intentions of agency leadership, a high value placed on personal loyalty among staff who "had each other's backs," and a reluctance to work in the riskiest parts of the agency matched by a preference for areas such as adoption that were seen as less risky. I thought the history of finger-pointing had also contributed to the focus on emergencies. The stories I heard about social workers' and supervisors' positive experiences all involved emergencies, which seemed to be the only times they felt reasonably protected from second-guessing: they couldn't have been doing something else because they were dealing with a crisis. Finally, recruitment to CFSA, always a challenge, became even harder after a tragedy.

In Utah, when enforcement of the settlement's hundreds of performance measures seemed harsh and arbitrary, staff reactions included despair and reluctance to put their ideas forward (the clinical experts who chose to "hide out" until things got better). In addition, the pattern Ken Patterson saw when he arrived, where workers followed the lead of lawyers, judges, and experts rather than thinking for themselves, may have reflected a climate that felt arbitrary and dangerous. In all the cases, the kind of social work practices encouraged by the QSRs—creativity, engagement with the child and family, leadership rather than passivity, thinking ahead rather than waiting for an emergency—are likely far harder when workers also feel obligated to cover themselves in case bad luck strikes.

With partial success, the leaders in the turnaround sites took several steps to counter the damaging historical patterns. They sought to clarify expectations up front, most comprehensively in the Utah practice model. Similarly, in the District's adoption policy, we responded to worker requests for guidance about when to push back against a judicial action. The leaders also briefed the press about the context and the reasons systems rather than individual workers were at fault and sought to make personnel decisions fairly and based on evidence over a period of time. Finally, to make these strategies stick, they usually relied on strong relationships with the mayor or governor built on prior discussions and information-sharing.

Despite these good faith efforts, I found myself only partly successful at countering the past history. For one thing, media, legislative, and public indignation directed at individual social workers, often named in public coverage, can be searing despite high-level support. John Mattingly in New York City puts the consequences for workers this way:

> The daily pressure of the media takes a terrible toll. A worker who was suspended in one of the cases went home and her door had a sign "child killer." An older worker, one of our best, was taking the bus back from a visit and wearing her agency ID—she had to leave the bus between stops because people were yelling at her.

For another, even if leaders do try to honestly judge whether a worker is at fault, social workers will often hear a different message shaped by their own experience. Where the leader sees a clear pattern of failed performance, social workers may see an arbitrary decision to penalize a worker who just got unlucky. Worse, they may see higher-ups protecting themselves by scapegoating workers. And, as I look back at my own decisions, the social workers may be right, for it is hard to be confident that decisions are made well when information is skimpy and mixed and outside pressure to take tough action is intense.

Culture Change in Child Welfare Must Reach across Organizational Boundaries

The child welfare system's complexity means that culture change on the front lines often must reach far more people than the agency's social workers. Colleagues in other systems such as lawyers and judges, community agency staff, and substance abuse counselors need to change their values and practices in parallel to social workers, supported by systems changes and clear expectations consistent with those in the child welfare agency. Not surprisingly, such linked changes are difficult, and successes in the sites are partial and reflect intensive effort.

In the District, the most successful example of paired culture change across two systems was our work with the local judges, aimed at a clearer focus on permanent homes for children, a stronger preference for families rather than group homes, and a commitment to engaging the child's family up front. While certainly a work in progress, the accomplishments of this partnership—from family team meetings to increased adoption and guardianships—were significant for children. To achieve these results, though, many strands had to come together: the parallel reforms (Family Court Act and CFSA Establishment Act) that jump-started change in each system around the same time, the personal partnership I established with the presiding judge, and the additional resources that both systems received to support the reforms.

Better meshing the work of social workers and the lawyers who represent the agency also came up as a reform strategy. In Utah, Ken Patterson thought the problems he saw on arrival partly emerged from a powerful legal culture, which dominated the thinking of new and inexperienced social workers, and led to social worker practices inconsistent with the new reform values. For example, lawyers sometimes urged social workers not to talk to parents before the court hearing, counter to the social work goal of engaging the family in protecting the child. Over the tenure of Patterson and his successor, Richard Anderson, these issues were resolved through the new practice model, which guided how the two professions should work together. In the District, the reform strategy was to meld government social workers and lawyers into a team that could plan together for children, a goal only partly achieved when I left.

Where the reform vision includes an emphasis on community, social workers need to reach out to community organizations—and those organizations in turn may need to modify their own culture or values in order to respond. In the District, while agency and community leaders agreed whole-heartedly on the broad vision, we did not manage during my years there to fully implement it, achieving neither clear expectations nor supportive administrative systems. While some of our problems were no doubt specific to the District's history, national experience suggests that meshing agency and community reforms may not be easy anywhere. An evaluation of community-based child welfare reform in four sites found that community partnerships' accomplishments were significant but hard to sustain and "figuring out how to consistently engage these partners in the ongoing work will be a continuing issue" (Center for Community Partnerships in Child Welfare and Center for the Study of Social Policy 2006, 21).

Unfinished Business: Linking Services Effectively

We've just seen that child welfare agencies can be successful at reforms that stretch across organizational boundaries, but only with difficulty. Such cross-cutting reforms demand parallel culture change, supportive administrative systems, and clear and consistent expectations in two or more organizations. These difficulties have big consequences for children's lives, because the services that they and their families need the most are generally funded and offered outside the child welfare agency, including education, early education, and health and mental health services for children and affordable stable housing, mental health, substance abuse, and domestic violence services for parents.

As the District and the other study sites illustrate, connections to these outside systems are often overwhelmingly complex to set up and maintain, and the services that children and families need may be unavailable or badly matched to their needs or location. Each service system has its own service delivery network, including a mix of public and contracted providers, its own federal and state fiscal structures, its own statutory framework (federal, state, and local), and its own quality standards. For the District, merging all these at once, on a tight deadline, with so many other demands competing for our attention, proved overwhelming. For example, we could not figure out how to give children initial and follow-up health care efficiently and responsively while billing appropriate costs to Medicaid and our CFSA appropriation for health coverage.

Why is linking these service systems so hard? First, organizational culture can defeat practice changes in service systems, as we have seen in child welfare. Therefore, if the cultures of all agencies involved do not initially align with the planned collaboration, it will be an uphill battle. If the mental health agency has historically given priority to the most seriously mentally ill, rather than to children whose distress results as much from trauma as from an underlying mental illness, then referrals that seem urgent to child welfare workers may languish at the end of the mental health agency's queue. Similarly, substance abuse counselors and child welfare workers will likely see the world differently in the absence of deliberate work to bring the organizational cultures together. "Although it is easy to understand how child welfare staff come to focus their attention primarily on the children and substance abuse counselors focus theirs primarily on the parents, isolating family members in this way tends to provoke tensions among service staff and anger and alienation among family members" (Young et al. 2007, 3–4).

Researchers studying how to implement the recent federal mandate that young children in child welfare be referred to early intervention services (for developmental disabilities) similarly note the need to bring the cultures and skills of the systems' caseworkers into alignment. They find that child welfare workers focus on the child's safety, while early intervention providers are "speech language therapists, occupational therapists, and physical therapists" who are used to providing a service highly valued by parents, not a court-ordered requirement that parents may see as intrusive or hostile (Barth et al. 2008, vii.).

At the same time, resources are a major constraint in all service systems. In fact, because child welfare can rely on substantial federal funding streams unavailable to many other services, the resource crunch may be far worse for its partner systems. Noting the ubiquity of these funding gaps, the four-site demonstration cited earlier found that

> the sites wrestled continuously with service availability. During the implementation period, states faced major fiscal crises that affected the budgets of the child welfare agencies and those of partners and providers. . . . Neighborhood networks found it difficult to generate the resources that could significantly expand the services available for families over the longer term. (Center for Community Partnerships in Child Welfare and Center for the Study of Social Policy 2006, 23)

These funding constraints can mean that no services are available for child welfare families. Or, almost as difficult, funding constraints can raise painful equity questions about whether child welfare families should move ahead of other clients in line. Such questions in turn push submerged tensions about mission to the forefront. When there are not enough housing vouchers or substance-abuse treatment slots to go around, should a mother who abuses her children have the first opportunity to access them? When resources are extremely inadequate, aligning agency missions to reach a shared view of who should be served is even more painful, politically sensitive, and time-consuming than if a larger share of people who need the service could be helped.

The partner services may also be misaligned with the needs of children in the child welfare system for a host of other reasons, such as provider skills, or geographic, linguistic, or cultural distribution of services. In our work on mental health services, we found too few trained providers willing to work with children who had experienced sexual abuse or children whose behavior was violent, particularly if Medicaid was paying. Either too few professionals were trained in the relevant specialties or not enough of them wanted to work with impoverished children or children in the child welfare system.

Adding to the difficulty of building effective collaborations between large systems is the extraordinary complexity of federal and state funding streams, budget rules, and laws that govern them. In the District story, this complexity particularly shadowed our efforts to link to health and mental health services. Most health and some mental health services for children in foster care are financially supported by Medicaid, a federal-state matching program with extremely complex rules about which services are available for which children for what period. Although Medicaid has more generous mental health coverage than many private plans, gaps are nonetheless frequent: "studies document difficulties finding providers, long delays in getting treatment, and difficult referral systems" for children with special health care needs (Aron and Loprest 2007, 81). Mental health services for parents are even scarcer and more complex to find and fund. For low-income parents, private insurance—if they have it—likely includes scant mental health coverage or none; Medicaid is available only for the very poorest parents, and its coverage of mental health services for adults may also be limited.

Scarce resources interact with complicated rules to redouble the difficulty of partnerships between child welfare and the other services families need. According to the four-site CPPC study,

> improved access and availability to essential services—especially mental health and domestic violence services—can be achieved . . . but remain a challenge to sustain. . . . Agency funding is limited and is often restricted to specified populations, presenting powerful barriers to effectively connecting families in the child welfare system to the services they need. (Center for Community Partnerships in Child Welfare and Center for the Study of Social Policy 2006, 21)

In the face of these challenges, what can a state or local child welfare agency do to link children and families to needed services? One approach is to focus internally on social worker practice, enhancing social workers' ability to create a team among providers working with a parent, to negotiate their own deals with colleagues in other agencies, and to improvise informal services—a neighbor to encourage a depressed mother when no clinician is available. While surely better than giving up, these solutions likely fall far short of what equally skilled social workers could accomplish if they had services and systems supporting them, not working at cross-purposes.

Another approach is for the child welfare agency to take control itself, which often tempted us in the District since designing and paying for a needed service was easier and quicker than linking to the health, mental health, or education systems. But such an approach is also more expensive, subject to criticism for being duplicative and wasteful, and most likely a guarantee that the new program will stay small because of dollar constraints. The successful drug court program, which CFSA funded at the court's request, was a small program that worked well but was unlikely to grow, absent a funding source beyond District appropriations. Similarly, we improved children's health care modestly by hiring a doctor and nurses at CFSA, but the bigger achievements that could have come from revamping the system eluded us.

A third possibility is for state agency leaders to work their way through these layers of complexity to reach partnership agreements across systems, jurisdiction by jurisdiction. Unfortunately, even if the obstacles described do not preclude effective partnership agreements, they certainly make them very hard. And the most troubled and overwhelmed child welfare agencies will be least able to spare the energy to untangle the knots. So the best opportunity to slice through this frustrating complexity lies with the federal government, which could fill national gaps in funding and revise complex rules for the top priority services.

The Fostering Connections to Success and Increasing Adoptions Act of 2008 includes provisions intended to improve child welfare agencies' links to health and education, although neither expanded funding nor simplification is a major focus. To improve links to health, the law requires that states, together with the state Medicaid agency, develop a plan for overseeing and coordinating health care services to children in foster care. Having this provision in federal law will likely improve state child welfare directors' ability to encourage state Medicaid directors to identify and resolve issues, but the provision does not change the underlying rules or budget constraints that make resolution difficult. To improve links to education, the law requires that each child in foster care have a plan for educational stability and that every school-age child for whom federal reimbursement is claimed be a full-time elementary or secondary school student (with very narrow exceptions). The law offers states some additional federal reimbursement for the cost of transporting children from their foster care placement to their original school (HHS, Children's Bureau 2008c). But, states can lose funding under the new provisions if children otherwise eligible for federal reimbursement are not in school full time; the Congressional Budget Office estimates that this provision will reduce federal reimbursements to states by more than $40 million a year (Congressional Budget Office 2008). Both the health and education provisions are worth tracking for future evidence of effectiveness.

Conclusion

This chapter has illustrated how the experiences of children in foster care can be improved by strengthening the capacity of front-line workers, including social workers, caregivers, and service providers. Improving front-line capacity is difficult, but the study sites offer examples of success in all these domains. Most often, agencies with a long history of failure require multifaceted strategies: no one program or one initiative can fix all the interrelated problems of culture and structure.

At the same time, the sites also hint at persistent failures, particularly in providing important services across several agencies and funding streams. Because this failure can be beyond the capacity of local and state programs to remedy alone, recommendations in the concluding chapter propose federal reform as well, to back up improved state and local leadership and service delivery.

10

Recommendations

M uch of this book has emphasized successful experiences of child welfare agency leaders who have changed systems for the better and improved children's and families' lives. In these examples, leaders' sense of responsibility for change and belief that their agencies can make a difference are important to their success. Without these qualities, agencies' view of themselves as powerless too often comes true. Yet important as it is for leaders to take responsibility, evidence from the study sites and the broader research also identifies obstacles in national policy and local politics that even the best and luckiest leaders rarely overcome completely.

This chapter addresses those obstacles. First is the absence of national investment in crucial and proven prevention and treatment services for parents and children. Second, while the expansion of federal adoption subsidies has paid off in increased adoptions from foster care, the federal policy framework for birth families has not improved in tandem, leaving the nation's child welfare system unprepared to ensure that all children grow up in permanent homes. Third, despite the intense public demand for children to be kept safe, the nation has not mounted a large-scale, national effort that would draw on the successful experience of safety initiatives in other fields to reduce deaths from child abuse and neglect. Fourth, federal financing remains ill-matched to the real problems of child welfare. Fifth, the local and state political context for child welfare reform is often turbulent, reactive to crisis or tragedy, and ill-suited to improving performance over the long haul. Sixth, agencies' ability to learn from quantitative and qualitative information, which is central to state and local improvement, can be enhanced by a national research agenda. Finally, the study sites suggest an important role for agency leadership, yet leaders cannot be developed solely from within.

The Rhythm of Reform: Progress, Failures, and Transition in the District

Many of these national issues, as well as progress and obstacles unique to the District, marked my third year there.

My Choice to Move On

Several times during my years in the District, I had felt exhausted and desperate to move on. I did not want to leave when the agency was unstable and progress so fragile, but I talked to a trusted colleague about what a transition might look like when the right moment came, and how to carry it out to enhance the agency's forward movement. Just envisioning that future helped me carry on.

As 2003 came to an end, with the management team now working smoothly together and positive reports from the court monitor, I thought I had finally accomplished what I came to do, the initial turnaround that gave the agency a strong base for continued improvement. About the same time, I identified a strong successor when CFSA's extremely talented chief of staff became willing to take on the role of director. The mayor was enthusiastic about appointing her, so we made the plan public in the winter, with my departure date set for the end of April 2004. We had a couple of months for what we hoped would be a smooth and well-planned transition.

Continuing Failures, Continuing Progress

In February 2004, two and a half years into the reforms, District police responded to a call about children left alone and found six children including a baby in a squalid apartment, "littered with dirty clothes and smell[ing] strongly of urine," with the children scrounging for raw food.[1] During the previous year, the mother had been under the agency's supervision as an in-home case (that is, her children lived with her) for several months while she was pregnant with the baby. After the baby's birth, the mother was again reported for neglect. Her mother (the children's grandmother) agreed to care for the children informally, but then returned the children to her daughter, telling the press afterwards that her daughter had said the agency approved the return. Shortly thereafter, the mother left the children alone.

The following month, the medical examiner reported that the recent death of a baby had been caused by her mother, who dipped her finger in the methadone she was receiving in a methadone maintenance program and gave it to the baby to stop her crying. CFSA and the public health agency had both been involved in the baby's early months because the baby was born addicted. After making sure that the mother and baby had appropriate services (such as the public health visiting nurse), CFSA had closed the case.

I reacted in two ways at the time, and a third in retrospect. First, I worried about the practices highlighted by the first case. We had worked closely with the mother while her case was open, providing more intensive casework than the pre-reform CFSA had; but the choice to close the case right after the baby's birth and the handling of the investigation undercut the work that had gone before. Even before the public attention, we had been planning to strengthen the quality of investigations and hold facilitated family team meetings, which I expect would have greatly improved the information available for decisionmaking—but the pace of improvement was still slow.

Second, I wanted to ensure that media attention to such cases would not push us toward less involvement with families. These cases occurred at a time when the Family Court judges and other legal advocates and attorneys were concerned that abuse and neglect court filings were down. Other jurisdictions, such as New York and Alabama, had seen much sharper declines in court cases and foster care caseloads after reform and interpreted them as successes. Judges and lawyers, however, traditionally worry that if parents are not brought to court—that is, if the agency handles reported abuse or neglect through other services and in-home supervision rather than a formal court filing—that children will not be safe. And the two cases occurring close together raised alarms in the press:

Is this [the left-alone case] an isolated case or just the tip of the iceberg? . . . . In light of the deplorable situation with [this] family, it is fair to ask whether the agency is exercising its best judgment. . . . how can the public be sure these children are out of danger? That is a question the mayor, the D.C. Council, and courts should be asking.[2]

Looking back now, I have a third reaction. In both cases, I wish we could have been closer to meeting the challenge described in chapter 9: achieving links and parallel reforms across crucial service systems like substance abuse, early childhood services, and mental health. For both mothers, substance abuse and a new baby were part of the equation, and perhaps depression as well. When the mother of a new baby and several young children leaves a filthy apartment to get high, clinical experts would likely see a mother self-medicating her postnatal depression. But CFSA's links to a mental health agency with an equally troubled past were still nascent when I left, and we had just begun to talk with the District's newly hired head of substance abuse programs about building a collaboration.

Around the same time these highly public cases showcased the agency's deficiencies, the court monitor issued two performance summaries that demonstrated substantial progress: the quality service review and an evaluation of how well the agency was meeting implementation plan requirements. The implementation plan report found that CFSA achieved 13 of the 15 required outcome standards for June and September 2003, completed 24 of 35 implementation strategies, and was making progress on the remaining 11.

As a result of these reports, the press covered the bigger context of progress as well as the troubling individual cases. The day after its editorial questioning CFSA's judgment about child safety, the *Washington Post* described the implementation plan report under the headline "Child Welfare Agency Showing Progress, Monitor's Report Says"[3] and quoted the court monitor's view that "The overall assessment is positive . . . The agency has demonstrated continued progress in many areas," including the large reduction in average caseload and the "incredible accomplishment" of licensing all group homes and independent living facilities "for the first time in the agency's history." She put the failures in the context of work still to be accomplished: "You still have cases where, despite the efforts of the agency, they're not making decisions that fully protect children and families."

Leadership Transition and Unfinished Business

My successor and I had a couple of months to plan a transition intended to maintain the momentum for reform. Because leadership turnover at

CFSA had typically been crisis-driven and led to turmoil and wholesale management departures, we needed to emphasize continuity of vision and of the team. But we couldn't afford complacency and had to make it clear that the next leader would keep CFSA on the same challenging path of dramatic change.

Unfortunately, just when I wanted to pass the job on to her with all the big problems under control, we realized that we had plunged backwards in our ability to conduct prompt and high-quality investigations of abuse and neglect reports. The backlog of investigations not completed in 30 days skyrocketed, reaching levels close to the court monitor's baseline finding of 800 back in May 2001. Most alarming was that we had not seen this failure coming. We didn't react to gradually worsening numbers until the court monitor highlighted investigations in the implementation plan report as the only indicator on which we were regressing. During the summer and fall, we knew that improvement in the timeliness of investigations had stalled, but we had expected as much while we worked full-tilt on quality and completeness, so no alarm bells went off. But we were not prepared when, in the winter, we planned training for every investigator and discovered that pulling staff out of the office for training was the last straw for timely investigations.

Recognizing the gravity of the problem, we set up a team to develop both emergency responses—such as temporarily assigning staff and managers from other offices to investigations—and longer-term fixes. We also stepped up recruitment for a director of investigations and hired an outside expert to take on the job temporarily until we found the permanent head. Progress in hiring was slow, however, and so was progress in erasing the backlog, because hundreds of new reports flooded in each month. Neither problem was solved by the time I left.

On my very last day, up until the moment I walked into my goodbye party, I was still negotiating with the lawyers and the mayor's office to resolve the disagreement over legal structure. I couldn't reach resolution and had to pass this problem on to my successor as well. Other loose ends and failures that remained for the new director included an agency budget request supported by community and provider organizations and the court monitor but met with mixed reactions from the District Council; a contract reform that still was not in place; an unfinished strategy for improving practice quality; and an incomplete response to the lessons from the two failed cases.

Yet, all these frustrations dimmed as I walked into the goodbye party. As each of my colleagues from inside and outside the agency spoke about what they took away from our three years of work together, I regained my hope that we had changed something important even if innumerable problems remained. CFSA and its partner organizations now had greater capacity to help children, because so many different people were energized by their shared commitment to ideals, practiced at turning that commitment into real, measurable change, and proud of the improvements already made in children's lives.

As I write this in spring 2009, CFSA is on its fourth director in the five years since I left. Many different reasons have prompted the turnover, including changes in political leadership, opportunities in other jurisdictions, and the toll that child tragedies take on an agency. All four directors were part of the management team that I had recruited, perhaps illustrating the strength of that team, or perhaps the difficulty of recruiting leaders to child welfare turnarounds. In retrospect, the time that my successor and I had to plan a careful transition seems a luxury.

The District's child welfare system has also had a difficult 2008. In January, after the bodies of four children were found murdered by their mother, Mayor Adrian Fenty dismissed six CFSA social workers and supervisors for mishandling the investigation of a child abuse report called in by a school social worker worried about the children. During the spring, reports of abuse and neglect shot up, at the same time as social worker vacancies increased and recruiting lagged. According to the mayor's chief lawyer, the backlog of overdue investigations had reached 1,600 cases by July.[4] In July 2008, the plaintiffs' attorney filed a contempt motion, arguing that "after years of planning, reorganization, investment of additional resources and capacity building to improve the system, the District's executive leadership has allowed the child welfare system to return to a dysfunctional state."[5]

By the fall, the District and the plaintiffs had signed an agreement to avert the contempt filing. At a November 2008 progress hearing, U.S. District Judge Hogan "said he was pleased to hear good news" from the agency, though noting that the progress was "a temporary shoring up of the agency," not a complete resolution.[6] A few months later, the flurry of legal activity resumed, with the District arguing that it should be released from court supervision and the plaintiffs arguing that the District should be held in contempt. At a court hearing in

February 2009, Hogan "scolded the District's attorney general . . . and told him that the city's child welfare agency is not ready to stand on its own."[7]

What happens next? The District's most recent approved implementation plan, agreed to by the parties in 2007, contemplated full compliance with the court's expectations by December 31, 2008. The District did not achieve that deadline, and the parties have not agreed on a new one or even on how to approach creating a new plan. While (according to one observer) the District's child welfare system has regained some of its balance after the turmoil of 2008 and functions better than before the reform began in 2001, it is still far from achieving the full hopes of reform. Reform in the District, as elsewhere, is clearly the work of many years, even decades.

Recommendations

What federal policy or investments, foundation interventions, or local political actions could help the District and other jurisdictions reach successful and stable reform with fewer detours along the way? The rest of this chapter makes recommendations to answer that question.

Taken together, and combined with strong agency performance, the recommendations would go a long way toward addressing the national child welfare failures described earlier. Individual recommendations target specific problems such as the stagnation of national efforts to reunite children safely with birth families and the unacceptably high level of child deaths from abuse and neglect. In combination, the recommendations could improve performance more broadly, addressing persistent child welfare problems that have multiple causes and treatments. For example, the combination of investment in substance abuse and mental health services, investment in high-quality early childhood development and parenting programs, and more extensive support for birth and extended families might reduce the overrepresentation of minority children in foster care. A more research-based approach to children's safety, more effective inclusion of governors and mayors, and an improved federal approach to funding and technical assistance might create a more hospitable environment for transforming troubled child welfare systems without court involvement.

National Investment in Proven Prevention and Treatment Services and Stronger Delivery Systems

As we have seen, persuasive research evidence demonstrates the payoffs of certain early services to families, including treatment for maternal depression and parental substance abuse, and two-generational services that counsel and support parents while providing early education to young children. It would seem natural to expect major federal investment in these proven services and easy access for families at risk of abuse or neglect, and those already in the system.

But those expectations would be wrong. The mental health, substance abuse treatment, and early childhood service systems are typically even more starved for resources than child welfare agencies, and access to them is difficult for child welfare families. This is partly because of the challenges of mission, culture, and administrative complexity, all intensified by lack of resources, that plague efforts to link large systems together. And it is partly because the child welfare agency, when it tries to go it alone and skip collaboration, is not only underfunded but also often poorly equipped to deliver the needed services. Its mission is too crisis-oriented to engage families early or keep them involved in services over time, and the focus on specific incidents makes it hard to diagnose such ongoing conditions as depression or substance abuse, or to think in the long-run terms required to attend to children's development.

Therefore, the recommendations below suggest strengthening the separate funding and delivery systems for three high-payoff interventions, linking them better to vulnerable families who have not yet abused or neglected a child, and linking them better to the child welfare system to help families already there. Also, because many families experience several problems concurrently (especially maternal depression, substance abuse, and domestic violence), the recommendations propose ways the federal government could enable states to bring different expertise together, by enhancing resources and promoting team approaches to working with families.

Maternal Depression. Recommendation: Build on clinical success in treating maternal depression and on promising state and local models for service delivery by (a) creating a federal funding stream to pay for services to uninsured or underinsured mothers and (b) providing incentives and expanded technical assistance for effective service delivery.

Depression is widespread among low-income mothers, harmful to children developmentally, and potentially threatening to children's safety. Although the condition is eminently treatable, two barriers stand in the way of early and effective treatment: the lack of a funding stream for services and the difficulty of engaging low-income mothers in these services because of stigma and mistrust as well as practical barriers like lack of child care and transportation (Knitzer et al. 2008).

States and communities are experimenting with good ideas for funding and for engaging mothers, so the urgent need is to take programs to scale. To ensure a funding stream, one approach is to follow the lead of North Carolina, which builds parental mental health services into the Medicaid package offered to eligible young children, since most low-income mothers who need to be reached have eligible children. (Income eligibility levels for children reach far higher than for adults.) The damage parental depression does to a child's health and development justifies including screening and services in a children's health package. The most ambitious plan, benefiting the most children, would be to require such Medicaid coverage as part of children's health services whenever screening shows that a parent is probably depressed. An alternative would be to provide a federal incentive to include this coverage, but leave it as a state option. The coverage could be limited to the first year of life, as in North Carolina, or it could be more expansive.

This funding strategy should be complemented by limited federal support for states and communities to build on the lessons learned about engaging low-income mothers in effective services. Once funding is available, providers will have a greater incentive for effective outreach without worrying that they won't be able to meet the needs. A forum for sharing lessons learned and expert technical assistance should also be included.

Substance Abuse. *Recommendation:* Intensify the federal emphasis on high-quality, two-generational substance abuse services for parents, as a strategy for preventing and responding to child abuse and neglect, by (a) expanding funding for services; (b) funding collaborative planning and service delivery in at least the substance abuse and child welfare systems; and (c) creating multiple points of entry for families into services, before, during, and after involvement with the child welfare agency.

Parental substance abuse is a major factor in child welfare cases, and workers' inability to identify it or to respond effectively frequently contributes to child deaths and other dangerous outcomes for children. Parental substance abuse also can lead to a chaotic environment that hinders children's healthy development. Rigorous evaluations of state child welfare experiments that pair substance abuse experts with social workers or enhanced substance abuse treatment resources show improvements in such outcomes as children's rates of reunification. Yet, as we have seen, states and localities are rarely able to deliver these improvements on their own, because of major gaps in resources and in the availability of substance abuse treatment—especially treatment that is suited to mothers with children and does not force their separation—as well as hurdles to ongoing, skilled collaboration between workers in such complex and overstressed systems.

Effectively deploying substance abuse treatment programs to prevent child abuse and neglect is even harder, because it requires collaboration among even more systems. Prevention requires that professionals (teachers, the child's pediatrician, the judge seeing the mother on a drug charge) who get to know a mother before maltreatment occurs feel responsible for connecting her to substance abuse treatment and know how to do it.

To fill in these glaring gaps, the federal government should expand resources for substance abuse treatment for parents. The substance abuse block grant could include targeted resources for this purpose, or (far more ambitiously) a young child's Medicaid benefits could include substance abuse treatment for a parent, as North Carolina has done for maternal depression services. At the same time, the federal government should provide resources jointly to the child welfare and substance abuse state directors to plan and implement treatment accessible to parents who are at risk of abusing or neglecting their children or who have already done so. Several existing and proposed models exist for federal resources to spark collaborative planning, including the Court Improvement Program that links child welfare agencies and the courts.

Early Childhood. *Recommendation:* Expand strong two-generational services for the poorest and most vulnerable babies and toddlers, using Early Head Start (and, potentially, other programs) as a platform.

A number of programs targeted to reach parents of babies and toddlers have demonstrated success for some groups of vulnerable families in improving parenting, reducing parents' depression and substance abuse in the home, improving children's cognitive and emotional development, and (in certain circumstances) reducing child abuse and neglect reports. Because babies represent a large share of the children who enter the child welfare system, and since the babies and toddlers reported to the system are doing badly on standard developmental scales, early services that help them stay at home and enhance their development could substantially improve children's future prospects and reduce the burden on the child welfare system.

After babies enter the system, high-quality early childhood programs could have another benefit. Today, babies and toddlers in foster care risk further developmental damage because multiple placements can jeopardize the sustained intimate, stable, nurturing connections crucial to their development. If enough high-risk families were already enrolled in high-quality early childhood programs before encountering the child welfare system, then the caregiver could offer a stable and loving relationship for the baby, even during changes in living arrangements. Ideally, the program would also provide a setting where the adults in the baby's life could talk together and with the program's caregiver about the baby's development.

Preventing child abuse and neglect, improving parenting, enhancing the development of the most at-risk babies and toddlers, and reducing the damage when babies come into care require an investment in staff and funding that is far above today's levels. For example, Early Head Start serves about 65,000 children nationwide, or barely 3 percent of eligible babies and toddlers (whose family income is under the poverty level). As part of the American Recovery and Reinvestment Act, Early Head Start will receive $1.1 billion, which will allow the program to serve 55,000 more babies and their families, almost doubling the program.[8] Doubling it again to reach over 10 percent of eligible children would cost several billion dollars more. Other evidence-supported early childhood programs now reach only a fraction of very low income babies and toddles, and would need comparable expansion.

Achieving the maximum improvement for babies and toddlers would require other enhancements as well, since early childhood and child welfare face the same administrative and mission-based barriers to collaboration as other large systems. The limited experiments described earlier in linking Early Head Start with child welfare illustrated these problems. Families typically participated for less than a year, and many children were referred too late or became ineligible for the pilot when the child welfare case ended. In addition, the experiments illustrated that we know much about how to provide high-quality services to willing parents, but less about how to engage and keep more reluctant parents involved.

Therefore, to improve collaboration and enhance effectiveness for these troubled families, eligibility for the newly funded programs should support continuity of involvement with the family over at least three years. Programs should also draw on the best knowledge and practices to attract and keep troubled parents engaged. Programs would also have to build knowledge and experience working with several caregivers—kin or foster parents as well as the biological mother—to support the baby. Retaining highly qualified caregivers, a goal of Early Head Start not often achieved under normal budget and salary pressures, would have to become an even higher priority. Ideally, the newly funded programs should test neighborhood saturation models, targeting services to all families with a pregnant mother or an infant so most families in these distressed, high-poverty neighborhoods enroll at or before birth and remain in the program throughout changes in the baby's living situation.

Strengthen Policy and Investment in Birth Families So Children Can Grow Up in Permanent Homes

Research demonstrates the importance of a permanent home to children's well-being and development. National policy has successfully increased children's chance for a permanent home if they cannot return to their biological families, through increases in adoptions and permanent subsidized guardianship, usually with kin.

But, there has been no progress for children whose plan calls for return to their birth families. Reunification has stalled, with no improvement in timeliness or safety. While those children who go home report they are glad to be there, some researchers find that they are not doing as well on developmental measures as children in other permanent settings—not surprising, given the correlation between family income and children's development, and the lack of money or services to resolve the parents' underlying problems.

For adoption and guardianship, the keys to success were increased funding and new legislation. Federal and state governments provide more than $1 billion annually to help subsidize the costs borne by adoptive families. The federal government also provides incentives to states for increasing adoptions, and the Adoption and Safe Families Act provided explicit federal direction about the role of adoption. For guardianship, early funding came from state governments and from federal waivers that allowed states to try out subsidies to families; the Fostering Connections to Success and Increasing Adoptions Act of 2008 provided federal funding.

Reunification has not benefited from either increased investment or legislation that clarifies expectations. The recommendations below suggest next steps to improve the alignment of federal resources and expectations with the underlying policy goal of achieving a permanent home for all children, including those who are going home.

Recommendation: Explore financial and health care supports to reunified birth families, including Medicaid coverage for children until age 18 (as with subsidized adoption and guardianship), alternative approaches to providing birth families with resources after a child returns home, and incentives for states to improve permanence through all means, including reunification.

Translating the lessons of the adoption and guardianship successes into new policy ideas to improve reunification is not easy. The earlier recommendations to invest substantially in treatment for maternal depression and parental substance abuse and in two-generational programs for parents of young children should help speed some reunifications. But going beyond those recommendations to heed the lessons about more resources and clearer policy is difficult, because subsidizing birth families, no matter how necessary to stable and successful reunification, raises worrisome issues of fairness. How can we consider rewarding birth families for abusing or neglecting a child, when other equally poor families raise their children successfully? Yet, the alternative is also unappealing: to ignore the urgency of reunification and keep raising children in care at today's rate until we solve the broad problem of families raising their children in deep poverty. This recommendation envisions three specific steps forward.

First is guaranteeing children who return to their birth families after foster care the same health care coverage through Medicaid until age 18 that children in adoptive and guardianship families receive. This coverage gives adopted foster care children access to treatment for any special health care needs (including those resulting from abuse, neglect, or the trauma of removal); it removes past incentives for families or children to stay in foster care just to ensure treatment. Similarly, children who go home should have health care that is not jeopardized by leaving foster care. Unfortunately, even though many children go home to poor families, they are not necessarily enrolled in Medicaid:

> [One study] . . . found that between one-third and one-half of children lost Medicaid coverage when they left foster care. Most likely, they were left with no health insurance. (Allen and Bissell 2004)

The second step is to explore various approaches for providing birth families with resources to address financial and service needs after a child returns home. One model would be federal reimbursement for a capped amount, with an individualized plan to guide the disbursement for each family. The amount might be set at the same total as one year of adoption or foster care subsidies; rather than paying the family cash, the plan could specify particular costs needed to meet the child's needs, such as a security deposit on an apartment, a year's tuition for a child's dance classes, or purchases required to bring a child home. Another approach would be to specify allowable purposes for federally reimbursed aftercare spending rather than a set amount.

The third step, modeled on the adoption incentive program, shifts funding toward goal achievement by targeting modest sums to states that make measurable progress toward permanence, including reunification. The shift would deliberately be small to avoid creating incentives to go after quantity at the expense of safety and stability. Congress could provide guidance for the incentives and require that HHS provide benchmarks for improvement in timeliness and safety of reunification through regulation. Total resources could be $10 million to $20 million a year, consistent with the adoption incentive program. Even though the amount earned by any one state would be small, a federal check and welcome positive publicity have successfully energized states to achieve important goals.

Reinvigorate the Safety Agenda

Despite the intense public attention that individual tragedies often generate, the national indicators of children's safety from abuse and neglect show mixed trends, with important measures not showing any recent improvement. Child deaths from abuse or neglect have risen, reaching almost 1,800 in 2007. The limited evidence about other safety measures suggests some decreases in children's rate of re-abuse but no improvement on measures of safe reunification. These stuck indicators suggest that the current practice of scrutinizing individual child fatalities to identify and punish fault is not working, and the ensuing turmoil and crisis mentality can take a severe toll on reform.

The evidence reviewed earlier suggests a better approach. The research and experience in health care and other fields indicate that focusing on individual actions as the cause of failure hinders safety improvements because retraining or punishing one person distracts attention from the inherent systems issues, making it more likely that the error will recur. Analyzing information on a large set of errors and near-misses (instead of investigating single cases in isolation) and creating the protections needed for effective reporting of mistakes also contribute to improved safety. The one effort to apply some of these lessons to child welfare, in Illinois, confirmed that this systems framework can suggest more practical fixes than focusing on the individuals who made the error (Rzepnicki and Johnson 2005).

But individual jurisdictions cannot fully benefit from these insights. They are likely too small to generate a sufficient universe of cases, and the political intensity of tragedy in any one jurisdiction may make it near-impossible to step back and propose a new way of studying child deaths. Therefore, these recommendations suggest a national approach, paired with state pilots to further explore the application of the national ideas.

Research-Driven National Framework for Data Analysis, Reporting, and Recommendations. Recommendation: Create a Federal-State Commission on Child Safety from Abuse and Neglect, charged with developing and implementing a plan that includes (a) analysis of child deaths and other serious incidents or near-misses; (b) a reporting structure for these incidents; (c) consensus around worker confidentiality or other protections needed for effective reporting; (d) regular provision of recommendations to federal and state governments based on the analysis of deaths and serious incidents, including recommendations for legislative, budget, and practice change; and (e) regular reporting and follow-up on the status of the recommendations and the status of key child-safety measures.[9]

The suggested elements of the commission's charge all reflect the lessons of successful patient safety initiatives. Because widespread reporting is so

crucial to accurate analysis and therefore to improving safety, these initiatives typically ensure that reporting doesn't lead to penalties, sometimes
going so far as to reach agreement among stakeholders that errors will not
be punished unless made deliberately or under the influence of alcohol or
drugs. In contrast to child welfare, where recommendations to improve
safety often hinge on one big idea, such as more sophisticated risk analysis,
what emerges from these data-driven initiatives is more typically a host of
incremental changes. These might include new protocols for communication and teamwork, standardized treatments or services to help reduce confusion and ensure that patients get what they need, and improvements
in working conditions to support better decisionmaking. Most important, the health care model shows that analyzing the evidence and making these changes can lead to reductions in death and injury from medical
errors. Clinicians who believed beforehand that no improvement was
possible because they were doing their best, changed their minds once
they realized the effects of mutually reinforcing improvements throughout the system.

   If these approaches succeed in child welfare, they could break the log-
jam over safety, leading to palpable improvements for children and for
the political climate. Suppose that a broad analysis of deaths, like the
Illinois analysis, finds that workers' difficulty in identifying substance
abuse, mental health problems, and domestic violence with little information in the heat and rush of an investigation is a common theme.
Rather than persistently recommend that we should retrain workers to
do the impossible, an analysis using this safety framework might accept
the limits on human judgment and recommend instead ongoing consul-
tation with substance abuse experts in a large number of uncertain cases.
Or, going even further with the model of standardized service packages
used in the health care world, the analysis might recommend expanded
access to substance abuse services before and during a family's involvement with child protective services.

   Some argue that there are two problems with this vision. First, con-
centrating the commission's attention on fatalities and injuries could
lead to recommendations that damage many children to help a few, for
example, if it recommended more frequent removal of children from the
home, potentially damaging children who are removed unnecessarily.
To avoid this, the commission should explicitly consider its recommendations' benefits and risks to the broad group of children in foster care.
Second, child welfare agencies and leaders may worry that increased

public attention to deaths and injuries, let alone sharing information about the particulars of agency failures, will increase political blaming and turmoil, not ameliorate it. But given the failure of the status quo, it seems far better to draw on the lessons of success in another field than to hope against hope that public outrage about child tragedies will be eased by just not talking about it.

Pilot Programs to Gain Experience. Recommendation: Support state pilot projects to (a) use the commission's analysis and recommendations to support change and then track the results and (b) test alternative approaches to setting up confidentiality and reporting requirements that best promote accurate information provided without fear of reprisal.

State pilots would add experience directly related to child welfare, fine-tune the strategy, and potentially provide early evidence of results that could improve the public and political context. Pilots focused on the reporting issues would help address a thorny issue in child welfare since workers may be reluctant to surface near misses or even injuries. States might want to explore whether definitions of fault and no-fault situations that are useful in child welfare can possibly be worked out among stakeholders—analogous to the Veterans Health Administration stakeholders' agreement that health care workers should only be blamed if errors are made deliberately and knowingly or under the influence of alcohol or drugs (McCarthy and Blumenthal 2006). Such an agreement would reduce social workers' fear that an inadvertent and understandable error could lead to dismissal when viewed retrospectively.

Federal Financing Reform

Most child welfare commentators agree that the major federal funding streams too frequently get in the way of improved performance and reform. The biggest problems, many of which these case studies illustrate, are insufficient (and declining) federal funding, extremely complex rules, funding streams badly aligned with the child welfare system's goals, and difficulty meshing child welfare funding rules with those of other crucial service systems. Funding is badly aligned with child welfare goals because uncapped funding is dedicated to foster care, adoption, and permanent guardianship but not to prevention, services to birth families, or staffing and training.

States draw on five major federal funding streams and other smaller ones, each with its own rules, to support child welfare systems. For the two largest funding streams, Title IV-E of the Social Security Act (which is dwindling in its capacity to pay for needed programs)[10] and Medicaid, the rules for state claiming are not only complex but also subject to interpretation by the federal regional offices. The regional offices have made different decisions about what is allowed depending on the region, the state, and the historical moment. The Urban Institute concluded that variation in what the federal government has approved is one reason states that are otherwise similar (for example, in caseload, cost of living, and child poverty) nonetheless have different funding patterns (Scarcella et al. 2006). With such complexity and subjectivity, federal disallowances are hard to predict and can at any moment create a local or state firestorm. A simpler, less demanding system would help leaders stay focused on child welfare results.

Many proposals for reform, such as those put forward by the Pew Commission on Children in Foster Care, focus on titles IV-E and IV-B of the Social Security Act—the two federal funding sources that are dedicated to child welfare alone—and propose relatively modest funding increases, along with strategies to allow states to reallocate existing resources toward goals such as prevention, reunification, and more stable staffing. I take a somewhat more ambitious approach, arguing that we should devote considerable new resources to intensive services to address depression and substance abuse, enhance early childhood development, and improve the circumstances of birth families and that most of these resources should flow through funding streams not dedicated to child welfare, such as Medicaid.

The Need for Increased Investment. What evidence suggests that the child welfare system as a whole (rather than just the resource-starved turnaround sites) needs more funds to achieve better results? Why isn't a more flexible approach to reallocating dollars enough? The first piece of evidence is simply the size of the current gaps in important services nationwide: caseload ratios at twice the recommended level, little help for low-income women suffering from depression, gaps reported by most states in substance abuse services. Small gaps might be filled through reallocation, but probably not national gaps of this size. More broadly, HHS reports that some 40 percent of children nationally who are abused or neglected remain home with their families with no services at all. It seems unlikely that better results for these children can be achieved with no additional federal funds for services.

Second, where states have tried to reallocate, the record suggests limited success. Under HHS's demonstration authority, which allows states to carry out formally evaluated experiments, four states have implemented demonstrations to encourage counties to reallocate Title IV-E money to higher priority services (a fifth is about to commence), and five states tested managed care financing "to reduce child welfare costs while improving . . . outcomes." The results are mixed at best. Most of the managed care states "terminated their managed care demonstrations early because of problems with maintaining cost neutrality and other implementation problems," while among the states that tested capping Title IV-E, one found evidence of improved results for approximately the same cost, while another saw costs increase and required counties to terminate services.[11] Nationally, in the face of flat or shrinking federal funds, states have increased their own contribution, even in the recession year of 2002 and even more from 2002 to 2006. One reason appears to be that higher expectations for programs—whether from litigation, federally required child and family services reviews, or state scrutiny—made higher expenditures necessary. If reallocation were the short-run answer, state expenditures probably wouldn't be rising consistently.

In the long term, some savings could materialize as we invest in substantially more preventive and early intervention services. Jane Waldfogel's comparison of child abuse and neglect in the United Kingdom and the United States supports the idea that considerably larger investments in family services will eventually decrease child maltreatment rates, which should in turn lead to savings. The scanty evidence, therefore, suggests long-run savings if the nation invests much more up front in preventive services, but not short-run savings in response to small changes.

Other Problems with Federal Funding for Child Welfare. Even with the considerable investments I have proposed, other problems with the child welfare funding streams remain. The following recommendations to address these problems, while not identical in detail, build on recent recommendations by many groups, including the Partnership to Protect

Children and Strengthen Families, a coalition of policy and advocacy organizations concerned with child welfare.

Recommendation: To reduce the complexity of funding and the resulting uncertainty in state budgets and turmoil in child welfare leadership, consider "delinking" child welfare reimbursement from family income, at least for child welfare staffing and training.

Federal reimbursement under Title IV-E is only available for foster care when children's birth families fit certain income eligibility requirements, which are driven by history rather than logic (they relate to the state's standard for welfare eligibility in 1996).[12] That means states are only reimbursed for a portion of their foster care cases and, even more difficult and complex, they have to determine how much time social workers spend on those eligible cases out of a full caseload of eligible and ineligible cases. This complexity has several bad effects. It makes it hard for states to cover workers' salaries sensibly, which leads some to turn to riskier funding streams such as Medicaid targeted case management (whose applicability to child welfare is controversial). It also costs money, because it takes resources to set up the income eligibility system, and leads to state budget uncertainty, since the federal government in auditing Title IV-E cases can upend state estimates about revenue if it questions the accuracy of the income test or the test for how caseworkers spend their time. And such budget surprises, which take the form of federal disallowances and may come complete with headlines about incompetent record-keeping and wasteful claiming, make for another source of turnover in child welfare leadership. In some states, this distinction also leads to unequal treatment of children, with more resources available (for example) to kin caregivers of Title IV-E–eligible children.

For all these reasons, there is considerable consensus that some path to delinking would be a good thing. Unfortunately, there is no consensus about how to get there. It would be very costly for the federal government to reimburse all foster care children at the same rate it now reimburses Title IV-E–eligible children, yet reducing the rate to recoup some of the costs would have inequitable effects across states. Possible approaches include phasing in delinking over many years or starting with administrative costs (such as hiring and training social workers and licensors) to fix the worst complexity first and get strong systems to oversee the care of all children.

Recommendation: Continue to explore ways of allowing states to reinvest Title IV-E foster care reimbursement in prevention.

Title IV-E's current focus on foster care is a poor fit to the goals of child welfare, leaving out funding for prevention, early intervention in families, and reunification. While reallocating resources is not the sole solution to this problem, allowing such reallocation could still be a useful part of a broader package, especially once the crucial specialized services are better funded. Then, child welfare agencies will be better able to devote their own funds to the kind of informal, neighborhood-based services that complement formal services. Allowing reallocation would allow states that do reduce foster care through more effective services to keep the federal Title IV-E funding as long as they reinvest it—and, in some proposals, their state match as well—into child welfare prevention services. Nonetheless, while this idea is widely supported, it is challenging to operationalize, because it requires an estimate of what the state would have spent on Title IV-E foster care absent the reallocation.

Recommendation: Create a mechanism for holding the federal officials who oversee child welfare–related funding streams accountable for achieving child welfare goals.

A big challenge for state child welfare officials, as well as for federal officials with direct responsibility for child-welfare-only funding streams, is that no single person or group of people at the federal level has responsibility for all the funding streams that matter to child welfare—in particular, Medicaid and the separate funding for mental health and substance abuse services. For the federal officials who oversee these other programs, child welfare may be the last thing that Congress expects them to pay attention to. Congress may hold them accountable for cutting costs, improving their program's overall effectiveness, or any number of other purposes, but rarely for contributing in a powerful supporting role to children's permanence, safety, and well-being. As a result, federal policies may change without warning, with state practices seen as legitimate one day branded as near-fraudulent the next and state officials given conflicting signals about what kinds of financial partnership between agencies is allowed.

Several strategies hold promise for addressing this problem. Congress could require, for example, that the relevant federal agencies develop program and financing models for collaboration among these different service systems and funding streams and disseminate them widely. Congress could also fund joint technical assistance to help states link Medicaid, mental health, substance abuse, early childhood, and child welfare services. It could require regular reporting from all the agencies involved on the most frequent difficulties experienced by states and families in accessing services, on proposed solutions, and on progress in implementing the solutions. Finally, either Congress or the administration could create a cross-agency working group of federal officials charged with helping states use these funding sources effectively to achieve child welfare goals.

Stabilizing the Political Context for Performance Improvement

Achieving significant results in long-troubled child welfare agencies takes many years. Yet staying the course for long enough is traditionally very hard because of political turbulence in response to child tragedies, turnover of agency directors, and the desire to move on to other budget and management priorities. In the study sites, the federal court stabilized performance expectations to make ambitious multiyear reform plans possible, but without litigation, reform needs other partners. Therefore, the two recommendations in this section propose ways that state and local elected officials, foundations and outside experts, and the federal government can help create a context more conducive to significant reform.

Active Involvement of State and Local Elected Officials. Recommendation: Engage governors and mayors in certain key child welfare leadership roles, including selecting the commissioner or cabinet secretary who will direct the administration's child welfare agency; developing a shared understanding with the agency head about how to address crises and tragedies; becoming involved in performance measurement, quality improvement, and goal-setting; and solving problems beyond the scope of a single agency.

Agency reformers need far-reaching support from the chief elected official to succeed. Such support enables them to win crucial political battles, keep reform moving through crises, successfully realign performance expectations and keep expectations consistent over time, and gain backing for crucial budget investments.

Because few governors and their top staffs will have previously experienced child welfare reform, philanthropic and policy organizations should consider how best to provide early information about child welfare to newly elected officials, particularly in jurisdictions with the greatest need.[13]

For example, when a new team begins to recruit and staff an administration, the possibility of a child welfare tragedy on their watch may be the furthest thing from their minds; yet in a jurisdiction of any size, it is quite likely (NGA Center for Best Practices 2008). Improvising when a tragedy happens runs many risks: the risk of making snap judgments on insufficient information about whether to back the agency head and the risk of failing to seize an opportunity for major change, or, conversely, of creating turmoil where reform was on a good track. A first step in being prepared is to elevate the recruitment of the child welfare agency's director so the governor is involved and can pick a leader who has his personal trust and sufficient stature to do the job. A next step is an early, honest conversation about the new leader's assessment of the biggest risks in the agency, what the leader and the governor expect from each other should a tragedy occur, and the extent and limits of the governor's support. Such a conversation lays the groundwork for the next prerequisite: frequent communication between the agency head and the governor or his senior staff, to address both crises and the broader challenges of reform.

A second topic for explicit discussion is how to align the elected officials' and the agency leaders' time frames for reform, which are likely very different. The governor and his team need to understand the steps required and the time realistically involved. The agency leader needs to understand the governor's likely sense of urgency about early results. To meet in the middle, the agency leader will probably need to deliver short-term successes that will enable the governor to sustain long-term support for reform. Agency leaders will complain that such a demand for immediate results could pull them off course; to avoid such wrong turns, they should propose which short-term successes fit the reform plan, as stepping-stones to bigger reforms.

Third, a governor who cares about child welfare reform should expect that his team will work closely with the agency to understand and help define its measures of success and will regularly receive information to gauge progress and gaps. Both the site experience with child welfare reform, and the national experience with CitiStat and its state variants, suggest that the executive branch officials need to buy into a shared definition of success and measures for assessing progress. At the beginning of a reform, elected officials may need to accept the limitations of agency capacity to measure. But as that capacity grows, elected officials should ask for the data they need to gauge progress, and they should monitor and participate in the agency's quality assurance process.

In return, elected officials should consider the information seriously when making budget decisions. For example, in Utah after the federal court's involvement ends, the agency has committed to providing voluminous data to the governor's office and key legislators, and the governor's office has agreed to commit sufficient financial resources to achieve the goals.[14] Reform-oriented governors should also be alert to the costs that come with a focus on measurement—in particular, to potential investment in computer systems, in skilled staff to provide technical support, and in quality assurance staff to compile, analyze, and share the information. While less obvious and harder to sell than investing in social workers or services, no investment is more important than ensuring accurate, relevant data.

Finally, a governor who wants to achieve child welfare reform will need to help solve problems that go beyond the agency's jurisdiction and influence. The child welfare system's complexity means that reform requires active participation from many outside stakeholders, including administrative agencies that oversee personnel, contracting, budget, and information systems; other human services and criminal justice agencies; and the local judiciary, the legislature, and private agencies.

Beefed-up Federal Technical Assistance Role. Recommendation: Build a stronger capacity for targeted technical assistance to jurisdictions where children's well-being is endangered or there is great room for improvement, funded by the federal government and provided by one or more credible intermediary institutions. Revise the Child and Family Services Review penalty approach to encourage intensive efforts to turn around the most troubled agencies.

In the long-troubled study sites, the federal court monitors contributed to long-term reform by measuring success or failure against consistent standards, reporting on performance publicly and regularly, briefing the media and elected officials on performance and resource needs, and providing more conventional technical assistance such as connecting agency leaders to outside experts. Immersed in the particular circumstances of the sites, court monitors could gauge when it would be helpful to raise the level of concern and when to celebrate progress.

The federal government has the measurement capacity, long-term presence, and access to public attention to play these roles. Why, then, has it not been able to step into failing settings before litigation is necessary? One reason is that federal staff may not have the right skills for this particular job, lacking recent on-the-ground experience and understanding of local political nuances. Another reason is that singling out individual jurisdictions for intensive attention and resources is a hard role for the federal government, almost always leading to criticism and debate about the criteria for selection.

Two proposals could address these concerns, yet build on the federal government's advantages. The first is to implement a targeted technical assistance strategy through credible and experienced intermediary organizations (such as federally funded resource centers in universities or professional organizations, or a major foundation or consortium of foundations) supported by a mix of federal and philanthropic funding. The second proposal, which would likely require congressional action, is to modify the penalty process for federal reviews, so jurisdictions that require intensive assistance could have penalties waived or reinvested in reform once an agreed-on plan for reform is in place.

Under this approach, the criteria for selecting the targeted jurisdictions should combine present failure, as evidenced in the Child and Family Services Reviews and other sources of performance data, and future opportunity for improvement. Once a failing location is selected, the intermediary organization would seek agreement with key state or local officials on the broad goals and some elements of the reform plan. When such an agreement has been reached, the relationship could include both carrots and sticks, similar to court oversight, to ensure the pace of reform. Carrots could include temporary on-site staff assigned to fill gaps, a national advisory group to offer knowledge and backup for difficult decisions, technical assistance, opportunities for agency staff and key external stakeholders to visit other settings that work, and help to recruit the right leadership team. In addition, flexible but time-limited turnaround money—whether provided through reinvestment of penalties, or through separate federal or foundation channels—may well be needed to spark change in troubled jurisdictions. Understandably, they may need to improve many service systems at once, get immediate help with social worker recruitment, or be unable initially to manage resources effectively, or claim their full allocation of federal funds.

The intermediary organization should also track progress and use the information strategically to leverage reform. Especially when progress is visible but not publicly acknowledged, reporting to the media could be helpful in breaking down cynicism and resistance to reform. When progress is persistently inadequate, the intermediary needs access to elected officials, who may need to consider appointing new executive leadership.

Help Agencies Learn

Recommendation: Through federal or philanthropic funds, support research that helps agencies learn and increases the value of quality assurance and administrative data.

Improvement in all the study sites was data-driven, with major improvements in both quantitative and qualitative data fueling successful change. The right research investments could multiply the potential of these data-driven successes. Particularly helpful would be research that studies how to link the short-term measures that practitioners use—both quantitative measures, such as visits to children or timely investigations, and qualitative measures, such as observer rankings of casework quality—with results for children over the longer term. In the early childhood development field, researchers have studied links just like these and have reached a rough consensus about which immediate indicators say the most about children's long-term outcomes. Such research makes it much easier for the director of a child care program to make sound judgments about which improvements to pursue. In child welfare, on the other hand, there is no equivalent research base, so agency directors must use their own experience to make educated assumptions. More knowledge about links would improve agencies' ability to learn by doing and to fine-tune their work.

Other examples of research to help agencies learn include the Pew Commission's recommendation to develop "more and better measures" of child well-being (Pew Commission 2004, 29). Another recommendation of several researchers is that agencies and the federal government need to invest in information systems and improve their analytical methods to track "entry cohorts" of children in care, using forward- rather than only backwards-looking analysis as children exit the system (Courtney, Needell, and Wulcyzn 2004).

Identify, Develop, and Support Leaders

Recommendation: Create a Child Welfare Leadership Corps to develop promising leaders early in their careers and to give mid-career leaders opportunities to reflect and contribute to the field.

The study site experiences paint a picture of a complex leadership role that demands a wide range of skills not easily developed in typical child welfare careers or via any single-agency career path. As John Gardner points out, both large organizations and professional specialization tend to suppress the development of leaders: "Tomorrow's leaders will, very likely, have begun life as trained specialists, but to mature as leaders they must sooner or later climb out of the trenches of specialization. . . . to see how whole systems function and how interactions with neighboring systems may be constructively managed" (1990, 159–60).

A leadership development program for child welfare can address this need in two ways. It can offer talented potential leaders who work inside child welfare bureaucracies the boundary-crossing experiences and chance for reflection that will prepare them for leadership roles. At the same time, it can attract promising but unconventional candidates from other fields, affording them access to child welfare expertise and grounding in the field.

For mid-career leaders, the fellowship can address different but equally important needs. First, given the experience in the study sites, where many leaders came from other related fields, consider a conscious strategy to encourage leaders with turnaround successes in health, human services, criminal justice, and education to bring their skills and insights to the child welfare arena. Second, a mid-career leadership corps could address another finding from the sites: that in an environment as turbulent as the child welfare turnarounds, leaders do best when they are confident of career options outside their current jobs and can therefore consider risky but highly beneficial reform strategies more freely. The Child Welfare Leadership Corps could provide such career options, through six-month or one-year fellowships to child welfare leaders who have completed a tour of duty. Leaders leaving one job could take some time to reflect, coach emerging leaders, or develop new skills before plunging back into the next.

Conclusion

This book has concentrated above all on the day-to-day work of reform in large, troubled organizations. In so doing, it seeks to redress an imbalance: experts typically pay far more attention to policy ideas than to understanding how to change what complex bureaucracies in harsh political settings actually do. This final chapter has sought to bring the two strands of thought together, arguing that carefully chosen changes in policy, funding, and political context can remove persistent barriers and raise the bar for leaders' achievement.

The recommendations offered here create new possibilities for state and local agencies and leaders to achieve our hopes for children: that they will grow up safe, have a permanent family, and thrive along the way in good health and with a decent education. Imagine if the District mother who left her children alone scrounging for food had lived in a world where she had a family doctor who realized she was depressed after her baby's birth and made sure to find her mental health treatment (which her insurance paid for), and where everyone in her neighborhood enrolled their young children in Early Head Start. Perhaps the relief of ongoing help, support from other parents and professionals in the community, and her joy in the baby's development would have prevented neglect and put her children on a better developmental path.

But even with better policy and more resources, these results cannot be taken for granted. Without a clear vision and accountability for results, careful tracking of performance, administrative systems that support the vision, and a political climate that does not scapegoat in case of tragedy, child welfare agencies will still fail many families. They will still respond to crises over longer-term needs, delay decisions rather than be responsible for choosing, make wrong decisions and then fail to learn from them, find themselves at cross-purposes with other service systems, fail to ensure workers have clarity about their jobs or the skills to do them, and lose sight of the difficult balance between children's needs and family life that their mission imposes on them. For government to work as it should for children and families requires both good ideas and skilled, strategic, effective leadership.

As President Obama's administration brings a whole new pool of young people into public service, I hope that many will find a passion not only for ideas, politics, and policy but for the hard work of leadership within organizations. When I first joined HHS as a political appointee, the generation of political and career leaders 15 years older than me had been inspired to try hands-on agency management by President Kennedy and the Peace Corps. In my own generation, various individual sources of inspiration led each of us to find retooling large organizations more satisfying than proposing policy ideas: early personal experience that told us what we were good at, family influences, religious commitment to those in need (strong for many of my colleagues in the District), and the personal satisfactions of creativity (since there are no cookbook solutions) and the chance to see results.

I hope this book can contribute to attracting the next generation of leaders, by highlighting the importance of their work and sketching the terrain ahead. In a country that is coming to realize the importance of effective investment in children, we need more than ever the effective agency leaders who can get the most from those investments: who can deliver repeated short-term improvements aligned with a long-term vision; attend to the complex intersections of policy, politics, and organizational culture; and support the capacity of agency staff to learn and improve. The best opportunity for children is a self-reinforcing cycle of good ideas, stronger performance, and a more supportive political setting.

Notes

1. What Does It Take to Reform Child Welfare?

1. "DHHS Child Welfare Final Rule Executive Summary," *Federal Register,* Vol. 65, No. 16, January 25, 2000.

2. Lora is not her real name. Her story is excerpted from the report of the quality services review team, outside experts who reviewed a randomly selected group of about 40 CFSA cases in fall 2003 (Center for the Study of Social Policy 2004b, A30–A32).

3. Scott Higham and Sari Horowitz, "A Child Endangered, without a Lifeline: Mentally Ill Mother Threatened Her Son, but D.C. Police and Child Protection Agency Failed to Act," *Washington Post,* September 12, 2001, B01.

4. Ashley Estes, "Group Seeks Child Welfare Change; Advocates, Others Ask Utah Governor to Investigate 'Illegal' Removal of Kids; DCFS Response: Some Changes Are Under Way," *Salt Lake Tribune,* April 26, 2001, B1.

5. As commissioner of the Administration on Children, Youth, and Families (ACYF) from 1993 to 1996 and then as assistant secretary for children and families from 1997 to January 2001, I oversaw the core child welfare programs, policies, and funding streams located in the Children's Bureau of ACYF.

6. James Tucker, Alabama Disability Advocacy Program, quoted in Joey Kennedy, "Joey Kennedy's Blog and Column: Alabama's R.C. Case Is Over, Once and for All," May 4, 2008, http://blog.al.com/jkennedy/2008/05/alabamas_rc_case_is_over_once.html (accessed April 15, 2009).

7. *David C. et al. vs. John M. Huntsman Jr. et al.,* Agreement to Terminate the Lawsuit (Civil No: 2:93-CV-00206 TC), May 11, 2007, 2.

8. Judge Tena Campbell, Order of Dismissal with Prejudice, *David C. et al. vs. John M. Huntsman Jr. et al.,* January 5, 2009.

9. The Fostering Connections to Success and Increasing Adoptions Act of 2008, summarized on page 75.

2. Building the Airplane While Flying It: The District of Columbia

1. *Washington Post*, "Children Died as D.C. Did Little: Critical Mistakes by Protection System Found in 40 Fatalities in Eight Years," September 9, 2001. See also the follow-up articles on September 10, 11, and 12.

2. *Washington Post*, "The Seventh Child to Die," October 27, 2001.

3. For an account of the battle to close Junior Village, a huge children's institution where hundreds of children lived separated from siblings and parents for months or years during the 1960s and early 1970s, see Taylor (1999).

4. *LaShawn A. et al. v. Sharon Pratt Dixon et al.*, Civil Action No. 89-1754, United States District Court for the District of Columbia (762 F. Supp. 959; 1991 U.S. Dist. LEXIS 5300), page 6.

5. *Washington Post*, "D.C. Judge Jails Social Worker for Contempt: Woman Failed to Report on Neglected Children," October 6, 2001.

6. *Washington Post*, "D.C. Judge Jails Social Worker."

7. There were two presiding judges during my time at CFSA, Judge Reggie Walton, who began the meetings and then moved onto the federal bench early in the fall, and Judge Lee Satterfield, who was the first presiding judge of the Family Court and remained in that role for my whole time at CFSA.

8. *Washington Post* editorial, Oct 27, 2001.

9. This change had required negotiations with the court plaintiffs and the District Council that had been largely completed before I arrived. We completed the plan and put it into practice.

10. *Washington Post*, "Md. Threatens to Return Foster Children to District; Paperwork Backlog, Failure to Track Youths Cited," April 18, 2002, B5.

11. See, for example, testimony of Olivia A. Golden, director, D.C. Child and Family Services Agency, before the District of Columbia Committee on Human Services for the fiscal year 2001 and 2002 performance and spending oversight hearing, February 27, 2002.

12. See, for example, Scott Higham, "Trying to Mend the 'Frayed Trust': New Child Services Chief Tackles Job with No Guarantee of Success," *Washington Post*, September 9, 2001.

13. Adapted from testimony of Olivia A. Golden, nominee for appointment as director of the Child and Family Services Agency, before the Committee on Human Services, District Council, September 17, 2001, pp. 7–14. We made just two changes to the priorities themselves over the following three years. A few months later, I added "Meeting federal court requirements" as a seventh priority, and over the next year or two, as we fixed the agency's information system, we enlarged the sixth priority to cover the other critical administrative systems that were not yet fixed.

14. *Washington Post*, "Child and Family Disservice," August 27, 2002.

15. *Washington Post*, "D.C. Making Strides in Foster Care, Report Says: Monitor Urges End of Probation," October 4, 2002, B1.

3. Children, Families, and the Child Welfare System: Alabama and Utah in the National Context

1. Sandra Ross, "We All Should Take Some of the Blame for the Vacca Case," *Birmingham News*, August 8, 1993, 201.

2. In 2007, HHS found a somewhat lower rate (10.6 per 1,000), as a result of fewer reports, fewer substantiation determinations, and more cases that never received investigations (HHS, ACYF 2009). It is too soon to know if this change represents a trend.

3. Because children often spend several years in care, the total number of children in foster care is always larger than the number removed from their homes and entering care in that year.

4. Ken Mysogland, the director of the Stamford, Connecticut, child welfare office, quoted in Daniel Bergner, "Her Most Difficult Call," *New York Times Magazine*, July 23, 2006, 53.

5. Caregivers in this sample were the current caregivers of children who had been reported for abuse or neglect. A small proportion (about one-ninth) were foster parents, but the rest were largely mothers, with a small number of fathers or others. In the most extreme situations, where children were removed from the home, their biological mothers were not in the sample. So this number and others reported for this caregiver sample are conservative, cautious estimates: the likely incidence of major problems among all mothers involved with child welfare is even higher (HHS, Children's Bureau 2005a).

6. Daniel Bergner, "Her Most Difficult Call," *New York Times Magazine*, July 23, 2006, 53–54.

7. The Fostering Connections to Success and Increasing Adoptions Act of 2008, summarized on page 75.

8. Ron Casey "It's Fourth Down and the State Can't Afford to Punt," editorial, *Birmingham News*, June 20, 1997, 9A.

9. Paul Vincent, former director of the Division of Children and Family Services of the Alabama Department of Human Resources, discussion with the author, July 2005.

10. Robin DeMonia, "State Seeks to Improve Aid to Troubled Families," *Birmingham News*, October 27, 1993, 101.

11. Bob Carlton and Scottie Vickery, "While Children Wait: Real Change or More of the Same? Clock Is Ticking on DHR Reform: Agency Ordered to Revamp, but Problems Abound," *Birmingham News*, September 28, 1993, 101.

12. Robin DeMonia, "Services for Abused Children Improving in Some Counties," *Birmingham News*, November 29, 1994, 101.

13. Robin DeMonia, "Unhappy with Path Child Welfare Taking, Deputy Chief Retiring," *Birmingham News*, June 28, 1996, 6D.

14. Robin DeMonia, "James Seeks End to U.S. Suit That Guides Abused-Child Cases," *Birmingham News*, July 6, 1995, 4B.

15. *Birmingham News*, "An Honest Official at Least: Attorney General Pryor Said Out Loud What Most of the Others Are Thinking," editorial, May 8, 1997, 8A.

16. Robin DeMonia, "Girls' Deaths Highlight Gaps in DHR Safety Net, Report Says," *Birmingham News*, August 20, 1996, 1A.

17. Nina Bernstein, "A Tough Road for Siblings Who Survived Abuse," *New York Times*, January 15, 2006, 27.

18. *Birmingham News*, "Just the Facts: Gov. James Should Get His Information Right When It Comes to DHR and Court Orders," March 26, 1997, 8A.

19. *Birmingham News*, "Tuscaloosa DHR Board Asks James' Help," April 4, 1997, 5C.

20. Judge DeMent's opinion, quoted in Robin DeMonia, "Federal Judge Scolds DHR, Warns of Takeover," *Birmingham News*, June 17, 1997, 1A.

21. The fiscal data and the quotation are from Erik Eckholm, "Once Woeful, Alabama Is Model in Child Welfare," *New York Times*, August 20, 2005, 1. Other improvement data are from this article and the court monitor's report, "RC vs. Walley Consent Decree: Monitor's Report on Response to September 2, 2005 Order."

22. From "David C. v. Huntsman: An Overview," http://www.youthlaw.org/litigation/ncyl_cases/child_welfare/3, updated July 9, 2007 (accessed June 23, 2008).

23. Guardians *ad litem* are lawyers appointed by the court to act on behalf of another party (in this case, a child, who cannot represent him- or herself). In most states, guardians *ad litem* in child welfare cases are private lawyers rather than state employees.

24. James Thalman, "Group Rallies to Change Child Custody Policies: Many Youths Put in Foster Homes without Good Cause, Members Say," *Salt Lake Tribune*, December 25, 2000, D2.

25. Ashley Estes, "Group Targets DCFS Child Removal; Utah Families Say Many Kids Taken from Homes Needlessly; New Group Says DCFS Causing Families Pain," *Salt Lake Tribune*, March 1, 2001, D1.

26. For a fuller account of ASFA's provisions and state implementation, see Golden and Macomber (forthcoming).

27. This distinction holds true in all three jurisdictions I studied, but it is not precise, because state judges too may hear litigation that addresses flaws in the whole system. For example, several cases in California have been heard by state courts.

28. See Hilary Groutage, "DCFS to Still Work under Eye of Monitor," *Salt Lake Tribune*, November 9, 1999, C2.

29. HHS, "States SACWIS Status," http://www.acf.hhs.gov/programs/cb/systems/sacwis/statestatus_states.htm (accessed June 25, 2008).

30. HHS, ACF, "Overview," http://www.acf.hhs.gov/programs/opre/abuse_neglect/nscaw/nscaw_overview.html (accessed June 23, 2008).

31. National Center for Youth Law, "Utah Foster Care Lawsuit Ends: Child Welfare System Cited as National Model. Court Commends Parties for Their Success," June 29, 2007, http://www.youthlaw.org/press_room/press_releases/2007_press_releases/utah_foster_care (accessed June 23, 2008).

32. Judge Tena Campbell, Order of Dismissal with Prejudice, *David C. et al. vs. John M. Huntsman Jr. et al.*

4. What We Know: How Research Can Contribute to Reform

1. As noted in chapter 3, about 60 percent of children with substantiated reports receive services (the 20 percent who are placed in foster care and the roughly 40 percent who receive services at home). Thus, about 40 percent of children with substantiated reports receive no services (HHS, ACYF 2009).

2. Ian Urbina, "With Parents Absent, Trying to Keep Child Care in the Family," *New York Times,* July 23, 2006, Section 1, 16.

3. See Testa (2004) for historical context.

4. The brief actually identifies three types of arrangements: kin caregivers who are formally serving as foster parents of children who have been removed from their homes, others who are caring for children in contact with the child welfare system but not formally taken into state custody, and still others who are caring for children as a result of informal arrangements, without any involvement by the child welfare system. The first two groups are described as children in "public kinship care" and the third as "private kinship care" (Main et al. 2006).

5. For examples of these reform strategies, see Berg and Kelly (2000); Center for Community Partnerships and Center for the Study of Social Policy (2006); Pecora et al. (2000); and the Annie E. Casey Family to Family web site, http://www.aecf.org/Home/MajorInitiatives/Family%20to%20Family.aspx.

6. See, for example, Vincent (2006) and Center for Community Partnerships and Center for the Study of Social Policy (2006).

7. In this section, I draw on considerable personal involvement with Early Head Start's inception, as chair of the advisory group that designed the program and as the HHS official who oversaw implementation, including development of the regulations and the initial research design.

8. For discussions of how the ideas might apply to child welfare, see Munro (2005) and Gambrill and Shlonsky (2001). For a description of a project that applies techniques from the other systems to review of child deaths carried out through the Illinois Department of Children and Families (DCFS), Office of the Inspector General, see Rzepnicki and Johnson (2005) and Illinois DCFS Office of the Inspector General (2005).

9. Telephone conversation with Dr. Rzepnicki, 2008.

5. The Broad Brush: Vision, Strategy, and Action

1. Their commitment continued after implementation, according to an early evaluation by the American Humane Association (Edwards and Tinworth 2005).

2. *Washington Post,* "D.C. Making Strides" (see chap. 2, n. 15).

3. Arthur Santana, "Study Cites Progress in D.C. Foster Care; Children Get Permanent Homes Sooner," *Washington Post,* October 23, 2002, B8.

4. Groutage, "DCFS to Still Work" (see chap. 3, n. 28).

6. Information, Learning, and Performance Management as Keys to the Turnaround

1. See, for example, Behn (2004, 2006, 2007a, 2007b, 2008); Executive Session on Public Sector Performance Management (2001); Forsythe (2001); Metzenbaum (2007); Smith (2001); and Walters (2007).

2. Summarized from Center for the Study of Social Policy (2004b), case #18, A-83–A-87.

3. Harold Beebout, notes for a presentation to state child welfare systems directors, personal communication with the author, July 2005.

4. *David C. et al. v. John Huntsman Jr. et al.*, Agreement to Terminate, 13.

5. It was part of a multiyear contract signed by the receivership with the company that developed the system.

6. Harold Beebout, notes for a presentation to child welfare systems administrators, personal communication with the author, July 2005.

7. Accountability and the Politics of Performance Improvement

1. David Nakamura, "D.C. Agrees to Overhaul Child Welfare Agency," *Washington Post,* May 17, 2003, B02.

2. Sewell Chan and Scott Higham, "D.C. Foster Care Agency Criticized by Lawmakers; GAO Report Notes Progress, but Also Serious Problems," *Washington Post,* April 3, 2003, B04.

3. Thirty states entered into consent decrees or settlement agreements as a result of child welfare litigation between 1995 and 2005, according to the Child Welfare League of America and the ABA Center for Children and the Law (2005).

4. I did not interview the federal judges in these cases or gather information about their particular strengths (or weaknesses), so this section, in its focus on systemic lessons, may not do justice to the personal contributions of committed and talented individual judges.

5. Robin DeMonia, "Fees Mount in Alabama Child-Care Overhaul," *Birmingham News,* September 2, 1993, 101.

6. *David C. et al. v. John Huntsman Jr. et al.*, Agreement to Terminate, 11.

7. Robin DeMonia, "JeffCo Fund Overspent, DHR Claims State Probing Flexible Money Earmarked for Abused Children," *Birmingham News,* June 7, 1997, 1A.

8. *Birmingham News,* "Flexible Funding Overspending by County DHR Must Be Investigated, but Let's Not Have a Witch Hunt," editorial, June 11, 1997, 8A.

9. Erik Eckholm, "Once Woeful, Alabama Is Model in Child Welfare," *New York Times,* August 20, 2005.

10. *David C. et al. v. John Huntsman Jr. et al.*, Agreement to Terminate, 11.

8. Leadership

1. Unpublished letter to the director of CFSA from John Mattingly of the Annie E. Casey Foundation summarizing the team's recommendations, April 2003, pp. 2 and 3.

2. Jolie Bain Pillsbury, "Facilitating Action Accountability Conversations," unpublished paper, January 2007.

3. Marcia Calicchia, Cornell University, School of Industrial and Labor Relations, e-mail correspondence with the author, February 2008.

4. Peter Drucker (1995) argues that this problem of finding technical staff who can understand the programmatic, customer-focused side of the business and translate between the two worlds is crucial and too often underrated in the private sector as well.

5. For an extended analysis of an expert consultant's intervention, see Argyris (1993).

6. Marcia Calicchia, Cornell University, School of Industrial and Labor Relations, personal communication with the author, February 2008.

9. Taking Reform to the Front Lines

1. Patricia Dedrick, "Social Workers Await Reform, Decide Who to Help," *Birmingham News,* August 15, 1993, 1301.

10. Recommendations

1. David A. Fahrenthold, "Six Children Left Alone in Filthy SE Apartment," *Washington Post,* February 5, 2004, B3.

2. *Washington Post,* "Children in Danger," editorial, February 12, 2004, A36.

3. Arthur Santana, *Washington Post,* February 13, 2004, B04.

4. Nikita Stewart, "District Is Facing Contempt Order," *Washington Post,* July 25, 2008, B01.

5. Plaintiffs' Motion and Supporting Memorandum for a Finding of Civil Contempt 2008, 1.

6. Petula Dvorak, "Federal Court: Judge Credits Agency's Progress," *Washington Post,* November 21, 2008, B05.

7. Petula Dvorak, "CFSA Is 'Not Ready,' Judge Says; City Rebuffed in Bid to End Court Involvement in Agency," *Washington Post,* February 7, 2009, B02.

8. See U.S. Department of Health and Human Services, "Head Start, Early Head Start Programs to Receive Over $2 Billion in Recovery Act Funding," press release, April 2, 2009.

9. The Institute of Medicine recommends a Center for Patient Safety in health care that would bring together somewhat similar functions and includes a review of the offices that do this work in several different fields (IOM 2000).

10. This is partly because of a change in federal law in the mid-1990s that reduced year by year the income level at which children were eligible. For more on this change and the reduction in Title IV-E as a percentage of child welfare expenditures, see Scarcella et al. (2006).

11. The quotations are from James Bell Associates (2007, 9) and the summary of Title IV-E from both James Bell Associates (2007) and HHS, Children's Bureau (2005c).

12. Until the Fostering Connections to Success and Increasing Adoptions Act of 2008, federal reimbursement for adoption was also linked to these income eligibility requirements for children's birth families. FCSIAA delinks adoptions, with the added federal cost phased in over many years.

13. The National Governors Association (NGA) Center for Best Practices is currently developing materials on this topic for governors and their staffs. See NGA Center for Best Practices (2008).

14. *David C. et al. v. John Huntsman Jr. et al.*, Agreement to Terminate.

References

Adams, Gina, Martha Zaslow, and Kathryn Tout. 2007. *Early Care and Education for Children in Low-Income Families: Patterns of Use, Quality, and Potential Policy Implications.* Washington, DC: The Urban Institute.

Allen, MaryLee, and Mary Bissell. 2004. "Safety and Stability for Foster Children: The Policy Context." *The Future of Children* 14(1): 49–73.

Annie E. Casey Foundation, The. 2003. *The Unsolved Challenge of System Reform: The Condition of the Frontline Human Services Workforce.* Baltimore, MD: The Annie E. Casey Foundation.

Argyris, Chris. 1993. *Knowledge for Action: A Guide to Overcoming Barriers to Organizational Change.* San Francisco: Jossey-Bass Publishers.

Aron, Laudan Y., and Pamela J. Loprest. 2007. *Meeting the Needs of Children with Disabilities.* Washington, DC: Urban Institute Press.

Barth, Richard P. 2000. "What Works in Permanency Planning: Adoption." In *What Works in Child Welfare,* edited by Miriam P. Kluger, Gina Alexander, and Patrick A. Curtis (217–26). Washington, DC: CWLA Press.

———. 2005. "Child Welfare and Race: Models of Disproportionality." In *Race Matters in Child Welfare,* edited by Dennette M. Derezoles, John Poertner, and Mark F. Testa (25–46). Washington, DC: CWLA Press.

Barth, Richard P., Shenyang Guo, Rebecca L. Green, and Julie S. McCrae. 2007. "Kinship Care and Nonkinship Foster Care: Informing the New Debate." In *Child Protection: Using Research to Improve Policy and Practice,* edited by Ron Haskins, Fred Wulczyn, and Mary Bruce Webb (187–206).Washington, DC: Brookings Institution Press.

Barth, Richard P., E. Christopher Lloyd, Cecilia Casanueva, Anita A. Scarborough, Jan L. Losby, and Tammy Mann. 2008. *Developmental Status and Early Intervention Service Needs of Maltreated Children.* Washington, DC: U.S. Department of Health and Human Services, Office of the Assistant Secretary for Planning and Evaluation.

Baydar, Nazli, M. Jamila Reid, and Carolyn Webster-Stratton. 2003. "The Role of Mental Health Factors and Program Engagement in the Effectiveness of a Preventive Parenting Program for Head Start Mothers." *Child Development* 74(5): 1433–53.

Bazelon Center for Mental Health Law. 1998. *Making Child Welfare Work: How the R.C. Lawsuit Forged New Partnerships to Protect Children and Sustain Families.* Washington, DC: Bazelon Center for Mental Health Law.

Behn, Robert D. 2001. *Rethinking Democratic Accountability.* Washington, DC: Brookings Institution Press.

———. 2004. *Performance Leadership: 11 Better Practices That Can Ratchet Up Performance.* Washington, DC: IBM Center for the Business of Government.

———. 2006. "The Theory behind Baltimore's CitiStat." Paper prepared for the 28th Annual Research Conference of the Association for Public Policy Analysis and Management, Madison, Wisconsin.

———. 2007a. "Designing PerformanceStat: Or What Are the Key Strategic Choices That a Jurisdiction or Agency Must Make When Adapting the Compstat/CitiStat Class of Performance Strategies?" Paper prepared for the 29th Annual Research Conference of the Association for Public Policy Analysis and Management, Washington, D.C.

———. 2007b. *What All Mayors Would Like to Know about Baltimore's CitiStat Performance Strategy.* Washington, DC: IBM Center for the Business of Government.

———. 2008. *The Seven Big Errors of PerformanceStat.* Cambridge, MA: Rappaport Institute for Greater Boston, Taubman Center for State and Local Government.

Berg, Insoo Kim, and Susan Kelly. 2000. *Building Solutions in Child Protective Services.* New York: W.W. Norton and Company.

Bradley, Robert H., Robert F. Corwyn, Margaret Burchinal, Harriette Pipes McAdoo, and Cynthia García Coll. 2001. "The Home Environments of Children in the United States Part II: Relations with Behavioral Development through Age Thirteen." *Child Development* 72(6): 1868–86.

Cameron, Theresa. 2002. *Foster Care Odyssey: A Black Girl's Story.* Jackson: University Press of Mississippi.

Center for Community Partnerships in Child Welfare and Center for the Study of Social Policy. 2006. *Community Partnerships for Protecting Children: Lessons, Opportunities, and Challenges. A Report to the Field.* Washington, DC: Center for the Study of Social Policy.

Center for the Study of Social Policy. 2002. *Progress in Meeting Probationary Period Performance Standards for the District of Columbia Child and Family Services Agency (CFSA).* Washington, DC: Center for the Study of Social Policy.

———. 2004a. *LaShawn A. v. Williams: An Assessment of the District of Columbia's Progress as of September 30, 2003, in Meeting the Implementation and Outcome Benchmarks for Child Welfare Reform.* Washington, DC: Center for the Study of Social Policy.

———. 2004b. *LaShawn A. v. Williams Qualitative Review: Process, Results, and Recommendations.* Washington, DC: Center for the Study of Social Policy.

———. 2006. *Self Assessment Workbook for Building a Stable and Quality Child Welfare Workforce.* Washington, DC: Center for the Study of Social Policy.

Center on the Developing Child. 2007. *A Science-Based Framework for Early Childhood Policy: Using Evidence to Improve Outcomes in Learning, Behavior, and Health for Vulnerable Children.* Cambridge, MA: Harvard University.

Chase, Richard. 2002. *Minnesota Department of Health Home Visiting Program to Prevent Child Abuse and Neglect.* St. Paul: Minnesota Department of Health, Family Home Visiting Team, Division of Family Health, Maternal and Child Health Section.

Chazan-Cohen, Rachel, Catherine Ayoub, Barbara Alexander Pan, Lori Roggman, Helen Raikes, Lorraine McKelvey, Leanne Whiteside-Mansell, and Andrea Hart. 2007. "It Takes Time: Impacts of Early Head Start That Lead to Reductions in Maternal Depression Two Years Later." *Infant Mental Health Journal* 28(2): 151–70.

Child Welfare League of America and ABA Center on Children and the Law. 2005. *Child Welfare Consent Decrees: Analysis of Thirty-Five Court Actions from 1995 to 2005, with an Introduction by Shay Bilchik and Howard Davidson.* Washington, DC: Child Welfare League of America and ABA Center on Children and the Law.

Children's Defense Fund. 2004. *States' Subsidized Guardianship Laws at a Glance.* Washington, DC: Children's Defense Fund.

Congressional Budget Office. 2008. "H.R. 6893: Fostering Connections to Success and Increasing Adoptions Act of 2008." Cost estimate. Washington, DC: Congressional Budget Office.

Cornell University. School of Industrial and Labor Relations. 2005. " 'How I Actually Changed': Summary of Responses to a Survey of Human Services Staff." Ithaca, NY: Cornell University, School of Industrial and Labor Relations.

Courtney, Mark E., Barbara Needell, and Fred Wulczyn. 2004. "Unintended Consequences of the Push for Accountability: The Case of National Child Welfare Performance Standards." *Children and Youth Services Review* 26:1141–54.

Courtney, Mark E., Richard P. Barth, Jill Duerr Berrick, Devon Brooks, Barbara Needell, and Linda Park. 1996. "Race and Child Welfare Services: Past Research and Future Directions." *Child Welfare* 75(2): 99–137.

Courtney, Mark E., Amy Dworsky, Gretchen Ruth Cusick, Judy Havlicek, Alfred Perez, and Tom Keller. 2007. *Midwest Evaluation of the Adult Functioning of Former Foster Youth: Outcomes at Age 21.* Chicago: Chapin Hall Center for Children at the University of Chicago.

CSSP. See Center for the Study of Social Policy.

District of Columbia. Child and Family Services Agency. 2004. "2003 Needs Assessment: Report." Washington, DC: District of Columbia Child and Family Services Agency.

Drucker, Peter F. 1995. *Managing in a Time of Great Change.* New York: Penguin Group.

Edwards, Myles, and Kathleen Tinworth. 2005. *Family Team Meeting (FTM) Process, Outcome, and Impact Evaluation.* Englewood, CO: American Humane Association.

Erickson, Martha Farrell, and Byron Egeland. 2002. "Child Neglect." In *The APSAC Handbook on Child Maltreatment,* 2nd ed., edited by John E. B. Myers, Lucy Berliner, John Briere, C. Terry Hendrix, Carole Jenny, and Theresa Reid (3–20). Thousand Oaks, CA: SAGE Publications.

Executive Session on Public Sector Performance Management. 2001. "Re: Get Results through Performance Management. To: Government Executives." Cambridge, MA:

Visions of Governance in the 21st Century, Kennedy School of Government, Harvard University.

Forsythe, Dall, ed. 2001. *Quicker, Better, Cheaper? Managing Performance in American Government*. Albany, NY: The Rockefeller Institute Press.

Gabarro, John J. 1985. "When a New Manager Takes Charge." *Harvard Business Review* 63(3): 110–23.

Gambrill, Eileen, and Aron Shlonsky. 2000. "Risk Assessment in Context." *Children and Youth Services Review* 22(11/12): 813–36.

Gardner, John W. 1990. *On Leadership*. New York: The Free Press.

Gawande, Atul. 2007. *Better*. New York: Picador.

Golden, Olivia A. 2006. "Policy Looking to Research." In *Child Development and Social Policy: Knowledge for Action*, edited by J. Lawrence Aber, Sandra J. Bishop-Josef, Stephanie M. Jones, Kathryn Taaffe McLearn, and Deborah A. Phillips (29–41). Washington, DC: American Psychological Association.

Golden, Olivia, and Jennifer Macomber. Forthcoming. "The Adoption and Safe Families Act Framework Paper: ASFA a Decade Later (working title)." Washington, DC: The Urban Institute and Center for the Study of Social Policy.

Harden, Brenda Jones. 2004. "Safety and Stability for Foster Children: A Developmental Perspective." *The Future of Children* 14(1): 31–47.

Hazen, Andrea L., Cynthia D. Connelly, Kelly Kelleher, John Landsverk, and Richard Barth. 2004. "Intimate Partner Violence among Female Caregivers of Children Reported for Maltreatment." *Child Abuse & Neglect* 28(3): 301–19.

Heifetz, Ronald A. 1994. *Leadership without Easy Answers*. Cambridge, MA: The Belknap Press of Harvard University Press.

HHS. See U.S. Department of Health and Human Services.

Hill, Robert B. 2006. *Synthesis of Research on Disproportionality in Child Welfare: An Update*. Baltimore, MD: Casey Family Programs.

Hollinshead, Dana, and John Fluke. 2000. "What Works in Safety and Risk Assessment for Child Protective Services." In *What Works in Child Welfare*, edited by Miriam P. Kluger, Gina Alexander, and Patrick A. Curtis (67–74). Washington, DC: CWLA Press.

Hurlburt, Michael S., Richard P. Barth, Laurel K. Leslie, John A. Landsverk, and Julie S. McRae. 2007. "Building on Strengths: Current Status and Opportunities for Improvement of Parent Training for Families in Child Welfare." In *Child Protection: Using Research to Improve Policy and Practice*, edited by Ron Haskins, Fred Wulczyn, and Mary Bruce Webb (81–106). Washington, DC: Brookings Institution Press.

Illinois Department of Children and Family Services. Office of the Inspector General. 2005. *CERAP Investigation (Redacted Report)*. Chicago: Illinois Department of Children and Family Services.

Institute of Medicine. 2000. *To Err Is Human: Building a Safer Health System*. Linda T. Kohn, Janet M. Corrigan, and Molla S. Donaldson, eds. Committee on Quality of Health Care in America. Washington, DC: National Academy Press.

————. 2001. *Crossing the Quality Chasm: A New Health System for the 21st Century.* Committee on Quality of Health Care in America. Washington, DC: National Academy Press.

IOM. See Institute of Medicine.

Isaacs, Mareasa R. 2004. "Community Care Networks for Depression in Low-Income Communities and Communities of Color. A Review of the Literature." Washington, DC: Howard University School of Social Work and the National Alliance of Multiethnic Behavioral Health Associations.

James Bell Associates. 2006. *Synthesis Report on the Operations of Early Head Start/Child Welfare Services (EHS/CWS) Projects and Preliminary Outcome Findings.* Arlington, VA: James Bell Associates.

————. 2007. *Summary of the Title IV-E Child Welfare Waiver Demonstrations.* Washington, DC: Children's Bureau, Administration on Children, Youth, and Families, Administration on Children and Families, U.S. Department of Health and Human Services.

Jantz, Amy, Rob Geen, Roseana Bess, Cynthia Andrews, and Victoria Russell. 2002. "The Continuing Evolution of State Kinship Care Policies." *Assessing the New Federalism* Discussion Paper 02-11.Washington, DC: The Urban Institute.

Johnson, Michelle A., Susan Stone, Christine Lou, Jennifer Ling, Jennette Claassen, and Michael J. Austin. 2006. *Assessing Parent Education Programs for Families Involved with Child Welfare Services: Evidence and Implications. Full Report.* Berkeley, CA: Center for Social Services Research, Research Response Team of the Bay Area Social Services Consortium.

Jones, L. 2005. "The Prevalence and Characteristics of Substance Abusers in a Child Protective Services Sample." *Journal of Social Work Practice in Addiction* 4(2): 33–50.

Kluger, Miriam P., Gina Alexander, and Patrick A. Curtis, eds. 2000. *What Works in Child Welfare.* Washington, DC: CWLA Press.

Knitzer, Jane, and Jill Lefkowitz. 2006. "Helping the Most Vulnerable Infants, Toddlers, and Their Families." Pathways to Early School Success Issue Brief 1. New York: National Center for Children in Poverty, Columbia University, Mailman School of Public Health.

Knitzer, Jane, Suzanne Theberge, and Kay Johnson. 2008. "Reducing Maternal Depression and Its Impact on Young Children: Toward a Responsive Early Childhood Policy Framework." Project Thrive: Issue Brief 2. New York: National Center for Children in Poverty, Columbia University, Mailman School of Public Health.

Kohl, Patricia L., Richard P. Barth, Andrea L. Hazen, and John A. Landsverk. 2005. "Child Welfare as a Gateway to Domestic Violence Services." *Children and Youth Services Review* 27(11): 1203–21.

Kotch, Jonathan B., Dorothy C. Browne, Vincent Dufort, and Jane Winsor. 1999. "Predicting Child Maltreatment in the First 4 Years of Life from Characteristics Assessed in the Neonatal Period." *Child Abuse & Neglect* 23(4): 305–19.

Kotter, John P. 1996. *Leading Change.* Cambridge, MA: Harvard Business School Press.

Leventhal, J. M. 1996. "Twenty Years Later: We Do Know How to Prevent Child Abuse and Neglect." *Child Abuse & Neglect* 20(8): 647–53.

Macomber, Jennifer. 2006. "An Overview of Selected Data on Children in Vulnerable Families." Washington, DC: The Urban Institute

Main, Regan, Jennifer Ehrle Macomber, and Rob Geen. 2006. "Trends in Service Receipt: Children in Kinship Care Gaining Some Ground." *Assessing the New Federalism* Brief B-68. Washington, DC: The Urban Institute.

Maluccio, A. N. 1991. "Response: Eagerly Awaiting a Child . . . " *Child and Youth Care Forum* 20(1): 23–37.

McCarthy, Douglas, and David Blumenthal. 2006. "Stories from the Sharp End: Case Studies in Safety Improvement." *Milbank Quarterly* 84(1): 165–200.

McGlynn, E. A., S. M. Asch, J. Adams, J. Keesey, J. Hicks, A. DeCristofaro, and E. A. Kerr. 2003. "The Quality of Health Care Delivered to Adults in the United States." *New England Journal of Medicine* 348(26): 2,635–45.

Metzenbaum, Shelley, with Allison Watkins and Adenike Adeyeye. 2007. *A Memo on Measurement for Environmental Managers: Recommendation and Reference Manual.* 1st ed. College Park: Environmental Compliance Consortium, University of Maryland School of Public Policy.

Mintzberg, Henry. 1975. "The Manager's Job: Folklore and Fact." *Harvard Business Review* 53(4): 49–61.

Moore, Kristin Anderson, Sharon Vandivere, and Jennifer Ehrle. 2000. "Turbulence and Child Well-Being." *Assessing the New Federalism* Brief B-16. Washington, DC: The Urban Institute.

Moore, Mark H. 1995. *Creating Public Value: Strategic Management in Government.* Cambridge, MA: Harvard University Press.

Morgenstern, John, and Kimberly A. Blanchard. 2006. "Welfare Reform and Substance Abuse Treatment for Welfare Recipients." *Alcohol Research and Health* 29(1): 63–67.

Morgenstern, John, B. S. McCrady, Kimberly A. Blanchard, et al. 2003. "Barriers to Employability among Substance-Dependent and Nonsubstance-Affected Women on Federal Welfare: Implications for Program Design." *Journal of Studies on Alcohol* 64:239–46.

Munro, Eileen. 2005. "Improving Practice: Child Protection as a Systems Problem." *Children and Youth Services Review* 27:375–91.

Nadler, David A. 2007. "The CEO's 2nd Act." *Harvard Business Review* 85(1): 66–72.

National Governors Association. Center for Best Practices. 2008. "Nine Things Governors Can Do to Build a Strong Child Welfare System." Issue brief. Washington, DC: National Governors Association.

Onunaku, Ngozi. 2005. *Improving Maternal and Infant Mental Health: Focus on Maternal Depression.* Los Angeles: National Center for Infant and Early Childhood Health Policy at UCLA.

Pecora, Peter J., and Anthony N. Maluccio. 2000. "What Works in Family Foster Care." In *What Works in Child Welfare,* edited by Miriam P. Kluger, Gina Alexander, and Patrick A. Curtis (139–56). Washington, DC: CWLA Press.

Pecora, Peter J., James K. Whittaker, Anthony N. Maluccio, and Richard P. Barth, with Robert D. Plotnick. 2000. *The Child Welfare Challenge: Policy, Practice, and Research.* 2nd ed. New York: Walter de Gruyter, Inc.

Pecora, Peter J., R. C. Kessler, J. Williams, A. C. Downs, D. English, J. White, C. Roller White, T. Wiggins, and K. Holmes. 2005. *Improving Family Foster Care: Findings from the Northwest Alumni Study.* Seattle, WA: Casey Family Programs.

The Pew Commission on Children in Foster Care. 2004. *Fostering the Future: Safety, Permanence, and Well-Being for Children in Foster Care.* Washington, DC: The Pew Commission on Children in Foster Care.

Reardon, Kathleen K. 2007. "Courage as a Skill." *Harvard Business Review* 85(1): 58–64.

Reder, Peter, and Sylvia Duncan. 2000. "Child Abuse and Parental Mental Health." In *Family Matters: Interfaces between Child and Adult Mental Health,* edited by Peter Reder, Mike McClure, and Anthony Jolley (171–84). Philadelphia, PA: Taylor and Francis, Inc.

Rosenberg, Steven, Elliot G. Smith, and Arnold Levinson. 2007. "Identifying Young Maltreated Children with Developmental Delays." In *Child Protection: Using Research to Improve Policy and Practice,* edited by Ron Haskins, Fred Wulczyn, and Mary Bruce Webb (34–43). Washington, DC: Brookings Institution Press.

Rubin, David M., Amanda L. R. O'Reilly, Lauren Hafner, Xianqun Luan, and A. Russell Localio. 2007. "Placement Stability and Early Behavioral Outcomes among Children in Out-of-Home Care." In *Child Protection: Using Research to Improve Policy and Practice,* edited by Ron Haskins, Fred Wulczyn, and Mary Bruce Webb (171–86). Washington, DC: Brookings Institution Press.

Rzepnicki, Tina L., and P. R. Johnson. 2005. "Examining Decision Errors in Child Protection Cases: A New Application of Root Cause Analysis." *Children and Youth Services Review* 27:393–407.

Sandler, Ross, and David Schoenbrod. 2003. *Democracy by Decree: What Happens When Courts Run Government.* New Haven, CT: Yale University Press.

Scarcella, Cynthia Andrews, Roseana Bess, Erica Hecht Zielewski, and Rob Geen. 2006. *The Cost of Protecting Vulnerable Children V: Understanding State Variation in Child Welfare Financing.* Washington, DC: The Urban Institute.

Scarcella, Cynthia Andrews, Roseana Bess, Erica Hecht Zielewski, Lindsay Warner, and Rob Geen. 2004. *The Cost of Protecting Vulnerable Children IV: How Child Welfare Funding Fared during the Recession.* Washington, DC: The Urban Institute.

Schene, Patricia. 1996. *Chronic Neglect in St. Louis City.* St. Louis: Missouri Department of Social Services, Division of Family Services.

Schon, Donald A. 1983. *The Reflective Practitioner: How Professionals Think in Action.* New York: Basic Books.

Senge, Peter M. 1990. *The Fifth Discipline: The Art and Practice of the Learning Organization.* New York: Doubleday.

Shlonsky, Aron. 2007. "Initial Construction of an Actuarial Risk Assessment Measure Using the National Survey of Child and Adolescent Wellbeing." In *Child Protection: Using Research to Improve Policy and Practice,* edited by Ron Haskins, Fred Wulczyn, and Mary Bruce Webb (62–80). Washington, DC: Brookings Institution Press.

Shonkoff, Jack P., and Deborah A. Phillips, eds. 2000. *From Neurons to Neighborhoods: The Science of Early Childhood Development.* Washington, DC: National Academies Press.

Smith, Dennis C., with William J. Bratton. 2001. "Performance Management in New York City: Compstat and the Revolution in Police Management." In *Quicker, Better, Cheaper? Managing Performance in American Government*, edited by Dall Forsythe (453–82). Albany, NY: The Rockefeller Institute Press.

Smith, Susan L., Jeanne A. Howard, Phillip C. Garnier, and Scott D. Ryan. 2006. "Where Are We Now? A Post-ASFA Examination of Adoption Disruption." *Adoption Quarterly* 9(4): 19–44.

Taylor, Fred. 1999. *Roll Away the Stone: Saving America's Children*. Great Falls, VA: Information International.

Testa, Mark. 2004. "When Children Cannot Return Home: Adoption and Guardianship." *The Future of Children* 14(1): 115–29.

Tilman, H. W. 2003. *Everest, 1938*. In *The Seven Mountain Travel Books* (423–510). Seattle, WA: The Mountaineers.

U.S. Department of Health and Human Services. Administration for Children and Families. 2002. "Making a Difference in the Lives of Infants and Toddlers and Their Families: The Impacts of Early Head Start. Volume I: Final Technical Report." Early Head Start Research and Evaluation Project. Washington, DC: U.S. Department of Health and Human Services.

———. 2006. *Preliminary Findings from the Early Head Start Prekindergarten Follow-up*. Early Head Start Research and Evaluation Project. Washington, DC: U.S. Department of Health and Human Services.

———. Administration on Children, Youth and Families. 1994. *The Statement of the Advisory Committee on Services for Families with Infants and Toddlers*. Washington, DC: U.S. Department of Health and Human Services.

———. Administration on Children, Youth and Families. 2006. *Child Maltreatment 2004*. Washington, DC: U.S. Government Printing Office.

———. Administration on Children, Youth and Families. 2009. *Child Maltreatment 2007*. Washington, DC: U.S. Government Printing Office.

———. Administration on Children, Youth and Families. Children's Bureau. 2005a. *National Survey of Child and Adolescent Wellbeing (NSCAW). CPS Sample Component, Wave 1 Data Analysis Report*. Washington, DC: U.S. Department of Health and Human Services.

———. Administration on Children, Youth and Families. Children's Bureau. 2005b. *Synthesis of Findings from the Assisted Guardianship Child Welfare Waiver Demonstrations*. Washington, DC: U.S. Government Printing Office.

———. Administration on Children, Youth and Families. Children's Bureau. 2005c. *Synthesis of Findings from the Title IV-E Flexible Funding Child Welfare Waiver Demonstrations*. Washington, DC: U.S. Government Printing Office.

———. Administration on Children, Youth and Families. Children's Bureau. 2008a. *Child Welfare Outcomes 2002–2005*. Washington, DC: U.S. Department of Health and Human Services.

———. Administration on Children, Youth and Families. Children's Bureau. 2008b. "Preliminary Estimates for FY 2006 as of January 2008 (14)." Washington, DC: U.S. Department of Health and Human Services.

_____. Administration on Children, Youth and Families. Children's Bureau. 2008c. "Program Instruction: New Legislation—The Fostering Connections to Success and Increasing Adoptions Act of 2008 (Public Law (P.L.) 110-351)." Washington, DC: U.S. Department of Health and Human Services.

Vincent, Paul. 2006. *Implementation of Alabama's R.C. Consent Decree: Creating a New Culture of Practice.* Montgomery, AL: The Child Welfare Policy and Practice Group.

Waldfogel, Jane. 1998. *The Future of Child Protection: How to Break the Cycle of Abuse and Neglect.* Cambridge, MA: Harvard University Press.

Walley, Page B. 2007. "The Next Step: Alabama Officials Hope to Continue Improving Child Welfare System." *State News* 50(4): 9–11.

Walters, Jonathan. 2007. *Measuring Up 2.0.* Washington, DC: Governing Books.

Wilson, Dee. 2005. "Can CPS Agencies Be Reformed?" Seattle: Northwest Institute for Children and Families, University of Washington School of Social Work.

Wilson, Timothy D. 2002. *Strangers to Ourselves: Discovering the Adaptive Unconscious.* Cambridge, MA, and London, England: The Belknap Press of Harvard University Press.

Wingfield, Katherine, and Todd Klempner. 2000. "What Works in Women-Oriented Treatment for Substance Abusing Mothers." In *What Works in Child Welfare,* edited by Miriam P. Kluger, Gina Alexander, and Patrick A. Curtis (113–24). Washington, DC: CWLA Press.

Wulczyn, Fred, Richard P. Barth, Ying-Ying T. Yuan, Brenda Jones Harden, and John Landsverk. 2005. *Beyond Common Sense: Child Welfare, Child Well-Being, and the Evidence for Policy Reform.* Piscataway, NJ: Transaction Publishers.

Young, Nancy K., Mary Nakashian, Shaila Yeh, and Sharon Amaretti. 2007. *Screening and Assessment for Family Engagement, Safety, and Recovery (SAFERR).* DHHS Publication (SMA) 07-4261. Rockville, MD: Substance Abuse and Mental Health Services Administration.

Young, Nancy K., Sidney L. Gardner, Brook Whitaker, Shaila Yeh, and Cathleen Otero. 2005. *A Review of Alcohol and Other Drug Issues in the States' Child and Family Services Reviews and Program Improvement Plans.* Version 20, updated November 2005. Irvine, CA: National Center on Substance Abuse and Child Welfare.

Zaleznik, Abraham. 1998. "Managers and Leaders: Are They Different?" In *Harvard Business Review on Leadership* (61–88). Boston, MA: Harvard Business School Press.

Zegans, Mark. 1997. "The Dilemma of the Modern Public Manager." In *Innovation in American Government: Challenges, Opportunities, Dilemmas,* edited by Alan A. Altshuler and Robert D. Behn (104–18). Washington, DC: Brookings Institution Press.

About the Author

Olivia Golden, an institute fellow at the Urban Institute, has led federal, state, and local child and family agencies and has written extensively on policies and programs affecting low-income families.

From 2001 to 2004, she was director of the Child and Family Services Agency of the District of Columbia, leading the agency out of federal court receivership. From 1993 to 2001, she served in two presidentially appointed positions within the U.S. Department of Health and Human Services, first as commissioner for children, youth, and families and then as assistant secretary for children and families. In these roles, she was responsible for more than 60 programs, including Head Start, Early Head Start, child care, the implementation of welfare reform, and child abuse and neglect.

In her most recent public-sector position, Dr. Golden served in 2007 as director of state operations for New York State, overseeing the management of all state government agencies and serving as the founding chair of the children's cabinet. Before her New York state position, she served as a senior fellow at the Urban Institute from 2004 to early 2007, leading the multimillion dollar *Assessing the New Federalism* project and overseeing its transition to a research focus on low-income working families.

Golden was also director of programs and policy at the Children's Defense Fund (1991–93), a lecturer in public policy at Harvard University's Kennedy School of Government (1987–91), and budget director of Massachusetts's Executive Office of Human Services (1983–85). Her book

Poor Children and Welfare Reform (1992) draws lessons from welfare programs around the country that tried to make a difference to families by serving two generations, both parent and child.

Golden holds a doctorate and a master's degree in public policy from the Kennedy School of Government at Harvard, where she earned a B.A. in philosophy and government. She lives in Washington, D.C.

Index